P9-CKR-411

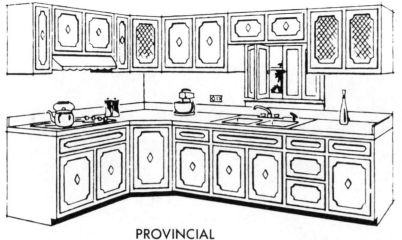

PROVINCIAL

Modern kitchen cabinets come in the three period stylings illustrated here—and many more. But construction is essentially the same for all cabinets. You achieve a particular style largely by your choice of hardware, face ornamentation (or lack of it), and the finish applied to the surfaces of the cabinets. Commercial cabinets, of course, are already finished. These sketches were supplied by the American Gas Association.

MODERN

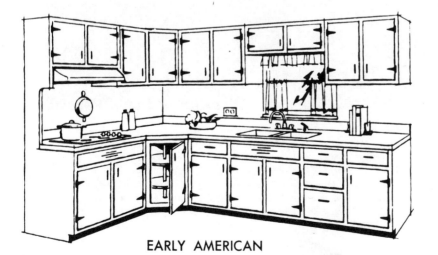

EARLY AMERICAN

In a questionnaire sent to a group of women planning new kitchens, all agreed emphatically on one point—they do not want to be shut away from the rest of the family like a prisoner in a cell. So, walls are coming down, opening the kitchen to large areas of the rest of the house—and kitchen planners are calling for everything possible to keep the former "prisoners" happy, including (on occasion) a cheerful open fireplace. Quaker Maid's new Clarion line of cabinets used in this kitchen are a "carefully crafted blend of pecan, oak, and softly polished brass." For more information, see a dealer or write to Quaker Maid Kitchens, Leesport, Pa. 19533.

How to Build Cabinets
and buy

for the
Modern Kitchen

Revised Edition

by Robert P. Stevenson

Working drawings by Richard J. Meyer

Arco Publishing Company, Inc.   New York

Sliding glass windows make this kitchen a part of the patio when the outdoor season arrives. Eating counters, with stools, are located just outside the windows. Photo by PPG Industries.

Second Printing, 1976

Published by Arco Publishing Company, Inc.
219 Park Avenue South, New York, N.Y. 10003

Copyright © 1974 by Robert P. Stevenson

All rights reserved

This book is a completely revised and enlarged edition of *How to Build Cabinets for the Modern Kitchen,* copyright 1954 by Simmons-Boardman Publishing Corp. and copyright © 1966 by Arco Publishing Company, Inc.

Library of Congress Catalog Card Number 72-85680

ISBN 0-668-03454-8

Printed in the United States of America

CONTENTS

Modern kitchen cabinets can have the appearance of fine furniture—as you can plainly see in these handsome units by commercial builders. Note the two effective ways to build in a wall oven. In the Caloric kitchen above, it's located across the corner; in the Tappan kitchen below, in a brick-faced structure in a line of cabinets.

KITCHEN REMODELING: BIG BUSINESS

The American Institute of Kitchen Dealers estimates that 2.44 million kitchens are remodeled each year. The cost averages between $3,500 and $5,000. Why are home owners so interested in making these improvements? *Time* magazine made a survey in conjunction with the Institute and found that most people gave several reasons. A total of 59 percent wanted new styling, 56 percent wanted up-to-date equipment and new features, 36 percent were replacing appliances, and 17 percent had moved to a new home. This book was written to help satisfy all of these needs.

Since the first edition appeared in 1954, important changes have come in kitchen planning and cabinet styles. Kitchens that were called modern a generation ago no longer are considered so by the new generation. Modern kitchens of the 'Fifties and 'Sixties need updating once again. Kitchens in the hundreds of new homes now being built sometimes fail to reflect the latest concepts in planning and cabinet design and are actually out of date before the first owner moves in.

Twenty or more years ago many home owners built their own cabinets, or had a local cabinetmaker do so, in order to get exactly what they wanted. Available commercial cabinets then left much to be desired. That is true no longer. Current commercial cabinets are both beautiful and functional.

This revised edition therefore offers a choice: buy your cabinets or build them. Typical examples of the beautiful cabinets available commercially are pictured and described in the book. References also are given to manufacturers' literature you may find helpful. For many people, buying cabinets is the surest and most satisfactory route to a modern kitchen. If, after reviewing the marketplace possibilities, you still want to go your own way, the book will help you build the modern cabinets you need or want. You may even decide to buy some and build others.

Surprisingly enough, the previous two editions of this book—both titled *How to Build Cabinets for the Modern Kitchen*—have contributed home-built cabinets to other rooms, too. Over the years, builders have let me know that they had adapted some designs for use in bathrooms, laundries, children's rooms, dining rooms, workshops, garages, and even living rooms. In the present edition, now carrying a new title, the emphasis remains on kitchens. But readers of this book should keep in mind that they may also find the cabinets they need for use elsewhere in the house.

In this Do-It-Yourself age, kitchen modernization offers rich possibilities to the amateur builder. As a rule, no other room in the house equals it in handyman opportunities. It is a rare kitchen, indeed, that fully satisfies the woman who uses it. Even if the room has a complete complement of up-to-date cabinets, arranged in an approved work-saving plan, there still may be knickknacks to build, or perhaps corner whatnots or other what-have-yous. Whatever it is that motivates an individual Do-It-Yourselfer—a desire to economize, an inherent need for a creative outlet, or perhaps just keeping up with the Joneses—a full or partial program of kitchen modernization will give him what he wants.

I am often asked how much a cabinet-building home owner can save. The answer obviously requires a basis for comparison. Will you compare your handiwork with the most expensive line of handsome commercial cabinets? Or will you stack them up against the unpainted cabinets you can buy with far less outlay? From this, it is evident that what you save will depend first of all on what would satisfy you if you were buying cabinets.

In building your own cabinets, lumber will be your major expense. Buying in small lots, you will pay more than the commercial builder. But, doing your own work, you will have no labor costs. Nor will there be tacked on to the item the mark-up that is part of a retail price. Considering all these points, it seems likely that home-built cabinets should cost you only about half as much as comparable commercial ones.

A book like this obviously can be written only with the help of others. I wish to thank here all of those who have given me a helping hand—and especially that kind lady who, returning part of the manuscript after reviewing it, wrote that she had become so absorbed that she let her dinner burn.

1

The Appliances You Want

In planning a new kitchen, or remodeling an existing one, it makes sense to decide first about the appliances. Then arrange these in a floor plan that will provide the utmost in convenience and happy use. Finally, choose the cabinets you want, both for style and function. The decisions you make about the appliances will determine to some extent what cabinets you must buy or build.

If you are now considering updating a kitchen, take a good hard look at *all* the appliances. Chances are some may be nearing the end of their useful life—and that could soon mean troublesome breakdowns and costly repairs. Besides, you will surely want the new features and improvements that have been developed in the appliance field in the past decade.

A range, a sink, and a refrigerator have long been considered the minimum appliances necessary in a kitchen. Now, who would consider a kitchen up-to-date without a dishwasher? Or perhaps a self-cleaning oven, an ice maker, a self-defrosting refrigerator/freezer, a garbage disposer, even an electronic oven? And that's just the beginning.

What about the sink? Will you settle for a single bowl? Anyone who has lived for awhile with a double-bowl sink will probably tell you she would not want to part with it. You'll find many choices to make, too, in the types of faucets, and most now come with a sink spray. Also, get the facts about a garbage disposer as well as a trash compactor. You may want to build in the compactor under the counter near the sink. Decide now.

Double-bowl sinks are available in many variations, some with drainboards attached. Use a disposer under one of the openings. In the Kohler line, the Trieste sink model has a third compartment, centrally located, for disposal, while the Lakefield model offers a specially fitted maple cutting board for use over the small disposal compartment. Kohler sinks have a pop-up knob to operate the drain. There is no need to reach into the water.

Some dishwashers come in combination with a sink. These may be a good choice for reasons of economy and space saving. Maytag has slip-in trim kit panels so you can match the dishwasher to drapes, cabinet paneling, or other appliances in your kitchen. A portable dishwasher is an acceptable choice where no under-counter space is available to build one in.

Women who still prefer to wash dishes by hand had better make a practice of removing their wedding bands first. The Journal of the American Medical Association has published findings that show a leading cause of "wedding ring dermatitis" is detergent trapped behind the band. Anne Williams, Westinghouse home economist, comments: "With a dishwasher, dishes are washed thoroughly in water hotter than the hands can stand, and there is no wedding ring dermatitis."

If you choose a free-standing range, you will be able to snug up base cabinets on either side and place a hood and exhaust fan over it. If you split up the range functions and choose a cooking top and wall oven, your cabinets must perforce be sized to accept them.

Be sure to consider two of the latest innovations in kitchen cooking—the microwave electronic oven and countertop cooking. Electronic cooking is becoming more and more popular. Complete meals can be prepared in a fraction of the time required in conventional ovens. Tappan notes, for example, that a baked ham dinner with all the trimmings can be cooked in less than half an hour. Foods are cooked with microwave

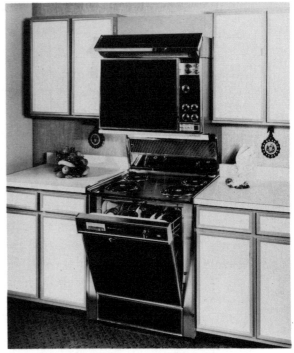

New idea! Set the kitchen sink at an angle as in this Quaker Maid showroom—and both dishwasher and dryer can stand beside the sink. Another idea: If there's no window, put a Marlite mural panel behind the sink as here.

There's a dishwasher, too, in this Cook-N-Clean Center developed by Modern Maid, Inc. (Chattanooga, Tenn. 37401). Think of the space it saves! The unit is available with both gas and electric ranges. Note flip-out hood above. The dishwasher includes a disposer.

Clean-up center in a modern kitchen includes a dishwasher and disposer. KitchenAid appliances here include a sink unit (right) that dispenses hot water at teakettle temperature whenever a cooking chore calls for it.

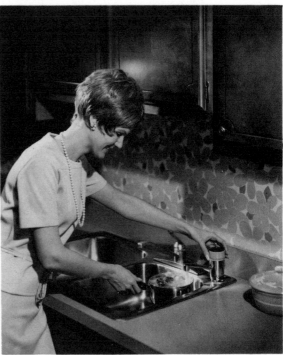

energy, not heat. The cooking can be done on paper or normal serving dishes, eliminating the pot cleanup chore. Several companies now offer portable microwave ovens.

As presented by Corning Glass Works, countertop cooking banishes conventional gas or electric burners. Instead, you see a flat sheet of glass-ceramic flush and smooth on the counter or range top with heating elements out of sight underneath. While not in use for cooking, the gleaming surface provides a convenient counter area that can be kept clean easily. Corning's original cooktops come with specially-designed cookware made of the same Pyroceramic brand glass-ceramic used in the cooktops. These Cookmates have ground and polished bottoms for maximum cooking efficiency. You buy them along with the Counter that Cooks or the Counterrange. Corning's newest models, however, enable you to use your own pots and pans.

Corning also offers the glass-ceramic surface as a Counter-Saver. The Counter-Saver is a built-in glass-ceramic work surface that won't burn, scorch, stain, or mar. Hot dishes or pans won't harm it. It's useful for carving, rolling out pie shells, chopping vegetables, or any of the chores that destroy ordinary counter surfaces. It is available in three sizes, with or without a mounting rim.

Keeping foods warm until serving time is a cook's problem that manufacturers have solved in various ways. Corning offers an infrared warmer for mounting under a wall cabinet to shine down on food placed on the counter below. Thermador (5119 District Blvd., Los Angeles, Ca. 90022) has a warming drawer you can build in where you will. Several Tappan ranges have a warming shelf located 18½ inches above the surface burners. Salton (519 E. 72nd St., New York, N.Y. 10021) offers a Hotray for building-in on a counter.

Hood ducts come in a variety of styles for use both on a wall or over an island or peninsula installation. To check out this variety, you may want to see the products of NuTone, Madison and Red Bank Roads, Cincinnati, Ohio 45227; Leigh Products, Coopersville, Mich. 49404; Berns Air King, 3050 North Rockwell, Chicago, Ill. 60618; Modern Maid Inc., Box 1111, Chattanooga, Tenn. 37401, as well as hood lines offered by major appliance makers. Most hoods include exhaust fans and lights. Where it is impossible to install ducts from a hood above a range or cooking top, a ductless hood is the answer.

Move your refrigerator? It's sometimes necessary to do so for cleaning or servicing. Frigidaire offers two ways to do it. This side-by-side unit has adjustable rollers factory-installed at all four corners. The doors can be decorated to match kitchen. For some other models, Frigidaire has an optional air-lifting device that you connect to a vacuum-cleaner blower to float the appliance on a film of compressed-air. Some General Electric refrigerators come with rollers for easy moving.

An automatic ice maker will make sure the ice supply outlasts the party. This Frigidaire machine measures less than 18 inches wide, 34 7/16 inches high, and 24½ inches from front to back.

Wall ovens here are placed beside the cooking top, but the two units can be separated and put anywhere in the kitchen that still suits good planning. Shown is Westinghouse double-oven. Townhouse kitchen cabinets are by IXL Furniture Co., a division of Westinghouse.

A microwave oven? This fast, space-age cooking facility comes as a part of Tappan's Electronic Cooking Center. The 30-inch range, model 77-1399, has a microwave oven above, a conventional self-cleaning oven below. Tappan also has a microwave oven in a double wall oven. Tappan, 250 Wayne St., Mansfield, Ohio 44902.

Hot water is on tap for instant use on this Frigidaire range. A kit comes with the 30-inch range for hooking up with the home's existing hot-water line. Pressing the lip of a cup or pan against the trigger below the tap releases the hot water into the container, a one-hand operation to speed up preparation of the many convenience foods that need hot water to start or complete the cooking. Range hood is by NuTone.

Range can be a drop-in, like this Hotpoint. At the left is a Hotpoint microwave oven on a roll-around cart.

Where are the burners? In the Corning Glass Works counter cooking system, thermostatically controlled heating elements are out of sight under the flat sheet of white glass-ceramic material. At right, a Counterrange. Below, the Counter that Cooks in the foreground. And Corning's wall ovens behind the model, shown working at a built-in food preparation surface also made of the glass-ceramic. Corning Glass Works, Corning, N. Y. 14830.

Twin-faced hoods (with fans) are available from NuTone for locating over cooking units placed on islands, peninsulas, or pass-through counters. This Heritage hood has two washable aluminum mesh grease filters.

Give extra thought to the hood and fan if you want to bring outdoor convenience indoors by installing a surface broiler. Waste King/Universal (3300 E. 50th St., Los Angeles, Ca. 90058) observes that when its Char-Glo grill is used indoors, the hood must be one designed for use over a gas broiler and capable of exhausting a certified rating of 600 C.F.M. If you are interested in an indoor grill, also investigate the Majestic "Char-Grill" (see photo), the Jenn-Air drop-in (see photo), as well as the products of Harvic Manufacturing Corp., 885-889 E. 149th St., Bronx, N.Y. 10455 (Chark-El).

In considering the third major kitchen appliance, the refrigerator/freezer, remember that ice has become an important home product. Will you be satisfied with the ice-cube capacity of the usual freezer-compartment trays? Probably not. Therefore, you should consider either a refrigerator with a built-in ice-cube maker or a separate appliance built for the purpose. Several appliance makers can now supply the latter and you might want to build one in under the counter. Other points to consider about the refrigerator/freezer: Some come with moldings

Built-in food preparation center brings together a variety of small appliances. At left is Ronson's Foodmatic, offering 14 standard attachments; at right NuTone's Food Center, with a stainless-steel counterplate and concealed power unit to which you attach seven appliances. For more information contact your dealer or Ronson Corp., Woodbridge, N. J. 07095, or NuTone, Cincinnati, Ohio 45227.

Corning Food Warmer mounts under a wall cabinet and delivers infrared heat at the countertop. The warmer plugs into a standard electrical outlet. Get more information from Corning Glass Works, Corning, N. Y. 14830.

Intercom puts home planning center in kitchen in touch with all other parts of the house—and provides radio and recorded music as well. Shown is a NuTone system.

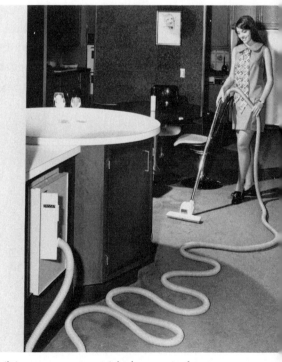

Kitchen corner becomes laundry center with space-saving two-in-one appliance developed by Frigidaire. Washer and dryer, vertically arranged in a two-foot-wide cabinet, may be operated independently or simultaneously.

Built-in vacuum system might be a part of your new kitchen planning, especially if you decide on carpeting as the floor covering. Photo shows a Tappan system.

that enable you to install front facing panels of your own choice (Admiral Corp., 3800 Cortland St., Chicago, Ill. 60647 is one); some have a special chill compartment for cooling down warm foods and drinks, a fan blowing cold air around the containers for a pre-set time; and several makers offer a compact refrigerator that might be used in addition to your regular appliance, even in a room other than the kitchen.

Unless you have space to spare in your home, it's sensible to provide a laundry center adjacent to the kitchen. When a washer and dryer are handy, laundry chores can go forward along with meal preparation. Locating the washer as near as possible to the kitchen sink, perhaps back to back with a wall between, reduces plumbing costs since both the water-supply and waste-water lines can be the same. A clothes dryer normally must be vented to the outside of the house. Westinghouse, however, offers a no-vent model. Moisture-laden air passes over a condenser which cools the air for recirculation in the drying system and condenses the moisture for removal through the waste line from the adjoining washer.

Before your plans progress too far, consider also a number of other conveniences that you may want either built into the cabinets or hidden in the walls. Among these are air conditioning, an intercom, a built-in toaster, or perhaps a built-in coffee maker.

In choosing your appliances, consider color. The trend is away from the laboratory look that came in years ago.

You get all of the outdoor flavor and fun of charcoal from Majestic's Char-Grill, installed in a kitchen base cabinet. Get information from the Majestic Company, Huntington, Ind. 46750.

No space for a wood-burning fireplace adjoining your kitchen? Look what was done with a Venus model from the Majestic Company, Huntington, Ind. 46750.

Smoke and odors vent downward from surface cooking on this 30-inch drop-in combination of range, oven, and grill from the Jenn-Air Corp., 3035 Shadeland, Indianapolis, Ind. 46226. A powerful fan draws smoke down through the opening at the center of the unit and exhausts it outdoors. The maker claims the grill "duplicates the flavor of outdoor charbroiling without the fuss."

Old-time warmth blends with today's conveniences in this modern kitchen, built to a step-saving U-plan. Cabinets were built of solid western hemlock and fitted with HL hinges. Note bricks behind cooktop. Photo by WWPA.

2

Your Very Own Kitchen Plan

Now that you have chosen your appliances, you can decide where to place each one to save steps and work in your new kitchen. To arrive at the most satisfactory arrangement, you should consider size and shape of the room, door and window location, where the kitchen is located in relation to other rooms, and the size of the family.

Strangely enough, some of today's most modern kitchens represent a return to grandmother's day in one respect. Work areas are compact, but the kitchen usually is open to other parts of the house. The cook can keep in touch with members of the family as she works, just as grandmother did in her large homey kitchen. Open fireplaces (perhaps with barbecue equipment) are sometimes located within the combined kitchen and family-living area these days to promote the same homey atmosphere. Folding doors and screens can close off the kitchen area when required.

You'll want to consider this open aspect of modern kitchen in your own planning. When it comes time to think about the floors, you'll want to know too that carpet manufacturers would like to tell you that new carpets, designed expressly for kitchen use, can be considered along with more conventional floor coverings. And keep in mind, as you make your plan, the latest research indicates every kitchen should have at least ten linear feet of base cabinets and ten of full-use wall cabinets.

Begin by deciding where to place the three fixtures common to all kitchens—sink, range, and refrigerator. These are commonly arranged with each at the point of a triangle. The sink, for instance,

Counters and cabinets in this modified U-kitchen are all surfaced with Formica laminates. In contemporary style, the kitchen has cabinets of Formica's Regency Walnut, matched by the laminate-surfaced beams that ornament the illuminated ceiling panels. Photo by Formica Corp.

might go at one end of the room and the range and refrigerator on opposite side walls. But not too far from each other. Some kitchen planners recommend that the sink and refrigerator be four to seven feet apart, the refrigerator and range four to nine, and the range and sink four to six—with the sum of the sides of the triangle being fifteen to twenty feet for greatest working efficiency.

This triangle arrangement remains a major planning goal even though you may want your floor plan to include more conveniences than the three major appliances.

No kitchen is complete nowadays without an automatic dishwasher, usually located just to the right of the sink. If the kitchen user is left-handed, locating the dishwasher to the left may be more convenient. You may want a food waste disposer in the sink, but before deciding be sure your local plumbing code permits one.

A wall oven and a cooking top may give more flexibility to your planning than a conventional range, for then you can place the two units

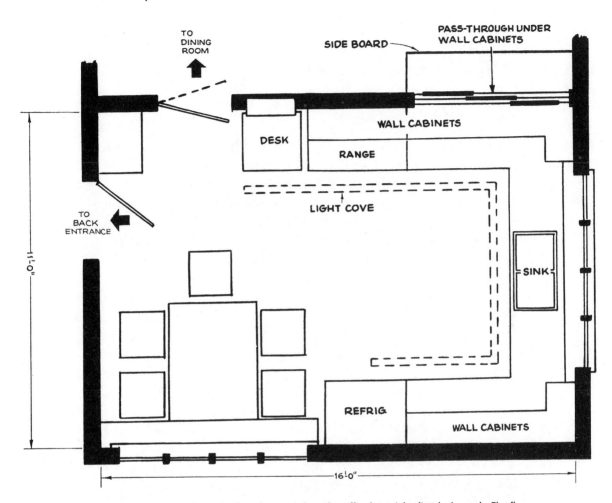

Because of its shape, the U-kitchen eliminates through traffic that might disturb the cook. The floor plan above shows a kitchen designed by Lenore Sater Thye of the Bureau of Human Nutrition and Home Economics in the U.S. Department of Agriculture. Note the step-saving triangular arrangement of the three basic kitchen appliances—sink, range, and refrigerator. A pass-through with sliding doors saves steps between the dining room and the food preparation area.

A peninsula separates the dining area from the work center of this model kitchen. The base cabinet at the left of the range has drawers opening on the side to make table mats, linens, etc., more accessible to the dining area. A corner base cabinet with revolving shelves stands between the range and sink. A peninsula often makes it possible to work out a compact kitchen plan and at the same time open up the kitchen to other areas of the house—a feature professional designers frequently strive for.

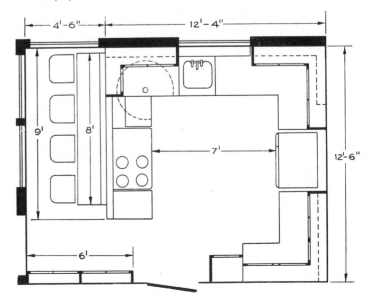

in different parts of the kitchen. Be sure, however, that you actually gain from this division and are not simply bowing to a whim of kitchen fashion. A single-unit range might be more convenient and economical.

Floor Plans and Work Centers

Soon after World War II university research studies found that a modern kitchen might follow any of four basic floor plans. This still holds true, even though some of the modern appliances mentioned in the preceding paragraph have come on the market since then. You can carry out the triangle arrangement of sink, range, and refrigerator in three of the basic floor plans—the U-kitchen, the L-shaped, and the corridor or two-wall plan. Where circumstances demand use of the fourth, or one-wall, plan, all three units are located in a line along the single wall. This should be avoided if possible, for the end units are forced too far apart if adequate counter space is provided beside each unit.

Efficient planning calls, too, for dividing your kitchen into work centers. Kitchen authorities usually recognize four distinct areas—the mix or food preparation center, sink center, range or cooking center, and the serve center. Two centers are sometimes combined.

Each center should store equipment and supplies used there, and have enough counter space to handle the activities pertaining to it. The refrigerator is a part of the mix center, the area where different food ingredients are combined. Baking, for instance, begins there. Vegetables, fruits, and other foods that require washing or water are placed at the sink center. Coffee, tea, and other foods that need boiling water go into the range center along with equipment used directly in cooking. In function, the serve center stands between the range and table. It stores cookies, dry cereals, bread, and the like. In the cabinet projects described later, you will find information under the "Uses" heading to suggest where the cabinet might go.

Kitchen planning has become a science. In this book we only summarize its major principles. Various kitchen appliance manufacturers offer you more detailed help.

Visit your local appliance store and ask the manager if he has kitchen-planning literature for you. Several planning kits include grid sheets and

The three major essentials of a modern kitchen—refrigerator, sink, and range—are all close together in this compact and efficient L-plan. Note also the dishwasher to the left of the sink, the most convenient location, and the intercom beyond the range. Kitchen designers now favor locating the cooking top at a slightly lower level than the normal counters—as in this case. Photo by General Electric.

An open hearth with rotisserie can adjoin a modern kitchen if a flue is available. Note also the high windows, an architectural feature that helps produce a cheerful kitchen. The wall above the hearth is panelled with Marlite Random Plank, a plastic surface hardboard. Such panelling is especially suitable for a kitchen since a sudsy cloth cleans it. Photo by Marsh Wall Products.

Where space is limited, perhaps in an apartment, a one-wall plan keeps the kitchen compact, with refrigerator, sink, and range in a row. Those who want a dishwasher could add it on either side of the sink. The Valencia-style kitchen cabinets in this photo are by Connor Forest Industries, Wausau, Wis. 54401.

appliance and cabinet cutouts that enable you to lay out your kitchen to scale. You can also get excellent planning literature by mail. Sometimes there is a charge. You may wish to write to one or more of the following firms and ask what they offer currently, and the charge they make, if any.

Hotpoint Division
General Electric Co.,
Appliance Park
Louisville, Ky. 40225

Long-Bell Division
International Paper Company
Longview, Wash. 98632

The Maytag Company
Newton, Iowa 50208

Mutschler Brothers Co.,
Nappanee, Ind. 46550

Rubbermaid Inc.
Wooster, Ohio 44691

St. Charles Manufacturing Co.
St. Charles, Ill. 60174

Tappan
Mansfield, Ohio 44901

Wood-Mode Kitchens
Kreamer, Pa. 17833

You'd have to try really hard to surpass this compact and efficient kitchen arrangement. Note the comfortable breakfast nook in the left foreground and then, reading clockwise, the sink, dishwasher, intercom, washer and dryer (behind sliding doors), range, and, in the right foreground, a breakfront refrigerator. The latter has eye-level fresh food storage above its own countertop and a huge roll-out freezer below. Photo by General Electric.

A peninsula or island is often a way of achieving a more compact kitchen arrangement. In this Georgia-Pacific model home, the sink is located in an island in the foreground and opposite it is a breakfast bar. The island was built of ¾'' hardwood plywood. The cabinets are stained ¼'' plywood on lumber frames. Birch plywood was used on the wall by the built-in oven. Photo by Georgia-Pacific.

In "The Kitchen Book," a commonsense and inspirational publication by Tappan, you will find five reasons why, and when, you might want to design a new kitchen—when your kitchen doesn't fit your personality, when your life style changes, when your family situation changes, when you need a new appliance, and when you move to a new home.

A Mutschler booklet lists the following "Handy Yardsticks," intended as rule-of-thumb measurements for minimum requirements:

1. Appliances, cabinets, etc., opposite each other should be at least four feet apart.

2. Distance between sink and refrigerator should be from four to seven feet.

3. Distance between range and refrigerator should be from four to nine feet.

4. Distance between sink and range should be from four to six feet. (Research has indicated this to be the most frequentl traveled path in almost every kitchen.)

5. Refrigerator should open to an adjoining countertop at least 15 inches wide.

6. Not less than 24 inches of heat resistant countertop should be provided next to range. (The same applies to the oven in kitchens using separate cooktop and oven.)

7. The mixing center should have counter space at least 36 inches wide. (Some planners stipulate a minimum of 42 inches.)

8. Dining area should have at least 24 inches of table or counter elbowroom per person; no less than 30 inches clearance around table for leeway in serving or moving chairs.

9. Minimum counter depth for breakfast bar is 15 inches; increase this to 24 inches if counter will be used for dinners.

10. Built-in seating and table area for a family of four requires no less than four feet by five and one-half feet.

Hotpoint's Kitchen Planning Service notes that ideally the sequence of work in a kitchen should move from storage to mix, on to preparation, then to cook and serve, and finally back to the sink for clean-up. Many

A modern kitchen usually is open to other areas of the home, and here is a fine example. When the family room in the foreground was added to this home, the wall of the kitchen area was knocked out. In its place the kitchen planners installed a peninsula arrangement of base cabinets and breakfast counter. Photo and floor by Armstrong Cork.

Ample countertop and cabinet space makes this kitchen easy to live with. Maintenance of the Formica-surfaced tops and cabinets is fast and easy with a damp cloth. Note that kitchen is open to rest of the house, too, including the patio through the sliding glass windows and doors at far left corner. Photo by Formica Corp.

otherwise excellent kitchen layouts fail to take the latter point into consideration—that the route from the eating site to sink should be as short as possible. Hotpoint divides each kitchen into three major work centers —refrigeration, sanitary, and cooking. It offers the following comments about each center:

Refrigeration: Built around the refrigerator, this center should be located near the door where supplies enter and should have sufficient drawer, shelf, and counter storage to handle the numerous kitchen utensils common in today's kitchen. There should be a minimum of 15 inches of work counter at the opening side of the refrigerator—more, if possible. Today's modern side-by-side refrigerator-freezer combinations function more efficiently with work space on both sides of the appliance.

Sanitary: This center handles both chores performed in the kitchen during preparation of daily meals and the subsequent clean-up. It is best when located between the range and refrigerator, and should have at least 24 inches of space on each side of the sink—whether the sink is double- or single-bowl.

In addition to the dishwasher, space must also be provided to store detergents, cleaning equipment and utensils, and to dispose of trash. A low-cost waste disposer is highly recommended to take care of "wet" garbage, while a trash compactor is an effective means of handling solid wastes such as milk containers, egg cartons, cereal boxes, bottles, and the like. Used together, a waste disposer and compactor will assure a neater, more sanitary, and odor-free kitchen.

Cooking: The best location for the cooking center is near the dining room and breakfast areas. A counter at each side of the range is important for efficiency as well as safety. There should be a minimum of 12 inches of counter on the side away from the sink, and 24 inches minimum between the sink and range. A large amount of storage is also required in this area for pots, pans, trays, utensils, dry foods, and condiments.

A planning and message center is also essential in today's modern kitchen. It can be as large as needed, or as small as an 8 x 10-inch shelf with telephone and recipe racks. If space permits, a bulletin board and intercom can be included.

Give thought to the windows when you remodel a kitchen; they're important. Double-hung windows above a sink or counter are difficult to reach and open. But a light touch with one hand opens a casement (above) or sliding window. Ask your dealer about the latest ponderosa pine windows with double glazing that make a storm sash unnecessary.

Window pass-through beyond sink at left makes it easy to serve meals on the deck that adjoins this kitchen. The paneling on wall is one-by-four tongue-and-groove western red cedar applied horizontally. One-by-four hemlock boards frame gypsum board above. Photo by WWPA.

An all-purpose bar is a handy addition that can be used for homework, buffet, snacks, serving, and many other functions. It can be an extension of one of the kitchen counters, part of a pass-through, or a shelf along one wall with added storage underneath as a useful option.

Another work center can be built around a home food freezer. A complete freezer center can be rather spacious, with storage for necessary packaging materials and tools, plus a place to sit and work at a sink. The freezer center can be located in the kitchen, a utility room, breeze-way, or wherever space permits.

3

Which Cabinets Do You Need?

The age of specialization has come to kitchen cabinets. In contrast to the old catchall cupboard, a modern cabinet is usually designed for a specific storage function, often in a particular part of the kitchen. Some have features that suit them especially to hold pots and pans, lids, seasonings, and other supplies used at the range. Some are fitted and equipped to ease the chore of baking a pie or cake—and even the electric mixer may have its own special niche. Some are solely for storing potatoes; some are just for keeping cleaning supplies handy to the sink; some are used only for storing and drying towels. Others have shelves just wide enough to store food supplies one-can deep, with none hidden behind and no waste space above.

The physical features of modern cabinets go far beyond the shelves and drawers that grandmother knew. As often as not, shelves now are adjustable up and down. Some shelves revolve; some slide in and out; some swing wide on doors; and some, turned on edge, support the stored equipment on hooks. Drawers may open in two directions, either into the kitchen or dining room. Dish cabinets, too, may have two fronts and no back—with the same double access. Work counters spread away in largely unbroken sweeps. Doors may slide back and forth instead of swinging on hinges.

Which cabinets do you need? What sizes? Where will you put them? How can you be sure of winding up with enough storage and counter space? How should you arrange the cabinets to save steps and work? Refer again to the floor layouts discussed in the previous chapter. Choosing the right cabinets for the right spot is an important part of developing an overall kitchen plan. Keep in mind that research indicates every kitchen should have at least ten linear feet of base cabinets and ten of wall cabinets.

Each cabinet should have a specific function—and this function ought to be fairly obvious. Rather than let your cabinets be catchalls for hit-and-miss storage, plan each one as to size and interior arrangement for complete utilization of the space. Ideally, you should choose the cabinet for the specific items you will store therein. In the kitchen as a whole, you should have a specific space for every piece of equipment and con-

A kitchen becomes most efficient when each cabinet has a specific storage function. So cabinet makers now offer a great variety of specialized cabinets. These photos, all showing cabinets made by the Long-Bell Division of International Paper Company, Longview, Wash. 98632, give you a hint of what's available. Slide-out racks store trays and large lids. A butcher block pulls out from a base-cabinet recess. Ventilated pans keep vegetables fresh. Revolving shelves help make corner space usable in both lower and upper cabinets, as well as in a full-height pantry cabinet. A tea table has its own storage place under the kitchen counter. Peninsula cabinets can open from both sides. See more on next pages.

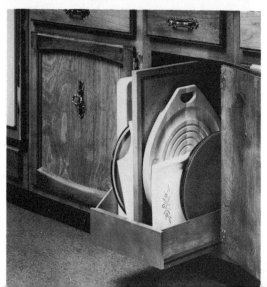

A few of the cabinet conveniences offered by Mutschler Kitchens, an American-Standard Company, are seen in these photos. A pull-out rack supports a plastic wastebasket, easily removed for emptying. Dish towels have their own niche behind a narrow base-cabinet door. A drawer is fitted with a metal liner for storage of bread.
Address Mutschler Kitchens at 320-358 South Madison, Nappanee, Ind. 46550.

tainer of foodstuffs.

Before you go further in your kitchen planning, make a list of everything you will want to keep and use in your new or remodeled kitchen. If you already have a kitchen, make an inventory of what it contains. Separate the inventory into lists of items that are related in use. For instance, make a list of what you need if you plan to bake a cake. Make a list of everything else you need when you clean up after a meal. List all the items you need in serving an average meal. What pantry items do you normally like to store, the number of cans of what canned goods, etc.? The objective is to plan storage for equipment and supplies as near as possible to the kitchen zone where you will use them. When items have overlapping functions of equal magnitude, it makes sense to keep the items midway between the two zones of use. Or you might want to solve the matter by storing duplicate items, one in each zone.

Think about the refrigerator/freezer as the zone for delivery of supplies from the market, and you'll see that this is a logical spot for cabinets

designed for storage of canned goods. But remember that you find considerable heat above a refrigerator—and this is not the best spot for food storage. Rather, aim to store there the products that may be benefitted by heat. If you have a choice, locate canned goods storage on the use path toward the sink, for it is there that you will want to open and prepare much of it.

When you can, keep pots and pans and aluminum foil cooking items handy to both the sink and range. Remember that the sink has two functions—food preparation and meal clean-up—and plan accordingly. Spices and condiments, of course, go near the cooking area, and dishes, placemats, tablecloths, silver, and the like as near as possible to the dining area or areas.

Accompanying photos show typical cabinets you can buy for specific functions. In the later chapters, you will find building plans for similar cabinets. Still another way to make full use of cabinet space is to buy special-function equipment designed for installation in open-space cabinets. Shelves that adjust up or down on metal standards also help you tailor each cabinet to a specific job.

Fitting Cabinets to the Housewife

If you build your own cabinets, or have them built, there is another aspect of planning worth considering—fitting them to the height and reach of the woman who will use them most. This will reduce stretching, stooping, and bending, all of which cause fatigue.

Motion studies show that a woman five feet four inches tall—approximately the average height of American women—usually can work best at a counter 36 inches high. But when she uses long-handled kitchen tools—an egg beater, long mixing spoon, and the like—her elbows tend to rise to an uncomfortable level. To eliminate this, model kitchens may drop the height of the work counter in the mix center to 32 inches—4 inches less than the other work counters where a housewife uses only short-handled tools or none at all.

A woman five feet four inches tall can reach to just above six feet without undue strain. Accordingly, constantly used shelves should be below that level. As suggested in the reach arcs in the accompanying sketch, articles should be stored within the comfort-

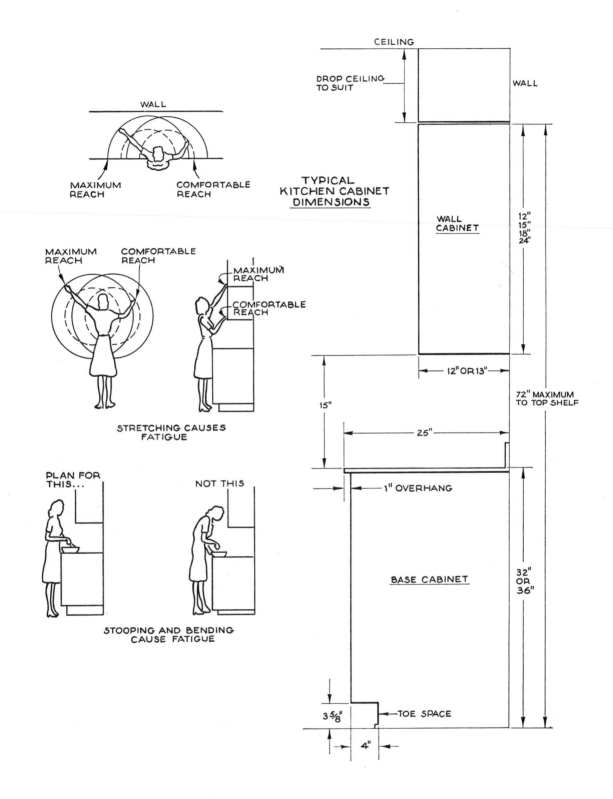

WALL

MAXIMUM REACH

COMFORTABLE REACH

MAXIMUM REACH

COMFORTABLE REACH

MAXIMUM REACH

COMFORTABLE REACH

STRETCHING CAUSES FATIGUE

PLAN FOR THIS...

NOT THIS

STOOPING AND BENDING CAUSE FATIGUE

TYPICAL KITCHEN CABINET DIMENSIONS

CEILING

DROP CEILING TO SUIT

WALL

WALL CABINET

12"
15"
18"
24"

12" OR 13"

72" MAXIMUM TO TOP SHELF

15"

25"

1" OVERHANG

BASE CABINET

32" OR 36"

3 5/8"

TOE SPACE

4"

able reach arc as often as possible. This is the circle described by the hand while the elbow is flexed. Maximum reach, of course, is attained by keeping the elbow straight.

You can stick to these dimensions if the housewife is about average height. But if she is only five feet, or if she nudges six, it would be advisable to lower or raise the cabinets to suit her. Adjusting the height of the toe space up or down also can bring the work counter to the proper level.

A mini-pantry behind the counter makes inches count in the wall between tall shuttered windows in a model kitchen developed by Western Wood Products Association, Portland, Oregon. The verticals framing the windows are two-by-fours, with standards and clips to support shelves of one-by-four pine. Boards this wide provide just enough space for visible storage one can deep.

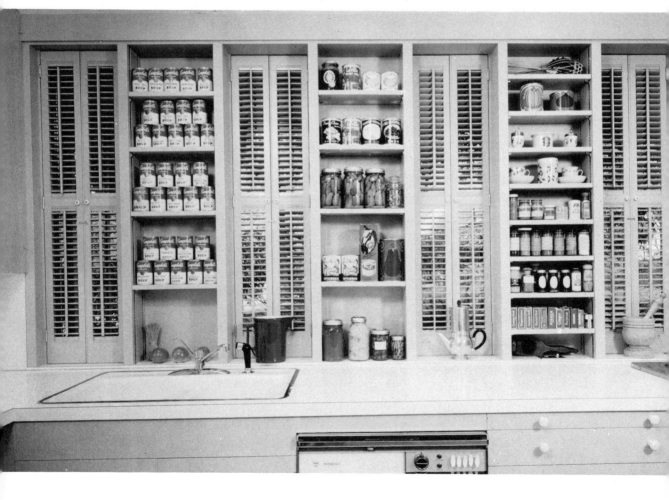

4

Buying an Entire Kitchen

To make your dream kitchen a reality, where do you turn for expert help if you decide to buy everything that goes into it—appliances, cabinets, wall and floor coverings, lighting fixtures, and all of the various accessories and ornaments? Who can mastermind the entire project and make sure all of the countless details go together into a complete kitchen satisfactory to you?

All communities now have kitchen shops with qualified people who make a business of solving problems like yours. Check the yellow pages of your telephone directory under the heading of "Kitchens." Look for such names as General Electric, Hotpoint, Kemper, KitchenAid, Maytag, Quaker Maid, St. Charles, Tappan, Youngstown, and many others. Go to local department stores. Check the catalogs and stores of major mail-order firms such as Sears Roebuck and Montgomery Ward. Write to some of the appliance and cabinet manufacturers whose names and addresses you will find throughout this book. Perhaps you will want to ask about some specific product or request a catalog or kitchen-planning book or kit. Find the location of the manufacturer's nearest retail outlet

The Stratford kitchen is a handsome example of what is available from major cabinet manufacturers. It's part of the line offered by Kemper (Richmond, Indiana), a division of the Tappan Company. The Stratford style is available in either dark or light finish and with decorative antiqued brass pulls. Doors and drawer fronts are deeply sculptured.

where you can actually see the products—or perhaps a model kitchen or two.

Make appointments with several kitchen advisers to visit your home for an on-site inspection. Let the experts make the recommendations. Decide beforehand that you will give the advisers just one of two answers: "I like it" or "I don't like it." If you really do not like a particular recommendation, stick to your guns. You are the one who will live in and with the kitchen—perhaps for years. You MUST be happy with your new kitchen. Let the expert *work* to make you so. That's his job.

Sleek walnut-finish cabinets contrast handsomely with white countertops in this functional corridor kitchen. The cabinet and counter surfaces are all Formica laminate for durability and easy maintenance. Photo by Formica.

Have you ever seen a military campaign trunk of the early days? That was the source of this kitchen style, created by Quaker Maid Division of the Tappan Company. Note the corner angles and recessed pulls, all in gleaming brass. You can get more information from Quaker Maid, Leesport, Pa. 19533. The ornamental railing atop the wall cabinets is a good idea for any kitchen.

5

Save With Unfinished Cabinets

Your new kitchen will cost considerably less if you are willing and able to start with unfinished wood cabinets. Some of these come unassembled and you must nail and glue the parts together. Others need only to be attached to the wall and a finish applied.

You can select these cabinets from a mail-order catalog or buy them from a cabinet shop, building-supply company, or other store. For the most part, you will have a choice of the same cabinets you see in this book. Before you buy you can plan on paper exactly what cabinets will fit into your kitchen. In some cases, filler units are available to fill gaps. Or you may want to use lumber or a finish molding.

The sources from which you get unfinished cabinets usually will also have countertops in sections, the topping already bonded to plywood or other backing. A curved splash board will usually be in place and a trim strip on the front edge. The sections can be cut to length and new edging applied to the ends. Clamping bolts draw sections snugly together. Make the sink cutout yourself or have it done at a local cabinet shop.

Want a new face fast for an old kitchen? Here's one way to get it—cement Marlite's Wormy Chestnut paneling to the fronts of the old cabinets. In the base cabinets, note that the textured wood grain hardboard was extended to cover even the cabinet frame. In such a renovation, new sliding doors cut from the paneling can be substituted for the old doors. Marlite paneling is ideal for kitchens since it can be damp-wiped clean. Both photos on this page were supplied by Marlite, Dover, Ohio.

To create the effect of a country kitchen, the owners of this kitchen first paneled the walls with Marlite's Wormy Chestnut planks. Then they applied decorative moldings to the plain faces of the old cabinets, and painted the cabinets a dark red.

6

Restyling an Old Kitchen

Styles change in kitchens, too, just as do our clothes, our cars, our homes, and our other possessions. Consequently, the kitchens that were modern when the first edition of this book was published in 1954 now need updating once again. The old kitchen still may be perfectly efficient and practical, but chances are it has begun to look its age, and a new generation of users will insist that the entire kitchen be redecorated in keeping with the times.

Restyling an old kitchen is a logical do-it-yourself endeavor. When you check the old kitchen against a newly installed one you may conclude that new cabinets must replace the old to get the restyling you want. But this is not the case. The old cabinets can easily be brought up-to-date both in appearance and function.

If restyling is the task *you* face, go back first to the opening chapters in this book. Before you begin a restyling, make sure you have the appliances you want to live with for the next five years or so and that they are located in the most convenient and approved spots. Ask yourself, too, whether you are satisfied with the relationship of the kitchen to the other rooms of your home. Would removal of all or part of a non-loadbearing wall, for instance, create the open effect that most home-makers now want in a kitchen?

You can approach cabinet restyling in a number of ways, and you will be happy to hear that a number of products are now available to make the job easier.

In some parts of the country you can now buy new drawer fronts and cabinet doors already ornamented in one of the new styles. These new fronts and doors may be molded from plastic, or made from wood. They come in a selection of standard sizes, and some can be trimmed slightly for a good fit. Measure your present doors and drawer fronts and then order the next larger size if the exact size is not available. Next remove the old drawer fronts and doors and spray or paint the front cabinet frames to match the finish you will apply to the new parts or the finish that may already be on the new parts. Then nail or cement the new facing parts in place. If you have not heard of the availability of such cabinet styling faces in your area, check a building supply house or one of the one-stop do-it-yourself stores that are spreading through-out the country. The parts may be just about to reach your region.

You may prefer, however, to leave the old doors and drawer fronts in place and simply apply new styling ornamentation. You can work wonders with standard materials from a lumber yard. Look at the variety of shapes in stock moldings available there. Apply a standard molding strip around all four edges of each drawer front or door, for instance. Perhaps center a raised panel on each one, too, after leveling the panel edges or ornamenting the edges with a router. Center a brass pull on the panel. Or you can change all of the hardware. Hinges, pulls, and knobs are far more decorative than they used to be. Look at photos of new cabinets for decorating ideas that you like and can duplicate in whole or part.

In recent years, several companies have introduced products especially designed for restyling kitchens. Check the mail-order catalogs for new moulding trim kits for cabinet doors. Visit your local building supply house and ask what they have available. How about self-adhesive vinyl panels that you simply peel and press to the doors and drawer fronts? The Decro-Wall Corporation, Executive Boulevard, Elmsford, N.Y. 10523, makes a line of such products in a variety of cabinet styles.

New kitchen styling is available in self-adhesive panels. Above left, Colonial Antique Birch; above right, Contemporary Walnut; bottom left, Continental Gold on White; bottom right, Country Classic Light Birch. These are products of Decro-Wall Corporation, Executive Boulevard, Elmsford, N.Y. 10523. Check to see if a local hardware or building supply store stocks them.

Paneling on the kitchen ceiling? That's an idea worth considering. Here are two situations where it was done. Paneling one or more walls is an easy do-it-yourself project. In one of these photos, the homeowner is installing tongue-and-groove Marlite planks; in the other, one-by-six V-groove Douglas fir paneling was used.

Repli-Carve by Emco, 300 New York Avenue, Des Moines, Iowa 50304, offers collections of decorator door panels, plaques, and moldings which you apply with a special adhesive in the kitchen, or other rooms of the house. Also look for the products of the Decra-Mold Division of Agee Products Corporation, P.O. Box 75248, Oklahoma City, Okla. 73107. These are made of solid wood—white pine, alder, northern beech. The decorative moldings include quarter circles as well as straight runs—ready made for cabinet doors. If you are building your own cabinets, the company's outside-corner lip molding for cabinet doors would be an ideal item for you. Your local store may stock these items or others similar to them. With them, you can restyle your kitchen between Saturday breakfast and lunch. It'll look good, too.

When you get the urge to redecorate a kitchen, don't overlook the great possibilities to be found in the prefinished wall panels available in plywood and hardboard. Use them on the cabinet fronts as well as the walls. In fact, if you build any of the cabinets described later in this book, consider facing your project with prefinished wall paneling instead of the plywood usually specified—or perhaps laminated to plywood. Finish off the edges with reverse corner molding.

Paint applied with a spray can (ventilate well!) or brush will also give you a new looking kitchen. Be daring with the paint. Use bold colors—but make sure first that you are doing it tastefully. If in doubt, consult a decorator or a friend who gets results that you always admire.

While you are doing over the cabinets, consider new wall and floor coverings also, perhaps even a new countertop of easy-to-care-for material. Is there an open space on one wall? Finish it off with a plate rail at about head height. Make the rail of stock molding. Place decorative plates along its upper edge. Hang fancy pots below.

Kitchen cabinets come in many styles. A few are seen
here, others throughout the book. Top left, sophisticated
styling by Formica, and right, Eton by Kemper. Get
more information from Formica Corp., 120 East Fourth
St., Cincinnati, Ohio 45202; and Kemper, Richmond,
Indiana.

7

The Basics of Cabinet Building

Now that you have reviewed what is involved in planning a kitchen and buying all of the cabinets for it, let's consider the other route you might take—building the cabinets from scratch. You will find examples of cabinets you could build presented in detail throughout the remainder of this book.

If you already are adept at cutting tenons or dadoes, by all means use them at the points where they should be used in the cabinets you select. If you are a beginning woodworker, you may want to master the advanced techniques for your own satisfaction—if for no other reason. But if you would rather not, you still can build kitchen cabinets, good ones too, using only butt joints.

A butt joint is made by smoothing two surfaces, fitting them together, and holding with glue, dowels, nails, or screws. To strengthen them, the hardware store will supply you with such things as corner irons, mending plates, and corrugated fasteners. Corner irons go inside a corner. Mending plates come in three shapes—straight, right-angle, or T—for use on the edges of the joined members.

A professional cabinetmaker might set shelves in dadoes. You can, too, if you wish. But cleats are a lot simpler, and functionally are just as satisfactory. However, the smart cabinet builder will use neither dadoes nor cleats except in special cases.

Instead, when he visits the hardware store, he will buy a batch of adjustable shelf standards, fasten the standards vertically inside the cabinet ends, and slip in the squared shelves. Some of the finest commercial cabinets have this feature. Not only do standards make cabinet building easier but they keep the cabinet in step with changes in storage needs. They are a logical substitute, too, for the peg-in-hole supports suggested in some of the cabinets in later chapters. If you wish, standards can be fastened directly to the cabinet ends. But setting them into vertical grooves cut in the cabinet ends, if you have the equipment for it, makes a more workmanlike job and reduces the width of the down cracks at the shelf ends.

Some Principles of Cabinet Building

Three of the drawing pages (I, II, and III) with this chapter illustrate some of the simple procedures that can be used in cabinet building. The drawings showing a wall cabinet and a base cabinet (I and II) came from Skil Corporation designs. They provide that the kitchen wall shall serve as the cabinet back. But it is easy enough to add thin plywood, hardboard, or a wallboard-type composition material if you want enclosed units.

The half-lap joint indicated at *A* in the base cabinet requires sawing half the thickness of the stock and chiseling out the waste. End lap joints (made the same way except that one or both joining members are cut on the end) can be used elsewhere on the front facing strips. The simple end rabbet shown on the flush-front drawer is a good one to master. A rabbet is a cut of right-angle section along the edge or end of a piece of wood. This joint usually is glued or nailed. Since glue does not hold well on end wood, it is better to use a rabbet than a butt when you join end wood. A rabbet gives the glue a better chance to do its job because some will be adhering to side wood.

An end rabbet like that shown can be cut by hand. Lay it out by gauging lines on the end, rear surface, and edges of the drawer front, making it half the thickness of the drawer-front stock. Suit the other

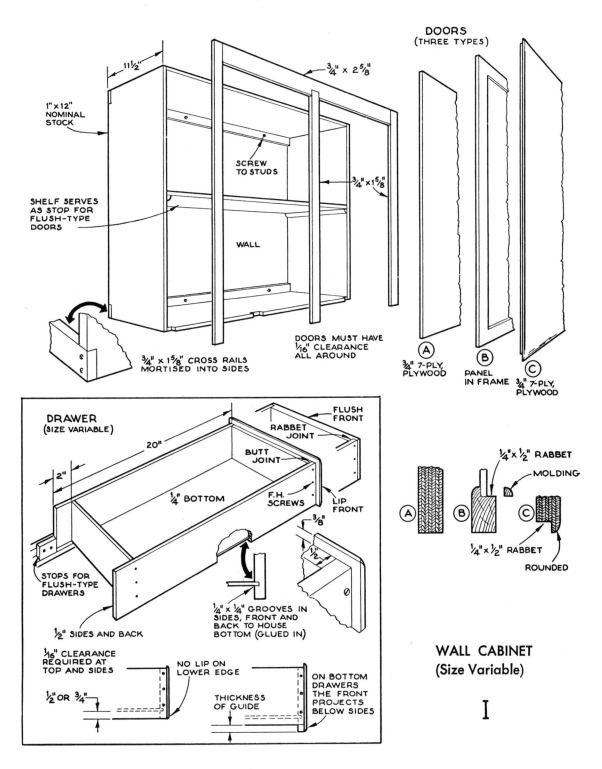

11½"

1" x 12"
NOMINAL
STOCK

¾" x 2⅝"

SCREW
TO STUDS

¾" x 1⅝"

SHELF SERVES
AS STOP FOR
FLUSH-TYPE
DOORS

WALL

¾" x 1⅝" CROSS RAILS
MORTISED INTO SIDES

DOORS MUST HAVE
1/16" CLEARANCE
ALL AROUND

DOORS
(THREE TYPES)

Ⓐ
¾" 7-PLY,
PLYWOOD

Ⓑ
PANEL
IN FRAME

Ⓒ
¾" 7-PLY,
PLYWOOD

DRAWER
(SIZE VARIABLE)

20"

2"

¼" BOTTOM

RABBET
JOINT

BUTT
JOINT

FLUSH
FRONT

F.H.
SCREWS

LIP
FRONT

⅜"

½"

STOPS FOR
FLUSH-TYPE
DRAWERS

½" SIDES AND BACK

¼" x ¼" GROOVES IN
SIDES, FRONT AND
BACK TO HOUSE
BOTTOM (GLUED IN)

1/16" CLEARANCE
REQUIRED AT
TOP AND SIDES

½" OR ¾"

NO LIP ON
LOWER EDGE

THICKNESS
OF GUIDE

ON BOTTOM
DRAWERS
THE FRONT
PROJECTS
BELOW SIDES

Ⓐ

Ⓑ
¼" x ½" RABBET

MOLDING

Ⓒ
¼" x ½" RABBET

ROUNDED

WALL CABINET
(Size Variable)

I

dimension to the thickness of the stock used for the side of the drawer. Clamp the drawer front in a vise with the end up. Then, using a back saw or rip saw, cut down through the end to the rabbet shoulder line, sawing in the waste area. Begin by nudging the saw into place with the thumb of your left hand. Start the saw in the corner and gradually level off. To cut the shoulder, remove the piece from the vise and clamp a guide block along the line. Again saw in the waste area.

A drawer bottom usually is set into grooves cut in the face and side pieces (and sometimes the back). But it doesn't have to be. It can rest on narrow cleats nailed and glued inside the side and end pieces.

Two types of doors are commonly used—flush and lipped. The flush type is mounted with its face even with the cabinet front. A lipped door has a rabbet around the edges of the rear surface, permitting the door to overlap its frame. A variation is a straight overlapping door without an inset. This usually is made of thin stock. The outer edges of a lipped door should be rounded off. If you want a lipped door, do not be scared away by the need for cutting a rabbet. Build up the door by gluing and bradding together two thin panels, one slightly larger than the other all around.

Sliding doors also are commonly used on cabinets. Plastic, metal, and wood mounting strips make them easy to install. You can get a few tips from most local hardware and building supply stores about what to buy to create doors that slide easily.

On some commercially made kitchen cabinets, you'll see a few accent doors with open fretwork panels, perhaps with glass behind. These are most often used in connection with Provincial and other newer cabinet styles. In larger cities, stores that specialize in cabinet hardware may handle such door inserts or the molding and other materials needed for them. You can achieve the same effect with gold anodized aluminum sheet available in open patterns. Check building supply houses, do-it-yourself hardware stores, or mail order houses or catalogs. For a door, you might enclose a panel within a frame of one-by-twos, much as you would frame a picture.

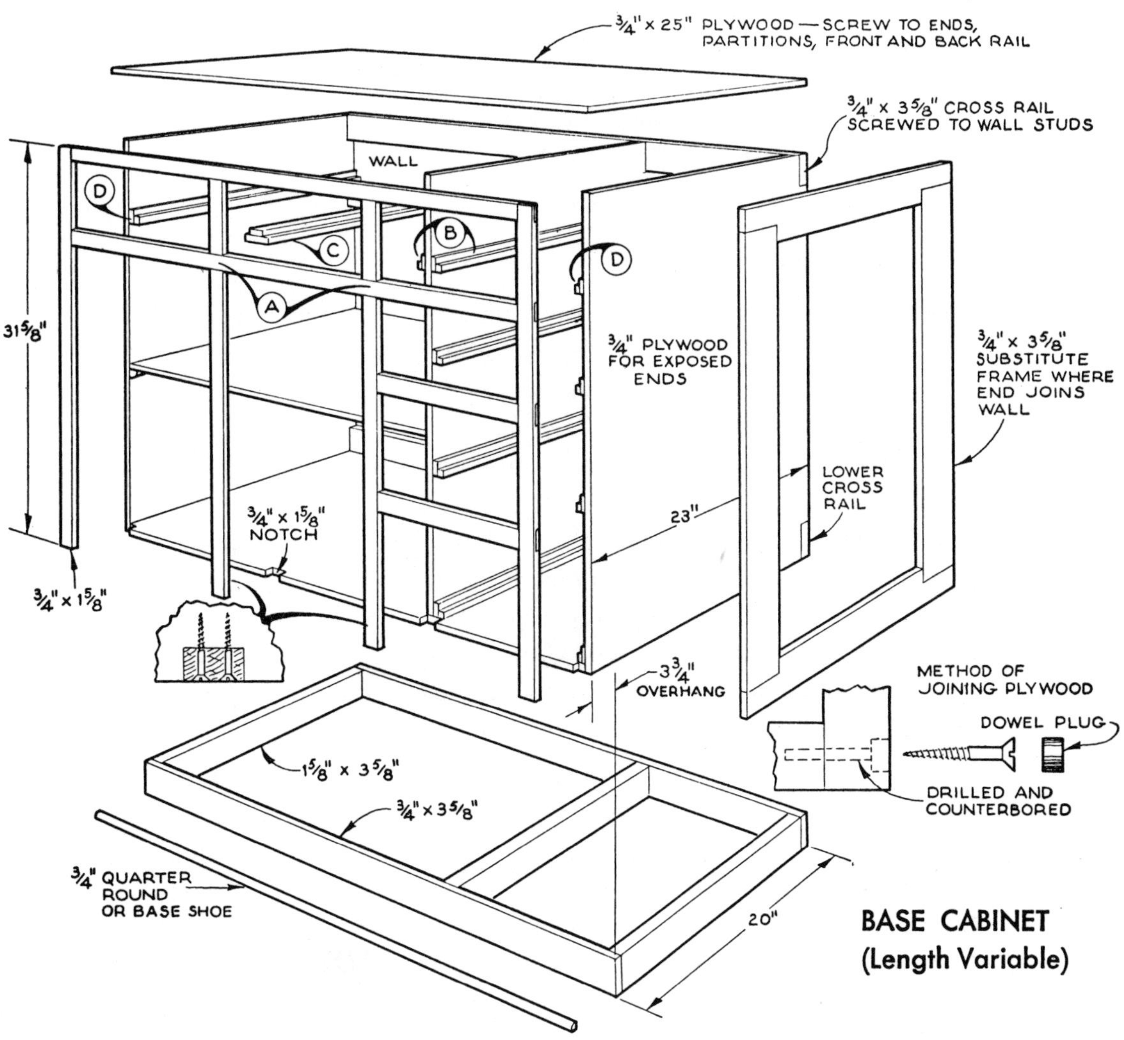
3/4" x 25" PLYWOOD — SCREW TO ENDS, PARTITIONS, FRONT AND BACK RAIL
3/4" x 3 5/8" CROSS RAIL SCREWED TO WALL STUDS
WALL
D
C
B
D
A
31 5/8"
3/4" PLYWOOD FOR EXPOSED ENDS
3/4" x 3 5/8" SUBSTITUTE FRAME WHERE END JOINS WALL
LOWER CROSS RAIL
23"
3/4" x 1 5/8" NOTCH
3/4" x 1 5/8"
3 3/4" OVERHANG
METHOD OF JOINING PLYWOOD
DOWEL PLUG
DRILLED AND COUNTERBORED
1 5/8" x 3 5/8"
3/4" x 3 5/8"
3/4" QUARTER ROUND OR BASE SHOE
20"

BASE CABINET
(Length Variable)

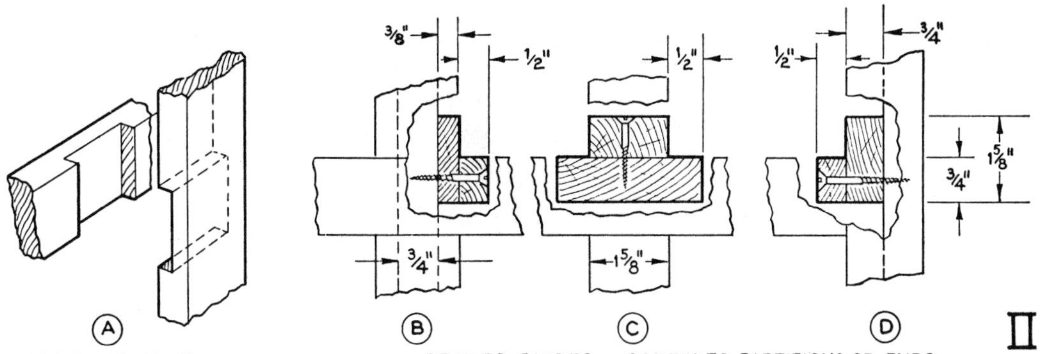
3/8"
1/2"
3/4"
1/2"
1 5/8"
1/2"
3/4"
1 5/8"
3/4"

Ⓐ HALF-LAP JOINT

Ⓑ Ⓒ Ⓓ

DRAWER GUIDES — SCREW TO PARTITIONS OR ENDS. DOUBLE GUIDE "C" IS SUPPORTED AT REAR ON CROSSRAILS (NOT SHOWN)

II

Cross rails on the back add strength and offer a means of screwing a cabinet to the wall. In standard stud walls, run screws through the rails, spacing them to suit the studs. For a hollow-tile wall, use toggle bolts; for a masonry wall, use bolts and expansion shields.

Installing Drawers in a Cabinet

Until only a few years ago, cabinetmakers commonly installed drawers in the cabinet (or case) by the method shown at A in the accompanying Fig. III. The bottom edge of each side piece of the drawer serves as a runner that moves along a guide screwed to the cabinet partition or end. You'll also find examples of this method in Figs. I and II.

The side runner-guide method still is acceptable (and especially good for heavy-duty drawers) but methods B and C may make it easier for the builder to get smooth drawer operation. Several firms make metal drawer guides and you should be able to get them from a hardware store. They require a minimum of one-half inch clearance between the sides of the drawer and the ends or framing of the cabinet.

The center guide method shown at C is widely used by cabinetmakers nowadays because of its simplicity of construction and ease of operation. There are several variations of this. Perhaps the simplest consists of a center guide strip mounted between front and rear framing members of the cabinet, plus a closely-mating slot centered in the bottom edge of the drawer back. That's all. The drawer is supported at three friction points—on the center guide (the slot at the rear makes it track on the guide) and on the front framing member under the face of the drawer. The bottom edges of the drawer sides (runners) rest on the frame piece. No side guides are needed.

As a variation, two parallel strips sometimes are attached to the drawer bottom, straddling the center guide secured to the cabinet frame—to serve with, or in place of, the slot in the drawer back. The construction also is sometimes reversed—a center strip being attached to the drawer bottom and two parallel strips on the frame to keep it aligned.

If you'll refer to an earlier chapter and the drawing accompanying the section, "Fitting Cabinets to the Housewife," you'll note that

THREE WAYS TO INSTALL A DRAWER

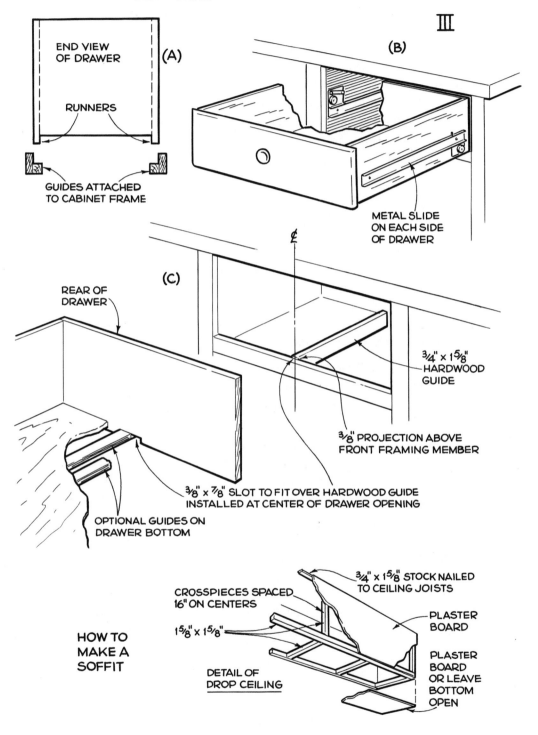

(A)

END VIEW
OF DRAWER

RUNNERS

GUIDES ATTACHED
TO CABINET FRAME

(B)

III

METAL SLIDE
ON EACH SIDE
OF DRAWER

(C)

REAR OF
DRAWER

℄

3/4" x 1 5/8"
HARDWOOD
GUIDE

3/8" PROJECTION ABOVE
FRONT FRAMING MEMBER

3/8" x 7/8" SLOT TO FIT OVER HARDWOOD GUIDE
INSTALLED AT CENTER OF DRAWER OPENING

OPTIONAL GUIDES ON
DRAWER BOTTOM

HOW TO
MAKE A
SOFFIT

CROSSPIECES SPACED
16" ON CENTERS

1 5/8" x 1 5/8"

3/4" x 1 5/8" STOCK NAILED
TO CEILING JOISTS

PLASTER
BOARD

PLASTER
BOARD
OR LEAVE
BOTTOM
OPEN

DETAIL OF
DROP CEILING

provision is made for a boxed-in section (soffit) between the top of the wall cabinets and the ceiling. This is done for the logical reason that space this far from the kitchen floor could not be used for storage of items the housewife frequently needs. She couldn't reach them without a stool. The popularity of the soffit also enables commercial cabinet builders to standardize the size of their cabinets.

But a soffit wastes space that might be put to use for dead storage. There's seldom enough of that kind of storage space in today's compact homes. In some modern kitchens, this area has simply been left open and used for display or ornamental kitchen items, with paint or paper on the wall above the cabinets. Construction probably will be easiest before the wall cabinets are in place. To make use of the space, install narrow drawers in place of the plaster-board facing—or custom design your wall cabinets to reach to the ceiling. Sliding doors are ideal for a soffit. At the sink area, where there usually are no wall cabinets above, overhead lighting can be concealed in the soffit.

Important Points About Wood

As a cabinet builder, you have a choice of three major materials— wood, plywood, and hardboard. You can build a complete cabinet of either wood or plywood—or combine plywood or hardboard with a wood frame. For cabinets, specify kiln-dried wood. Poorly seasoned stock will cause the best of joints to open up as it dries.

Some builders may want to limit their use of lumber stock in favor of the working ease provided by the panel materials, plywood and hardboard. But wood usually will still be needed for the framing members. Such parts call for 1 x 2's, 1 x 3's, 1 x 4's, and some 2 x 2's and 2 x 4's. These are nominal (or rough) size designations.

All dressed lumber is less than the rough size by which it usually is designated, the difference having been planed away in the process of dressing. Because of this, stock 1″ thick in its rough state actually measures nearer ¾″ after being dressed—and is frequently referred to as such. These variations, of course, do not apply to plywood.

Two Ways to Use the Soffit Area Decoratively

Rather than box in the wall space above wall cabinets, you can use it for display of decorative items — as shown above in the kitchen for a Georgia-Pacific model home, where the cabinets were made of flakeboard faced with red oak. Or if you prefer to enclose the soffit area, the Masonite Corporation suggests using its Pegboard as shown below.

Cabinet parts in the project drawings throughout this book usually are indicated in actual dimensions. In the materials lists, however, lumber stock is designated in nominal sizes as an aid to the builder in making lumber-yard purchases.

When possible, the cabinets utilize lumber stock in the width received to minimize ripping—or the need for jointing. For most wall cabinets, for example, 1″ x 12″ (nominal) stock will do nicely for sides, top, and bottom. Its actual dressed width of 11½″ gives adequate depth. Shelves, too, can often be made of stock widths.

Although most of the cabinets are presented as separate units, you will usually find it economical of material and time to frame and build adjoining ones as a single assembly. The sub-base on which a line of base cabinets rest should of course be a single unit. This can be made of 2 x 4's, 1 x 4's, or a combination of the two. The 3⅝″ actual dimension of the 4″ (nom.) stock establishes the height of the toe space. Combining several cabinets into one unit also may make it possible to use thin material, or perhaps nothing if partitions are not needed, in place of the ¾″ plywood generally specified for cabinet ends.

When combining two or more of the cabinet projects, it often will be possible to consolidate the separate materials lists into a more economical single one, making use of waste that may result from the individual lists. An hour spent with pencil and paper before buying materials should help you get only what you need. Lumber stock usually is sold in lengths in multiples of 2 feet up to about 16 feet. If your projects require 1″ x 4″ (nom.) stock in a total of, say 24 feet, you may wind up with less waste from one 8-foot length and one 16 than from two 12-foot lengths, or vice versa.

If you have facility with a sketching pencil, it would be well to assemble your complete kitchen visually before you begin to build. Choose the cabinets that you want, and then combine them into the space that you have available. An example of a completely sketched kitchen is found on the following two pages. These drawings originally appeared in "Flying Chips & Deltagram," a useful magazine for woodworkers published by Rockwell Manufacturing Company, Pittsburgh, Pa. The shallow sink drawer is one of several good ideas that you may want to borrow from these plans.

For most economical use of plywood panels, you should have a cutting plan before you pick up the saw. Squared paper will help you work this out. When ¾″ plywood is being used for a counter 25″ wide, the 23″ strip remaining from a 48″-wide panel can be utilized for the base cabinet ends. Make the cut so that the saw kerf falls within the 25″ width. The edging that you'll want to apply to the counter will compensate for the saw-kerf loss.

Facts to Remember About Plywood

There are two major types of plywood—lumber core and veneer. Lumber core has a fairly thick middle layer of solid wood with a ⅟₁₆″ layer on each side and a ⅟₂₈″ face veneer. In all ways except cost, this is the most desirable for cabinet work. On the edge, veneer plywood shows from three to seven layers. In thickness, it ranges from ⅛″ to ¾″. Lumber core usually begins at ½″ and goes up to 1⅜″.

Plywood is divided further into interior and exterior types, made with different kinds of adhesives. More expensive, the exterior type will stand up under permanent exposure without going to pieces. In a kitchen, this type would be a good choice for a sink counter. For other uses, the interior type would do.

Plywood is available in a series of grades with facings of fine hardwoods—birch, butternut, cherry, elm, gum, ash, mahogany, walnut, maple, oak, and many others. But fir plywood is the most common and most economical. The panels—usually 4′ x 8′, although you can get other sizes—are clearly marked as to type (interior or exterior) and grade.

Grade is determined by the quality of both faces. Faces are rated as good, sound, or utility. A good face is a perfect piece of veneer over the entire panel. A sound face may consist of two pieces of veneer per panel, perfectly joined but with small imperfections such as patches, stains, or sapwood. A utility face may have knots, pitch pockets, knot holes, and small splits that impair the strength but not the looks of the panel. Another grading system designates faces as A, B, C, and D. Under this, an A-A panel would have two good faces, an A-C panel a good face and utility back, and so on.

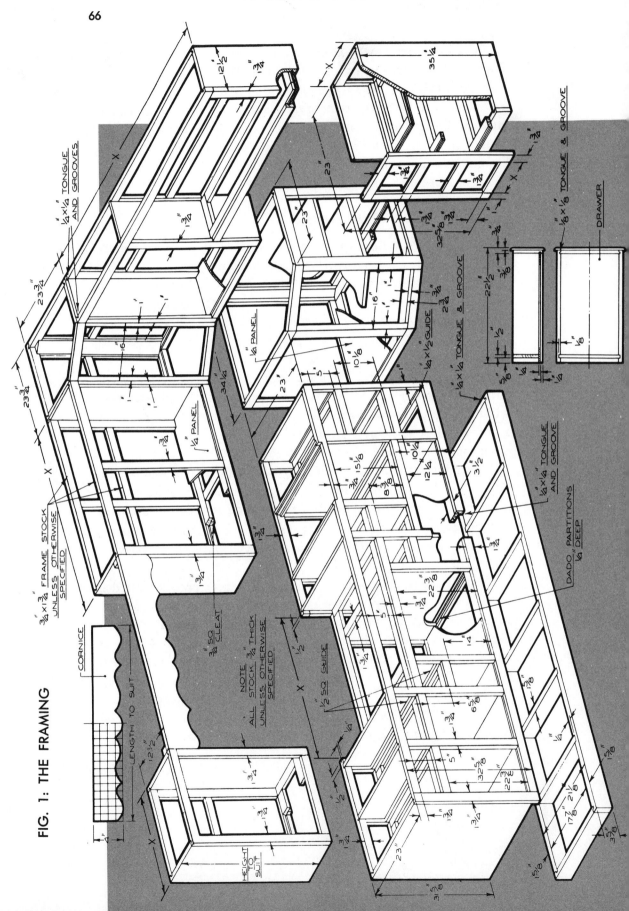

FIG. 1: THE FRAMING

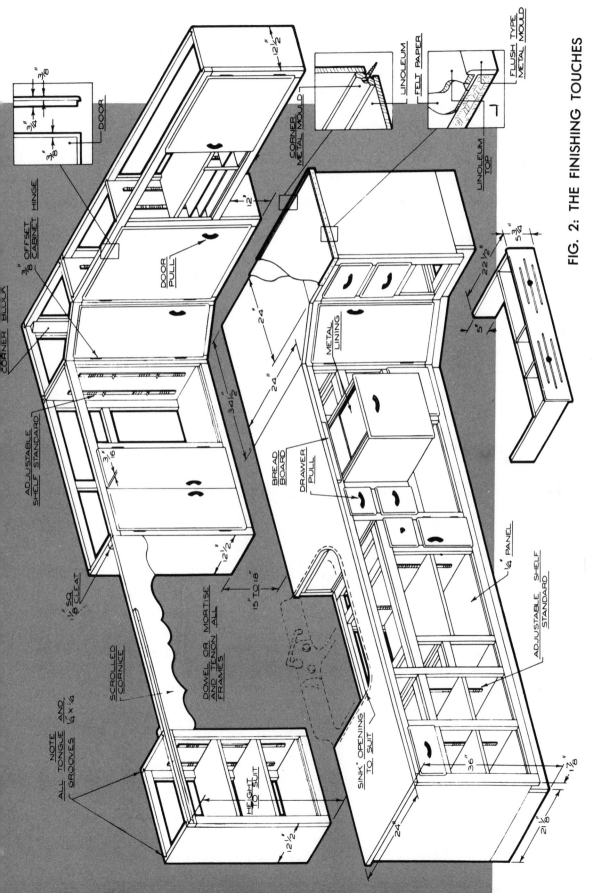

FIG. 2: THE FINISHING TOUCHES

Drawings courtesy of Rockwell Manufacturing Company

A fir plywood panel may have any combination of faces. The top grade has a good face on each side and may be marked G2S. Kitchen cabinets would rarely require this top grade. Even where both sides will show, as in a cabinet door, a money-saving alternate is G1S, good on one side and sound on the other. If cabinets are to be painted, the sound-two-sides (S2S) or even S1S will reduce the materials cost even more. The wallboard grade (WB), which has a sound face and a utility back, will do nicely for cabinet backs. Sheathing (SH) has two utility faces.

Plywood comes with many different surface treatments. You can also get it with hardboard bonded to the face. This combines the surface smoothness of hardboard with the strength of plywood. Other plywood panels have plastic impregnated or plastic sheet facings, making them especially suitable for counter tops, since grease, alcohol, ammonia, fruit juices, and boiling water will not mar the surface. In some cases, plastic sheets are laminated over hardwood plywood, providing a durable natural finish that needs no further attention. Laminates also come in a variety of colors.

Another material that has been attracting considerable attention in recent years for cabinet building is flakeboard overlaid with a hardwood veneer. This is substantially cheaper than most lumber-core plywood. It also has the advantage of being more stable than wood in the presence or absence of moisture.

How to Hide Plywood Edges

Because of the plies, exposed edges and corner joints in plywood construction present an appearance problem. You should tackle this first in the design stage, planning the cabinet to minimize the number of visible edges. Edge grain can be hidden in a number of ways. One procedure is to butt a wood strip (half round will do in some cases) to the edge with brads and glue. Or, if you have power equipment, lock the strip on with a tongue and groove. In addition, a strip of veneer can be glued in place. A triangular strip ripped off the edge at 45 degrees, with the cut slanting toward the rear, can be reversed and then bradded and glued back on the edge to bring the bottom surface to the front. A 90-degree V-cut underneath, starting from the panel edge, will yield a 45-degree strip that can be swung down from the top against the angled edge. This makes a front edge that matches the top. The method has some disadvantage, in that the width of the panel is reduced in an amount equal to its own thickness. But all such tricks are usually unnecessary if the plywood is to be painted. Just force plastic composition wood into the edge grain, let it set, and sand the surface smooth.

At corners, the plies can be hidden by using a miter joint, splined or reinforced with corner blocks. A rabbet joint with a single-ply overlap looks good enough for even the finest construction. Quarter-round can be used to hide two plywood edges at a corner. Assemble the plywood panels over a frame or support them with inside corner blocks. Stop the edges of the panels short before they reach the corner. Then fill the corner with the quarter-round, butting one of its flat faces against each plywood edge. Similarly, the plywood can be joined to a corner post with tongue and groove.

Types of Hardboard

Hardboard, the other major panel material, comes in various types, but only two, standard and tempered, are of major interest to the cabinet builder. The tempered type is recommended for use where hard wear is expected and where high or changing humidity conditions may prevail. A third type, with a smooth finish on both sides, would be an excellent choice for a single-panel cabinet door or for sliding doors. Standard and tempered hardboards come in thicknesses of $\frac{1}{8}''$, $\frac{3}{16}''$, $\frac{1}{4}''$, and $\frac{5}{16}''$, in panels 48" wide and in a choice of lengths. The two-faced type, $\frac{1}{8}''$ and $\frac{3}{16}''$ thick, is commonly available in panels 60" wide.

The accompanying page of sketches, adapted from plans drawn by the Masonite Corporation, shows how extensively tempered hardboard (Presdwood) can be used in cabinets. Supported by a wood frame, tempered hardboard serves as a counter covering. On a frame of (nom.) 1 x 2 material a sheet of hardboard becomes a shelf surface.

When a door is made by sandwiching a wood frame between two hardboard panels, ventilation slots should be cut in the frame as indicated. This allows air to circulate inside the door, causing the

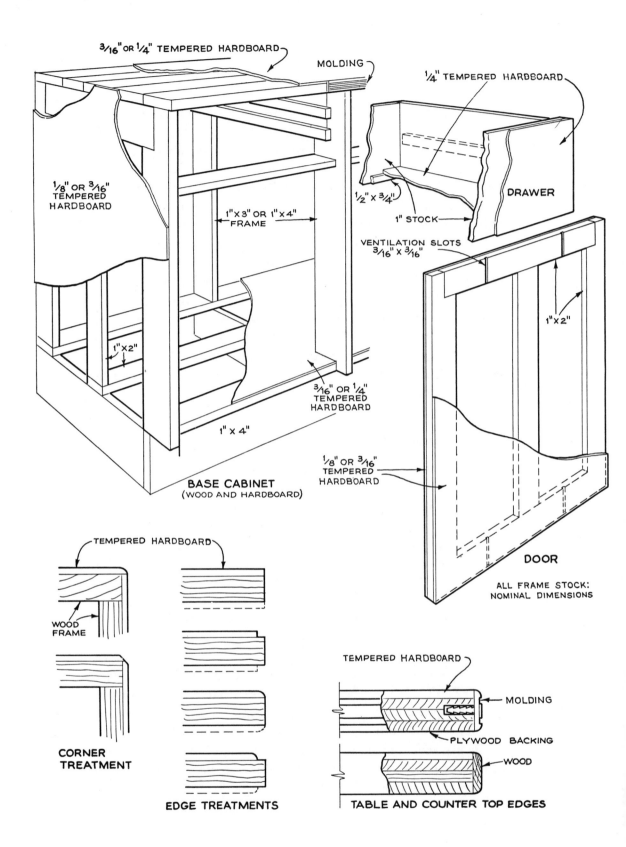

3/16" OR 1/4" TEMPERED HARDBOARD

MOLDING

1/4" TEMPERED HARDBOARD

1/8" OR 3/16" TEMPERED HARDBOARD

1"x3" OR 1"x4" FRAME

DRAWER

1/2" x 3/4"

1" STOCK

VENTILATION SLOTS
3/16" x 3/16"

1"x2"

1"x2"

3/16" OR 1/4" TEMPERED HARDBOARD

1" X 4"

BASE CABINET
(WOOD AND HARDBOARD)

1/8" OR 3/16" TEMPERED HARDBOARD

DOOR

ALL FRAME STOCK:
NOMINAL DIMENSIONS

TEMPERED HARDBOARD

WOOD FRAME

CORNER TREATMENT

EDGE TREATMENTS

TEMPERED HARDBOARD

MOLDING

PLYWOOD BACKING

WOOD

TABLE AND COUNTER TOP EDGES

hardboard to react equally on both surfaces to humidity changes. In the plans, drawer construction calls for a box of 1″ (nom.) stock with a hardboard bottom and facing. The drawer rides on wood slides that fit between parallel guides in the cabinet. Corners or exposed edges of hardboard can be beveled or rounded with sandpaper or a plane.

When sawing hardboard, turn up the surface that will be exposed. This will avoid scratches if the panel should slide on the supports. A sharper edge is also obtained on the upturned face. If you use a hand saw, the crosscut type with 8 to 12 points per inch and a No. 6 set is usually the most suitable for straight cutting. For most drilling operations, a twist drill is preferred to an auger bit.

(Since this book was first written, decorative lip moldings have become available to solve the plywood and hardboard edge problem. One is made by the Decra-Mold Division of Agee Products Corp., P.O. Box 75248, Oklahoma City, Okla. 73107.)

What About the Counters?

Durable counters can be provided for base cabinets in a number of ways and using a variety of materials. Least expensive of available materials is linoleum, followed closely by vinyl plastic. Both of these are attractive and easily installed, but they lack the durability of such other coverings as stainless steel, ceramic tile, wood, and laminated plastic (Formica, Micarta, Textolite, Nevamar).

Whatever material you choose, you'd do well to include at least a small section of hard maple in your counter as a cutting board. You can now buy these boards as prefab counters in various short lengths, the maple being laminated from strips 1½″ thick, including a 4″ backsplash. If your local building-supply house can't help you, try a Sears Roebuck store or catalogue.

You can also get, from the same sources, several types of prefab plastic countertops with a rear splash and front lip molded in. These come in stock sizes for straight counter runs, corners, and with sink cutouts. Matching end caps and splash strips finish off the counter.

Lumber dealers can sell you some of the laminated plastic materials already bonded to ¾″ plywood or other material, sometimes with the top and backsplash combined in one unbroken piece. You then apply a metal molding or piece of matching plastic to the edges of the counter and the top of the backsplash. You may also want to attempt the bonding yourself. Your lumber dealer may have printed instructions from one of the companies that make laminated plastics.

What About Installing the Sink?

A supplier should be able to furnish a countertop with an opening to suit the sink you have chosen, or perhaps he'll cut it for you. If you install the sink yourself, ask for instructions when you buy it.

8

Special-Purpose Wall Cabinets

Wall cabinets are the device by which real economy of floor space is achieved and the kitchen is drawn together into a unit small enough to cut down the housewife's steps. The list of supplies and equipment needed in the ordinary kitchen is so extensive that only by stacking up part of them in cupboards or shelves, at or above chest height, can the working area be kept compact. Important too is the fact that wall cabinets can offer storage at a height where the housewife needs only to reach forward and up. The more she can store in wall cabinets the less bending she will have to do in pulling what she needs from a base cabinet. The easy reach arc of a housewife standing at work normally embraces only the first row of drawers under the work counter. Storage below that level therefore may require extra effort. Bear these points in mind as you do your planning, and try to arrange for the most convenient and work-saving storage areas.

Include all the wall cabinets you can in your kitchen. The following pages offer various types, each designed for a specialized job.

OVER-REFRIGERATOR CABINET

Uses

This cabinet is a convenient place to store canned juices that eventually will go into the refrigerator for chilling. Large economy-size cans fit nicely at the rear of the bottom shelf, smaller sizes go above and on the two door shelves. Jellies and jams can be kept here too. Since the cans are aligned only one deep, everything in the cabinet comes into view when the doors swing open. Even though the refrigerator top is high, the cabinet door shelves bring their contents within reach.

Materials

1″ x 12″ (nom.) stock (12 linear feet) to make—

    2 pc. 14½″ long — ends.

    2 pc. 26″ long — top and bottom.

    1 pc. 5½″ x 24½″ — shelf.

    4 pc. 5¼″ x 9½″ — door-shelf bottoms.

¼″ plywood or hardboard to make—

    8 pc. 1½″ x 5¼″⎫
                    ⎬ door-shelf sides.
    4 pc. 1½″ x 10″⎭

1″ x 2″ (nom.) stock (10 linear feet) to make—

    2 pc. 16″ long — facing strips.

    4 pc. 10″ long — door battens.

    2 pc. 6″ long — shelf cleats.

    1 pc. 26″ long — cross rail.

1″ x 4″ (nom.) pine tongue-and-groove (12 linear feet) to make—

    8 pc. 16″ long — doors.

2 pr. H-hinges.

2 door knobs.

2 pr. cabinet spring catches.

4 corner braces 2″ x 2″.

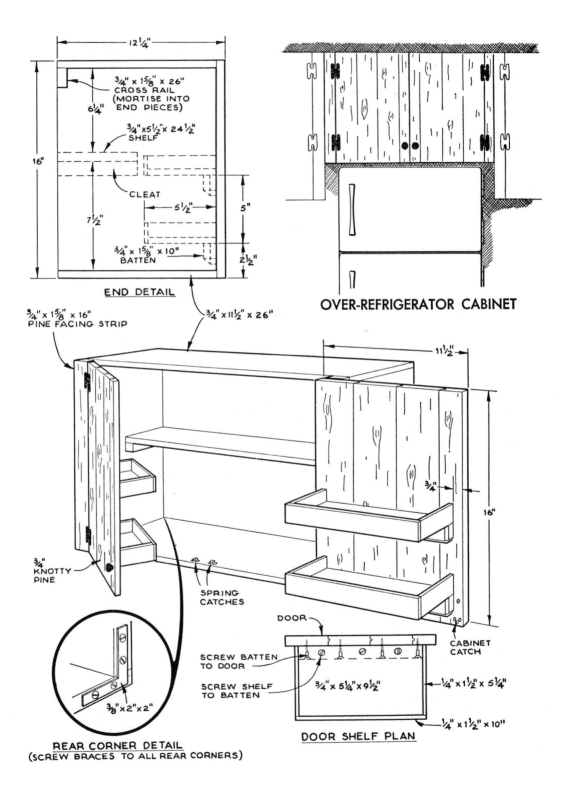

12¼"

¾" x 1⅝" x 26"
CROSS RAIL
(MORTISE INTO
END PIECES)

6¼"

¾" x 5½" x 24½"
SHELF

16"

CLEAT

5½"

5"

7½"

¾" x 1⅝" x 10"
BATTEN

2½"

END DETAIL

OVER-REFRIGERATOR CABINET

¾" x 1⅝" x 16"
PINE FACING STRIP

¾" x 11½" x 26"

11½"

¾"

16"

¾"
KNOTTY
PINE

SPRING
CATCHES

CABINET
CATCH

REAR CORNER DETAIL
(SCREW BRACES TO ALL REAR CORNERS)

⅜" x 2" x 2"

DOOR

SCREW BATTEN
TO DOOR

SCREW SHELF
TO BATTEN

¾" x 5¼" x 9½"

¼" x 1½" x 5¼"

¼" x 1½" x 10"

DOOR SHELF PLAN

Pointers for Building

A cabinet as simple as this can be built with a hammer, saw, square, screwdriver, and twist drill. In sawing the pieces, be careful to make square cuts. Mortise the ends for the cross rail by marking with the squared end of the rail and sawing inside the lines. All assembly can be with wood screws, countersunk and filled, although glue can be used if desired. Position and attach the two cleats for the middle shelf before assembling the cabinet proper. Screw the bottom to the ends, the middle shelf to the cleats, and the top to the ends, in that order. After making sure the assembly is square, screw a metal brace to each rear corner for extra strength if you wish. These will not be needed if you nail on a back of thin plywood or hardboard. The back can be set into rabbets cut in the rear edges of the cabinet top, bottom, and sides. But it actually is not necessary for you to go to the trouble of cutting rabbets. Just nail the back on, making its edges flush with the cabinet sides.

If you plan to give the doors a natural finish, use dowel plugs to hide the heads of the screws with which you attach the two pine facing strips. Two of the door strips will have to be ripped to make the desired 11½" width. Battens serve the double function of holding the door sections together and providing a base for the shelves. Beveling the edges of the battens will give the job a more professional look. Because the door shelves must support considerable weight, it would be advisable to use both glue and screws to attach them to the battens.

Alternate Construction

As you might expect, any cabinet can be built in different ways. The second page of drawings shows variations you may prefer in this case. All parts can be cut from a 4' x 4' panel of plywood. The wide shelf will probably turn the rear area into dead storage space, but some housewives may prefer this.

Polished and lacquered, the brass sash rod suggested for the door shelf would add an attractive touch to natural pine doors. Use a hacksaw to cut it to the desired lengths. Screw the dowel posts to the shelf after the rods have been forced into holes drilled for them.

The sketch of the rabbet joint illustrates a principle often used to

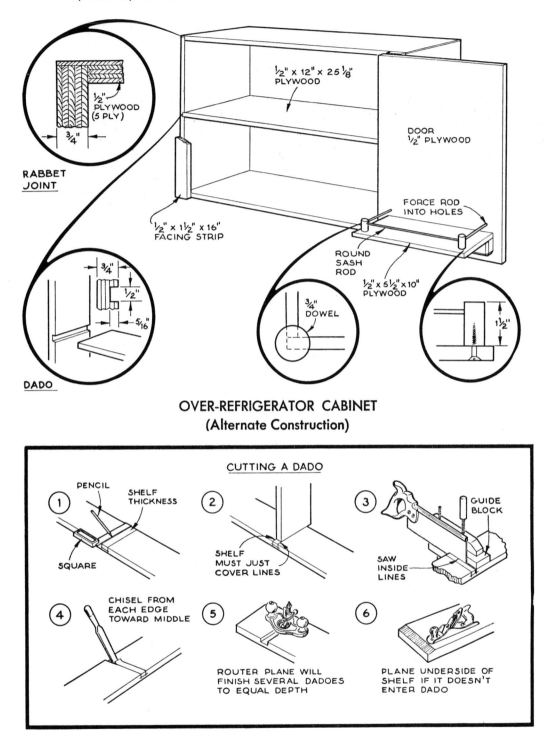

½" PLYWOOD (5 PLY)

¾"

RABBET JOINT

½" x 12" x 25 ⅛" PLYWOOD

DOOR ½" PLYWOOD

FORCE ROD INTO HOLES

½" x 1½" x 16" FACING STRIP

ROUND SASH ROD

½" x 5½" x 10" PLYWOOD

¾" ½" 5/16"

DADO

¾" DOWEL

1½"

OVER-REFRIGERATOR CABINET
(Alternate Construction)

CUTTING A DADO

PENCIL SHELF THICKNESS

① SQUARE

② SHELF MUST JUST COVER LINES

③ GUIDE BLOCK   SAW INSIDE LINES

④ CHISEL FROM EACH EDGE TOWARD MIDDLE

⑤ ROUTER PLANE WILL FINISH SEVERAL DADOES TO EQUAL DEPTH

⑥ PLANE UNDERSIDE OF SHELF IF IT DOESN'T ENTER DADO

disguise a plywood edge. Only one ply is left when the rabbet is cut. When the joint is fitted, this results in just a thin line showing along the edge. The joint can be glued and nailed after being carefully fitted together.

Cutting a dado to support a shelf is a more difficult bit of construction than tacking on a cleat, but a dado eliminates the down cracks left at the shelf ends when cleats are used. Food particles collect in such cracks and attract insects. (A dado runs across the wood grain, a groove runs with it.) With care, a dado in solid stock can be completed with a chisel after being sawed to depth, but a router plane will give a surer fit. In plywood, the chisel must be used cautiously or it may chip out a ply to an unwanted depth. Everything considered, a dado cutter on a circular saw is a worthwhile investment for the man who expects to do any extensive dado cutting. A dado should be a tight fit. Join the two members with glue, holding them with clamps until the glue has set.

In the sequence of dado-cutting operations shown in the sketches on the preceding page, you can finish the job with the use of a chisel as shown in step 4. A router plane is a useful tool, but you can get by without it. If the end of the shelf doesn't quite enter the dado, plane or sand off the under edge until it does.

LID AND PAN RACK

Uses

Since this cabinet could go either near the range or in the mixing center, you may want one for each location. Lids and flat pans such as pie tins or small cooky sheets are stored upright. Storage bins of two different widths offer a choice for pans and lids of different thickness. The shelves slant downward to the rear to keep round tins from falling out. The spice rack and storage area on the bottom shelf can be used for other items frequently needed at the range or mixing center. This cabinet was adapted from a design of the makers of Malarkey plywoods.

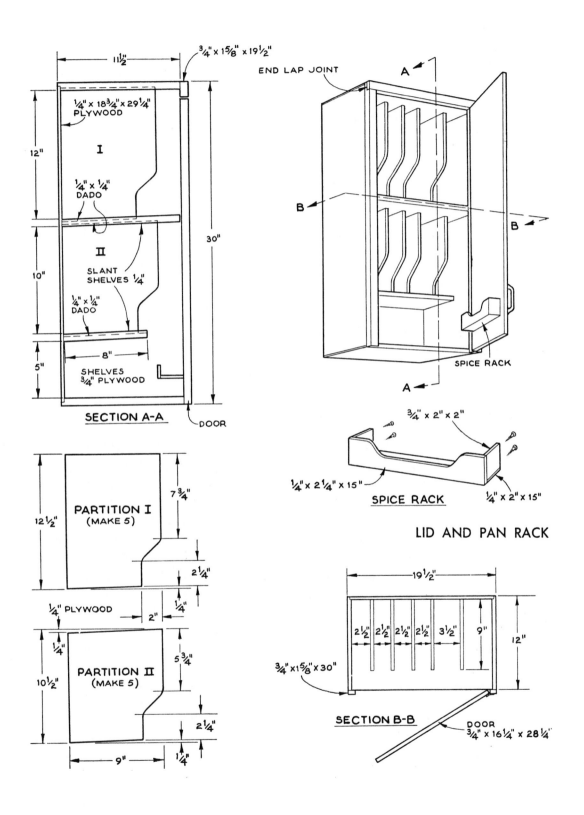

$\frac{3}{4}$" x 1$\frac{5}{8}$" x 19$\frac{1}{2}$"

END LAP JOINT

A

11$\frac{1}{2}$"

$\frac{1}{4}$" x 18$\frac{3}{4}$" x 29$\frac{1}{4}$"
PLYWOOD

I

12"

$\frac{1}{4}$" x $\frac{1}{4}$"
DADO

II

10"

SLANT
SHELVES $\frac{1}{4}$"

$\frac{1}{4}$" x $\frac{1}{4}$"
DADO

30"

8"

5"

SHELVES
$\frac{3}{4}$" PLYWOOD

SECTION A-A

DOOR

B

B

SPICE RACK

A

$\frac{3}{4}$" x 2" x 2"

$\frac{1}{4}$" x 2$\frac{1}{4}$" x 15"

SPICE RACK

$\frac{1}{4}$" x 2" x 15"

LID AND PAN RACK

7$\frac{3}{4}$"

12$\frac{1}{2}$"

PARTITION I
(MAKE 5)

2$\frac{1}{4}$"

$\frac{1}{4}$"

$\frac{1}{4}$" PLYWOOD

2"

$\frac{1}{4}$"

10$\frac{1}{2}$"

PARTITION II
(MAKE 5)

5$\frac{3}{4}$"

2$\frac{1}{4}$"

9"

$\frac{1}{4}$"

19$\frac{1}{2}$"

2$\frac{1}{2}$" 2$\frac{1}{2}$" 2$\frac{1}{2}$" 2$\frac{1}{2}$" 3$\frac{1}{2}$"

9"

12"

$\frac{3}{4}$" x 1$\frac{5}{8}$" x 30"

SECTION B-B

DOOR
$\frac{3}{4}$" x 16$\frac{1}{4}$" x 28$\frac{1}{4}$"

Materials

¾″ plywood (4′ x 4′ panel) to make—

   2 pc. 12″ x 30″ — sides.

   2 pc. 12″ x 19½″ — top and bottom.

   1 pc. 12″ x 18½″ — top shelf.

   1 pc.   8″ x 18½″ — bottom shelf.

   1 pc. 16¼″ x 28¼″ — door.

   2 pc.   2″ x 2″ — rack ends.

¼″ plywood (4′ x 4′ panel) to make—

   1 pc. 18¾″ x 29¼″ — back.

   5 pc.   9″ x 10½″ — lower partitions.

   5 pc.   9″ x 12½″ — upper partitions.

   1 pc.   2¼″ x 15″ — rack front.

   1 pc.   2″ x 15″ — rack bottom.

2 pc. ¾″ x 1⅝″ x 30″ pine — front facing strips.

1 pc. ¾″ x 1⅝″ x 19½″ pine — top facing strip.

Pointers for Building

Cut ⅜″ x ¾″ rabbets in the ends of the top and bottom pieces to take the side pieces. Rabbet all four of these pieces ¼″ x ⅜″ for the ¼″ plywood back. Cut ¾″ dadoes ¼″ deep in the sides for the two shelves, slanting them as shown. Stopped dadoes are indicated in both the top and bottom surface of the upper shelf for the partitions, but these can be full dadoes if you want the partitions to be adjustable. Corresponding dadoes also are needed in the 8″ bottom shelf and the under side of the cabinet top. Cut the partitions ¼″ off square as indicated in the drawing. To get exactly the same angle on all the partitions, clamp them together and cut them all at once. After fitting the partitions into the dadoes, position the shelves between the sides of the cabinet and you will find that they slant downward toward the rear as desired.

The spice rack can be attached with flathead screws sunk in the face of the door. Hide the screw heads with putty or other filler.

Special-Purpose Wall Cabinets

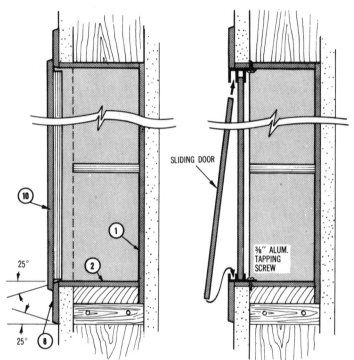

HINGED DOOR SECTION A-A

10

1

2

25°

25°

8

SLIDING DOOR SECTION

SLIDING DOOR

⅜" ALUM.
TAPPING
SCREW

RECESSED WALL CABINET

Here's a real space saver. The cabinet is located in the wall, between the studs. The depth is just right for storage of small and medium cans. You can install either swinging or sliding doors, use plastic-finished paneling to line the cabinet or make the doors. For complete plans and instructions, send a post card to Handyman Plans, Marlite Paneling, P.O. Box 250, Dover, Ohio 44622. Ask for Plan No. 105.

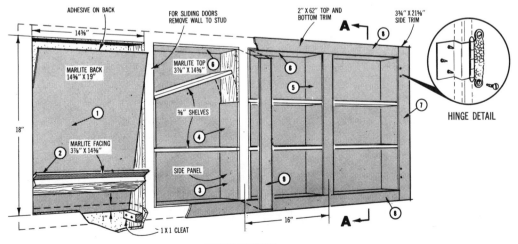

ADHESIVE ON BACK

14⅜"

MARLITE BACK
14⅜" X 19"

1

MARLITE FACING
3⅞" X 14⅜"

2

18"

1"

1 X 1 CLEAT

FOR SLIDING DOORS
REMOVE WALL TO STUD

MARLITE TOP
3⅞" X 14⅜" 6

⅜" SHELVES

4

SIDE PANEL

3

2" X 62" TOP AND
BOTTOM TRIM

A

6

5

5

9

16"

A

3¾" X 21⅝"
SIDE TRIM

8

7

9

HINGE DETAIL

CABINET ASSEMBLY

SLIDING-RACK CABINET

This easily-built special-purpose cabinet is a good candidate for installing above a hood/fan unit over a range, above a wall oven or refrigerator, or over a sink. In these top-of-the-wall locations, shown in the handsome Tappan kitchen on the facing page, the housewife would have finger-tip access to items stored in the sliding rack. Other seldom-used items can go into the tuckaway shelf, and tall bottles fit into the compartment at the left. Adjust the cabinet dimensions to fit the space available, that is the overall height and width.

Spice rack slides back and forth to uncover the larger items stored in tuckaway shelf behind it.

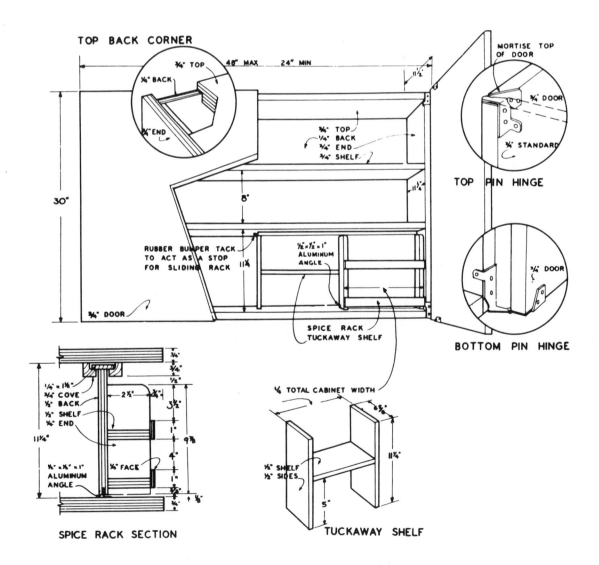

TOP BACK CORNER

MORTISE TOP OF DOOR

TOP PIN HINGE

BOTTOM PIN HINGE

RUBBER BUMPER TACK TO ACT AS A STOP FOR SLIDING RACK

SPICE RACK TUCKAWAY SHELF

SPICE RACK SECTION

TUCKAWAY SHELF

Three locations are seen in the Tappan kitchen above where the sliding rack wall cabinet on the facing page might be installed—above the sink, above the range hood, and above a wall oven. If you already have cabinets there, build in spice rack and tuckaway shelf.

SLIDING DOOR CABINET

Uses

Because swinging doors on wall cabinets frequently present a head-bumping hazard, cabinets with sliding doors are preferred by many home owners. In some cases, too, sliding doors offer a solution to a space problem where conventional doors would not open fully. The cabinet shown could be used for general utility anywhere in the kitchen. If desired, sliding doors could be adapted to many other cabinets in this book. This one is presented only as an example of what it is possible to do. The same principles can be used on base cabinets too where that may be desirable.

Materials

1″ x 12″ (nom.) stock (16 linear feet) to make—

    2 pc. 36″ long — top and bottom.

    2 pc. 30″ long — ends.

    2 pc. 10″ x 35″ — shelves.

1/4″ plywood or hardboard (4′ x 4′ panel) to make—

    2 pc. 18″ x 29″ — doors.

    1 pc. 30″ x 36″ — back (if desired).

11′ 3/4″ x 7/8″ cove.

1 pc. 1/4″ x 1/2″ x 28″ pine — door strip.

2 door pulls.

Pointers for Building

The cabinet itself can be built by any conventional construction method. Rabbet or butt joints can be used at the corners, with cleats, dadoes, metal standards or movable pegs supporting the shelves.

Plastic or metal door tracks made sliding doors a cinch. But you can also make the tracks. If power equipment is available, cut a 1/4″ x 5/16″ rabbet on the front edge of the bottom, and 1/4″ behind this cut a 1/4″ x 5/16″ groove. Cove mold or a 1/4″ x 7/8″

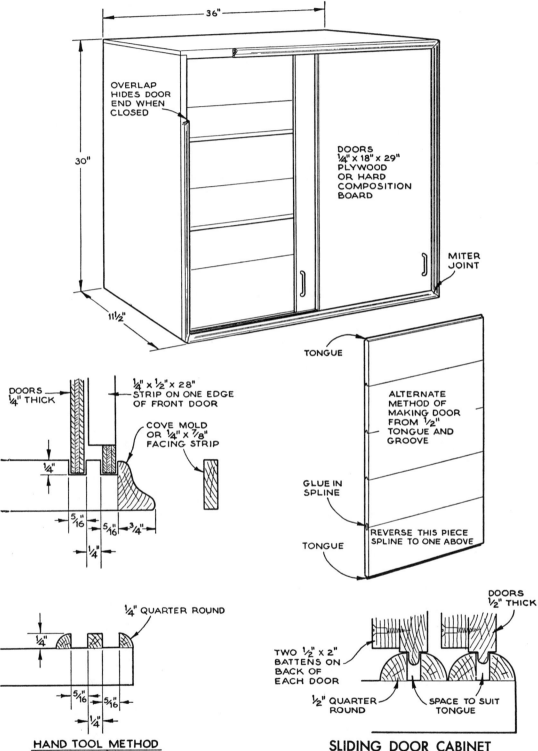

36"

OVERLAP
HIDES DOOR
END WHEN
CLOSED

30"

DOORS
1/4" x 18" x 29"
PLYWOOD
OR HARD
COMPOSITION
BOARD

MITER
JOINT

11½"

DOORS
1/4" THICK

1/4" x 1/2" x 28"
STRIP ON ONE EDGE
OF FRONT DOOR

COVE MOLD
OR 1/4" x 7/8"
FACING STRIP

1/4"

5/16"   5/16" 3/4"

1/4"

TONGUE

ALTERNATE
METHOD OF
MAKING DOOR
FROM 1/2"
TONGUE AND
GROOVE

GLUE IN
SPLINE

TONGUE

REVERSE THIS PIECE
SPLINE TO ONE ABOVE

1/4" QUARTER ROUND

1/4"

5/16"   5/16"

1/4"

HAND TOOL METHOD

DOORS
1/2" THICK

TWO 1/2" x 2"
BATTENS ON
BACK OF
EACH DOOR

1/2" QUARTER
ROUND

SPACE TO SUIT
TONGUE

SLIDING DOOR CABINET

pine facing strip nailed and glued to the edge closes up the rabbet as a track for the front door. Some may choose to dispense with the cove or face strips and cut two grooves as the door tracks. On the under side of the cabinet top, cut corresponding tracks—but make these $\frac{1}{16}''$ deeper. Thus, when the doors at rest are just high enough to rise $\frac{1}{32}''$ into the upper tracks, it will be possible to lift up and pull them out of the cabinet to clean dust or food particles from the tracks. Cut enough off the 29'' indicated length of the doors to make this possible.

The hand-tool method of making the tracks is equally satisfactory. In this case, cut the doors first, making them $\frac{1}{16}''$ shorter than the inside vertical dimension of the cabinet. Then use the doors as a guide in positioning the track strips, putting a thin piece of cardboard between door and strip to assure good clearance for sliding. Using a sanding block, reduce the height of the lower track members sufficiently to allow the doors to be pressed into place—or pulled out for cleaning of the grooves. The chance of dirt collecting in the grooves is a disadvantage of sliding doors.

Make the sliding doors $1\frac{1}{2}''$ wider than half the inside width of the cabinet. This allows adequate overlap when they are closed, and provides space for mounting the pull on the inside door. For smooth operation, sand the door edges with progressively finer paper. Finish with two coats of shellac, each well rubbed with the finest steel wool. Then rub a light coating of candle wax on them. Smooth and wax the tracks in the same way.

Making the doors from tongue-and-groove lumber results in a heavier construction, and the method is best suited to large cabinets. But some people may pick it for the sake of appearance. Vertical battens, screwed in place, join the door parts together. Tracks might be made of $\frac{1}{4}''$ quarter-round instead of $\frac{1}{2}''$.

Many builders may prefer to use $\frac{1}{8}''$ hardboard for the doors instead of the $\frac{1}{4}''$ shown. In a cabinet this size, the $\frac{1}{8}''$ material will have sufficient rigidity for easy use. The smooth surface of hardboard makes it ideal for sliding-door use.

Rather than build his own sliding doors from scratch, the builder may find it an advantage to shop around and see if he can make use of one of the commercial sliding-door assemblies, especially the hardware.

ADJUSTABLE SHELF CABINET

Uses

Shelves that adjust up and down permit a housewife to make more efficient use of available cabinet space. If items of equal height are grouped, dead space above can be eliminated and devoted to an upper or lower shelf. In the cabinet shown, you could have two or even three movable shelves supported on pegs, instead of only one. Kitchen planners would be smart to settle on adjustable shelves for every cabinet in the room. In this case, the shelf dividers also are adjustable.

The cabinet's place in the kitchen would depend on what is to be stored in it, but the dividers make it a good candidate for the lids and flat pans required at the range or mix center. Without the dividers and open shelf below, and with shelf pegs or metal standards running the full height, the cabinet could be used as the design for all the general-purpose units in the kitchen.

Materials

1″ x 12″ (nom.) stock (22 linear feet) to make—

 2 pc. 36″ long — sides.

 3 pc. 22½″ long — shelves and bottom.

 2 pc. 10½″ x 35¼″ — doors.

 1 pc. 12¼″ x 22½″ — top (nail or glue ¾″ x ¾″ strip to rear edge).

 1 pc. 5½″ x 22½″ — open shelf.

 2 pc. 5½″ x 8¾″ — shelf ends.

2 pc. 1″ x 2″ (nom.) stock 36″ long — face strips.

¼″ plywood (4′ x 4′ panel) to make—

 1 pc. 24″ x 36″ — back.

 7 pc. 11″ x 16″ — dividers.

2 pc. 2″ x 4″ stock 5″ long — shelf supports.

¼″ dowel 5″ long.

2 pr. hinges. 2 door pulls. 2 cabinet catches.

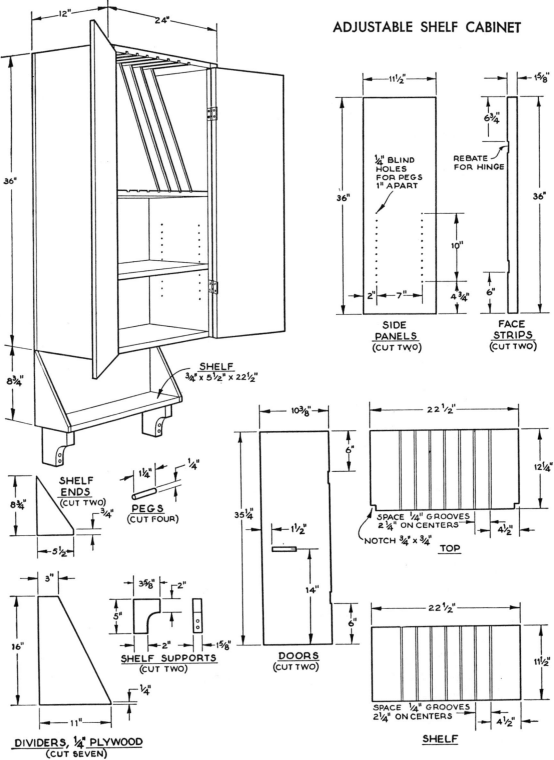

ADJUSTABLE SHELF CABINET

12"

24"

36"

8¾"

SHELF
¾" x 5½" x 22½"

SIDE PANELS
(CUT TWO)

11½"

36"

¼" BLIND HOLES FOR PEGS 1" APART

10"

2" 7" 4¾"

FACE STRIPS
(CUT TWO)

1⅝"

6¾"

REBATE FOR HINGE

36"

6"

SHELF ENDS
(CUT TWO)

8¾"

¾"

5½"

PEGS
(CUT FOUR)

1¼" ¼"

DIVIDERS, ¼" PLYWOOD
(CUT SEVEN)

3"

16"

11"

¼"

SHELF SUPPORTS
(CUT TWO)

3⅝" 2"

5"

2" 1⅝"

DOORS
(CUT TWO)

10⅜"

35¼"

1½"

14"

6"

6"

TOP

22½"

12¼"

SPACE ¼" GROOVES 2¼" ON CENTERS

4½"

NOTCH ¾" x ¾"

SHELF

22½"

11½"

SPACE ¼" GROOVES 2¼" ON CENTERS

4½"

Pointers for Building

The top, notched ¾″ x ¾″ at the front corners for the face strips, is butted between the sides, extending ¾″ in front of them. The shelves can be cut to identical 22½″ lengths and the fixed one butted between the sides or supported on cleats. The fixed shelf could also be cut 23″ long and dadoed in place. Grooves for the dividers under the cabinet top and on the upper surface of the fixed shelf must match exactly as to spacing. Locate the top edge of the fixed shelf 16½″ from the upper end of the side pieces. Locate the holes for the adjustable shelf pegs with a sharp pencil and center-punch them for exact drilling. Drill the holes ½″ deep. Screwed in place, or simply nailed, the ¼″ plywood back gives rigidity to the entire cabinet. But here, as in many other cabinets in the book, you may find it possible to omit a back to conserve material and cut costs, letting the kitchen wall serve as the back.

The open shelf below the main cabinet is built as a separate unit. After cutting the parts, nail them together. Four screws about 3″ long will attach the shelf to the wall. If you wish, this shelf can be used elsewhere in the kitchen.

COMBINATION WALL CABINET

Uses

This wide wall cabinet combines storage facilities sometimes found in two separate units. Its adjustable vertical dividers keep pie and cake pans and pot lids handy and tidy. Its lower shelves, adjustable for height, serve as a cupboard for packaged baking and cooking supplies and a variety of staples. Set between the sink and refrigerator, the wall cabinet and a companion base cabinet form an efficient baking and mixing center.

Materials

1″ x 12″ (nom.) stock (36 linear feet) to make—

  2 pc. 36″ long — sides.

  1 pc. 38½″ long — top (with ¾″ x ¾″ strip glued to rear).

  4 pc. 38½″ long — shelves.

  4 pc. 35¼″ long — doors.

  1 pc. 8¾″ long — support for dividers.

1″ x 2″ (nom.) stock (12 linear feet) to make—

  3 pc. 36″ long — hinging strips.

  2 pc. ¾″ x ⅞″ x 11″ — shelf cleats.

¼″ plywood (4′ x 4′ panel) to make—

  1 pc. 36″ x 40″ — cabinet back.

  5 pc. 8¼″ x 9¾″ — shelf dividers.

10 dowels ¼″ x 1¼″ — shelf pegs.

3 pr. 1½″ x 1½″ cabinet hinges.

Pointers for Building

To save work, this cabinet uses the shelving full width for the sides, the bottom and the shelves. The width of the top board can be increased by 3/4″ to bring its front edge out flush with the upright hinging strips by tacking or gluing a fill strip on the rear edge.

When the sides are in place, the notches form a recess for the top ends of the far left and far right hinging strips. Setting the strips back this way provides an overhang for the doors. Front edges of the shelves below serve as door stops.

Cleats support the one fixed shelf. In boring the peg holes for the other shelves, be careful about horizontal alignment of each pair or the shelves will not rest level.

If available, a dado plane will make quick work of the grooves in which the dividers rest in the fixed shelf and the upright piece set into the rear edge. For an easier job, and as satisfactory one, use the alternative method of forming grooves by tacking down parallel strips.

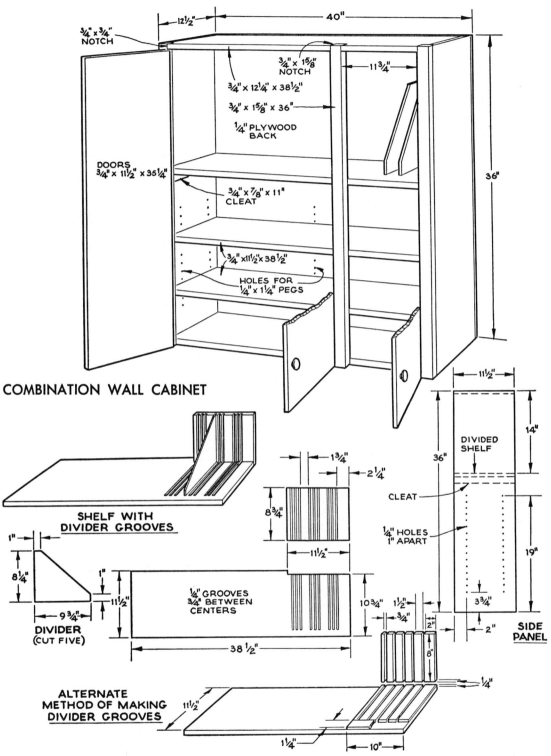

COMBINATION WALL CABINET

¾" x ¾" NOTCH

12½"

40"

¾" x 1⅝" NOTCH

11¾"

¾" x 12¼" x 38½"

¾" x 1⅝" x 36"

¼" PLYWOOD BACK

36"

DOORS ¾" x 11½" x 35¼"

¾" x ⅞" x 11" CLEAT

¾" x 11½" x 38½"

HOLES FOR ¼" x 1¼" PEGS

SHELF WITH DIVIDER GROOVES

1¾"

2¼"

8¾"

11½"

11½"

36"

14"

DIVIDED SHELF

CLEAT

¼" HOLES 1" APART

19"

3¾"

2"

2"

SIDE PANEL

1"

8¼"

9¾"

1"

11½"

DIVIDER (CUT FIVE)

¼" GROOVES ¾" BETWEEN CENTERS

10¾"

1½"

¾"

2"

38½"

8"

ALTERNATE METHOD OF MAKING DIVIDER GROOVES

11½"

1¼"

10"

¼"

MIX CENTER WALL CABINET

Uses

Supplies for making cookies, cakes, pies, and other baked goods some-times present a storage problem. But not so if your kitchen has this cabinet. Its bins not only store good amounts of flour, sugar, meal, etc., but the housewife can get what she wants without fuss and bother. The large storage bin holds about 40 pounds of flour, and a metal shutter feeds it into a small bin below. This and other small bins, all removable for cleaning, take the place of the conventional row of canisters.

Shelves provide space for several mixing bowls, measuring spoons and cups, casseroles, and custard cups. Pie, cake, muffin, and bread pans can be filed between the dividers on the top shelf. Another vertical file (not adjustable in height) can be placed above the flour bin for such articles as a pudding pan, tube cake pan, and salad mold.

Materials

1″ x 12″ (nom.) stock (40 linear feet) to make—
   2 pc. 52″ long — cabinet ends.
   2 pc. 48″ long — top and bottom.
   1 pc. 35½″ long — partition.
   3 pc. 30¾″ long — adjustable shelves.
   1 pc. 14″ long — fixed shelf.
   1 pc. 5¾″ x 45½″ — bin framing (back).
   4 pc. 6¾″ x 8″ — bin partitions.
   1 pc. 5½″ x 45½″ — bin framing (bottom).
1″ x 2″ (nom.) stock (12 linear feet) to make—
   1 pc. 48″ long — top facing strip.
   3 pc. 36″ long — facing strips.
   1 pc. 45½″ long — bin framing.
1 strip ½″ x ¾″ x 45½″ — bin molding.

¾″ plywood (4′ x 4′ panel) to make—

    2 pc. 14¾″ x 35¼″ — doors.

    1 pc. 14″ x 20½″ — flour bin facing.

    1 pc. 14″ x 14¾″ — upper door.

¼″ plywood (4′ x 6′ panel) to make—

    1 pc. 44¾″ x 47¼″ — cabinet back.

  10 pc. 7⅝″ x 9″ — shelf dividers.

    1 pc. 9″ x 30½″ — divider backing.

About 18 square feet 24- or 26-gauge galvanized iron — small bins.

About 7 square feet 16-oz. copper — flour bin.

1 pc. ¹⁄₁₆″ strap iron 1″ x 25″ (approx.) — flour bin arm.

4 pr. hinges.

8 door or drawer pulls.

Pointers for Building

The ends of the cabinet may be extended down to the work counter or may be stopped flush with the lower edge of the bins. This decision will mostly depend on what the cabinet adjoins. In the original layout, which you can see in the picture of the step-saving U-kitchen shown in the first chapter, a merry-go-round corner cupboard is located on the left, and the full-length side of the wall cabinet is common to the corner unit.

All shelves are adjustable except the 14″ one above the flour bin. After cutting the ends and vertical partition, drill holes for the shelf pegs. Rabbet the ¼″ plywood back to the rear edges of the top and ends to help give rigidity to the cabinet. Corner irons or blocks also are desirable. The shelf dividers are similar to those used in the range wall cabinet (No. 2) previously described. Dividers may be placed above the flour bin or the space may be left clear, depending on the needs of your particular kitchen.

To make the flour bin, first lay out a full-size pattern on wrapping paper or cardboard, taking your dimensions from Section C-C and the front elevation. You will need a sheet of metal approximately 20″ x 50″, the greater dimension being used for bending the metal at three of the vertical corners and making the seam at the fourth.

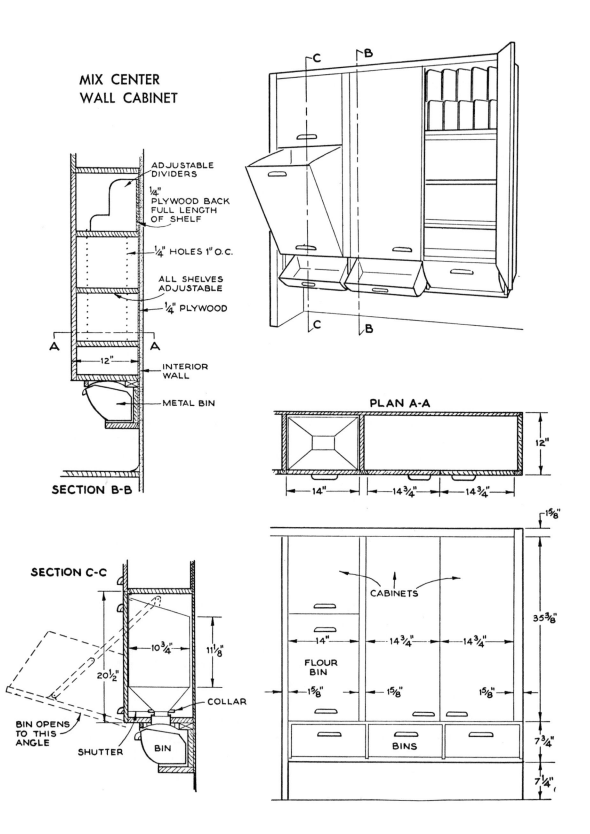

MIX CENTER
WALL CABINET

ADJUSTABLE
DIVIDERS

¼"
PLYWOOD BACK
FULL LENGTH
OF SHELF

¼" HOLES 1" O.C.

ALL SHELVES
ADJUSTABLE

¼" PLYWOOD

12"

INTERIOR
WALL

METAL BIN

SECTION B-B

A — A

SECTION C-C

10¾"

11⅛"

20½"

COLLAR

BIN OPENS
TO THIS
ANGLE

SHUTTER   BIN

PLAN A-A

12"

14"   14¾"   14¾"

1⅝"

CABINETS

35⅜"

14"   14¾"   14¾"

FLOUR
BIN

1⅝"   1⅝"   1⅝"

BINS

7¾"

7¼"

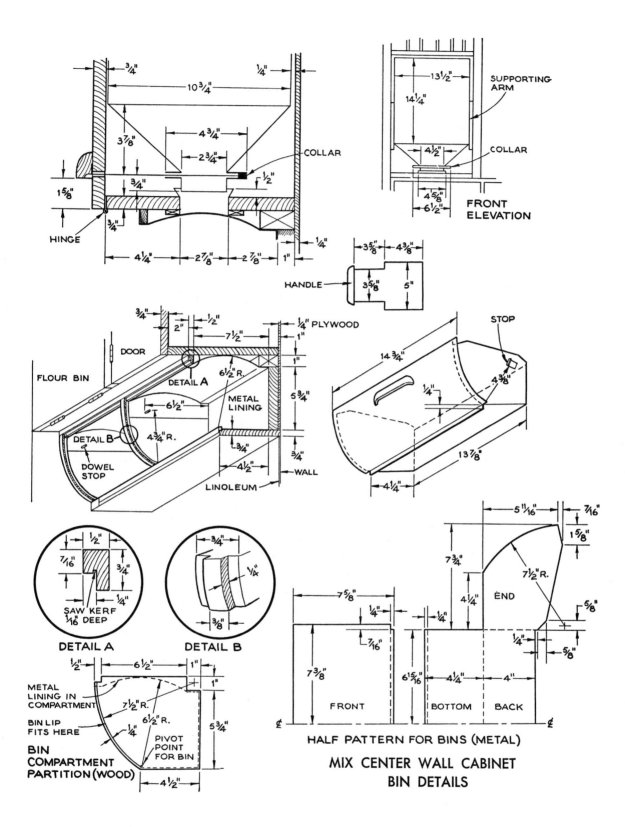

3/4"   **10 3/4"**   **1/4"**

3 7/8"   **4 3/4"**   **2 3/4"**   **1/2"**

COLLAR

3/4"   **1 5/8"**   **3/4"**

HINGE

4 1/4"   **2 7/8"**   **2 7/8"**   **1"**   **1/4"**

13 1/2"   SUPPORTING ARM

14 1/4"   **4 1/2"**   COLLAR

4 5/8"   **6 1/2"**

FRONT ELEVATION

HANDLE   **3 5/8"**   **4 3/8"**   **3 5/8"**   **5"**

3/4"   **2"**   **1/2"**   **7 1/2"**   **1/4" PLYWOOD**   **1"**

DOOR   **1"**

FLOUR BIN   DETAIL A   **6 1/2" R.**   **5 3/4"**

6 1/2"   METAL LINING

DETAIL B   **4 3/4" R.**   **3/4"**   **3/4"**

DOWEL STOP   **4 1/2"**   WALL

LINOLEUM

STOP

14 3/4"   **1/4"**   **4 3/8"**

13 7/8"   **4 1/4"**

1/2"   **3/4"**

7/16"   **3/4"**

SAW KERF 1/16" DEEP   **1/4"**

DETAIL A

3/4"   **1/4"**   **3/8"**

DETAIL B

5 11/16"   **7/16"**

1 5/8"

7 3/4"   **4 1/4"**   **7 1/2" R.**   END

5/8"

1/4"   **5/8"**

1/2"   **6 1/2"**   **1"**

METAL LINING IN COMPARTMENT   **7 1/2" R.**   **1"**

BIN LIP FITS HERE   **6 1/2" R.**

1/4"   PIVOT POINT FOR BIN   **5 3/4"**

BIN COMPARTMENT PARTITION (WOOD)

4 1/2"

7 5/8"   **1/4"**   **7/16"**

7 3/8"   **6 15/16"**   **4 1/4"**   **4"**

FRONT   BOTTOM   BACK

HALF PATTERN FOR BINS (METAL)

MIX CENTER WALL CABINET
BIN DETAILS

The funnel bottom can be shaped in one of two ways: either by extending the bin sides down, cutting the extensions to the indicated triangles, and soldering the corners; or by making the funnel separately and attaching it to the body of the bin. You will note that the mouth of the funnel fits into a flared chute that carries flour through the wood bottom of the compartment and into the smaller bin below. The collar into which the shutter slides consists of two rectangular pieces of metal (with openings to match the funnel mouth), joined at the edges so as to allow enough clearance for the shutter to slide in and out between them at the fourth edge. The shutter passes through a thin slot cut in the bin door. Two pieces of strap iron, joined with a pin to give an elbow action, limit the opening of the bin when it is to be filled. The bin itself is attached to the wood facing, which is hinged at the bottom.

The framing for the small bins is simple but requires careful work to assure a smooth bin fit and operation. First attach the strengthening (nom.) 1″ x 2″ member that runs under the rear corner of the main cabinet. Then cut the four wood partitions. Detail B shows the curving rabbets against which the bin lips fit when the bins are closed. Detail A is a section of the ½″ x ¾″ molding that faces the front top edge. The ¹⁄₁₆″ saw kerf in this is designed to receive one end of the metal that lines the compartment. After the framing is in place, one sheet of metal can be run from this slot across the top (curving as indicated), down the back, and out the floor to the metal edging that finishes off the front of the compartment. Other pieces of sheet metal can be placed over the wood partitions at the ends of each compartment.

As the half pattern shows, each bin can be shaped from two pieces of metal. A slightly flaring V formed by the ¼″ edges of the bottom and back supports the bin on the metal shelf edging and allows the necessary pivoting action. A metal stop, aligned with a projecting dowel pin, keeps each bin from falling out.

Instead of using the galvanized iron and sheet copper specified in the materials list for the bins, the builder might, with a little ingenuity, substitute sheet aluminum in whole or in part. This is now available as a "do-it-yourself" item in hardware stores. Just cut it, shape it, and tack it in place as you would the other metal.

WALL VEGETABLE BIN

Uses

Set into the wall back of the sink area, this bin stores vegetables and fruits within reach of the sink where they will be cleaned for cooking. A row of the bins, located under a wide casement window, is a feature of a functional U-shaped kitchen designed by Lenore Sater Thye of the U.S. Bureau of Human Nutrition and Home Economics. Behind the bin compartments, a sheet of rigid insulation is substituted for the sheathing normally placed under house siding. This keeps winter temperatures from nipping the stored vegetables—and prevents house heat from escaping. Each bin lifts out so both it and the wall compartment can be easily cleaned. A stool (window base) 10″ wide above the bins can be used for house plants. Although the drawings show the bin located under a window, a row of them could also be placed below a line of wall cabinets at the back edge of a wide working counter, either set into the wall or built against it.

Materials

FOR ONE BIN:

⅝″ plywood (2′ x 4′ panel) to make—

    1 pc. 10¼″ x 17¾″ — front.

    3 pc. 1½″ x 17⅜″ — back.

    1 pc. 7¼″ x 17⅜″ — bottom ⎫
    2 pc. 6⅝″ x 9⅝″ — ends ⎬ for all wood construction.

24-gauge galvanized iron to make—

    1 pc. 9¾″ x 40″ — bin sides and bottom.

    1 pc. 18″ x 28″ ⎫
    2 pc. 8⅛″ x 10″ ⎬ compartment lining.

(Note: Instead of using galvanized iron for the bin and compartment lining, the builder could substitute sheet aluminum, available at most hardware stores. For this, however, it probably would be necessary to build a wood framework for the bin.)

WALL VEGETABLE BIN

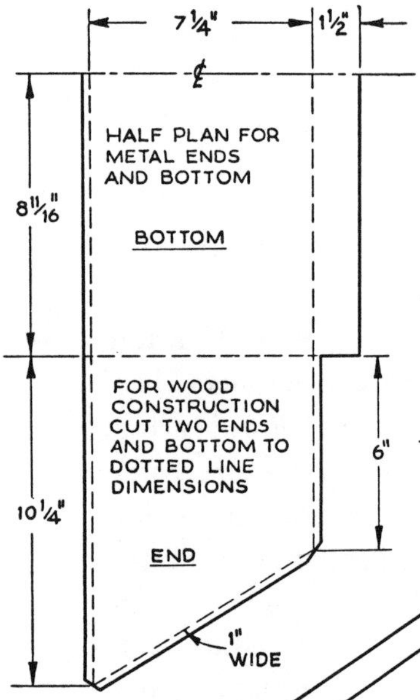

7¼"
1½"
HALF PLAN FOR METAL ENDS AND BOTTOM
BOTTOM
8 11/16"
FOR WOOD CONSTRUCTION CUT TWO ENDS AND BOTTOM TO DOTTED LINE DIMENSIONS
10¼"
6"
END
1" WIDE

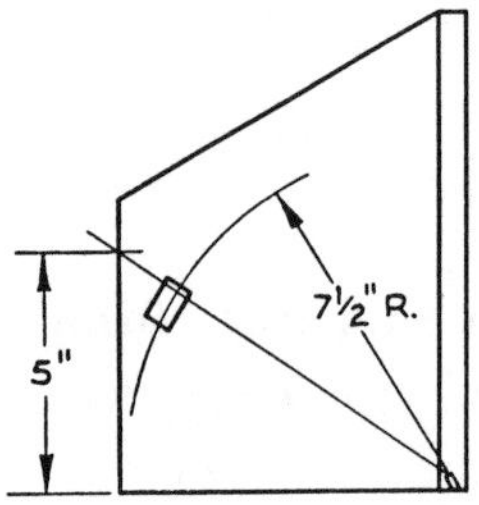

5"
7½" R.

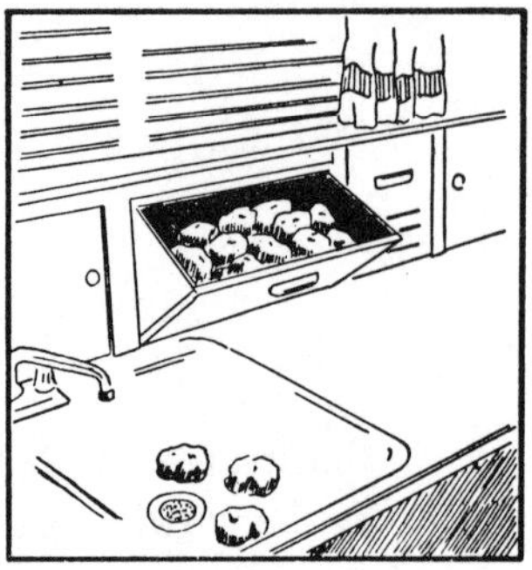

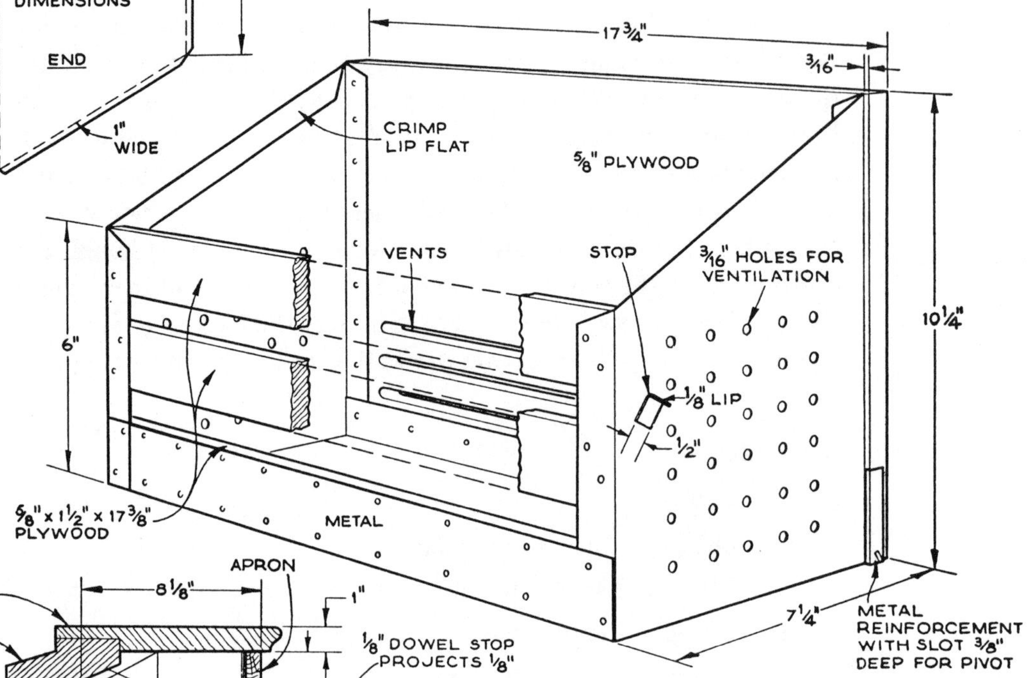

17¾"
3/16"
CRIMP LIP FLAT
5/8" PLYWOOD
10¼"
6"
VENTS
STOP
3/16" HOLES FOR VENTILATION
1/8" LIP
½"
5/8" x 1½" x 17⅜" PLYWOOD
METAL
7¼"
METAL REINFORCEMENT WITH SLOT 3/8" DEEP FOR PIVOT

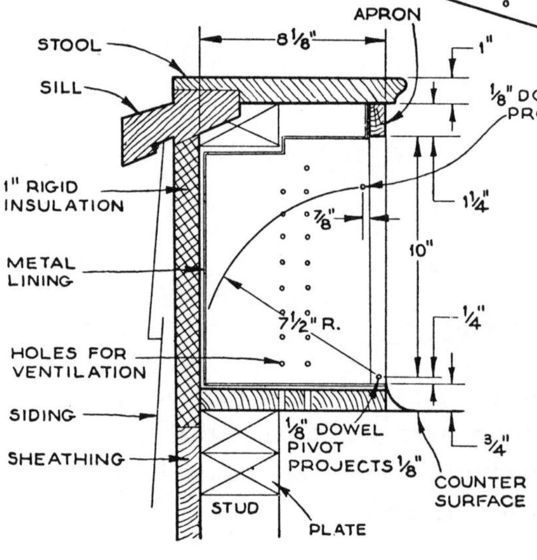

STOOL
SILL
APRON
8⅛"
1"
1/8" DOWEL STOP PROJECTS 1/8"
1" RIGID INSULATION
1¼"
7/8"
10"
METAL LINING
7½" R.
¼"
HOLES FOR VENTILATION
SIDING
1/8" DOWEL PIVOT PROJECTS 1/8"
¾"
SHEATHING
COUNTER SURFACE
STUD
PLATE

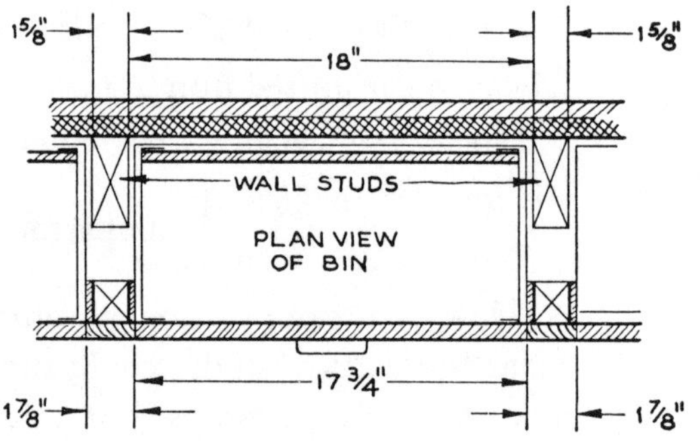

1⅝"
18"
1⅝"
WALL STUDS
PLAN VIEW OF BIN
17¾"
1⅞"
1⅞"

FRAMING FOR COMPARTMENT:

1 pc. 2″ x 4″ (nom.), length optional — window plate.

1 pc. 1″ x 10″ (nom.) length optional — window stool.

1 pc. ¾″ x 8⅛″ stock, length optional — compartment base.

1 sheet 1″ insulation board.

2 pc. 2″ x 4″ (nom.) stock, 10″ long — studs in each compartment.

2 pc. 2″ x 2″ (nom.), 11½″ long — front compartment uprights.

2 pc. ¾″ x 1⅞″ x 11½″ — vertical facing strips.

1 pc. ¾″ x 1¼″, length optional — window apron.

Pointers for Building

As shown, the framing for this bin ties in with the framing for the window and would be easiest if done by the contractor as part of the original house construction. In any case, you will have to adapt the framing to suit your circumstances, especially the length of the space available. In the model U-kitchen designed by Lenore Sater Thye, four bins—two 17¾″ wide and two 10½″ wide—and a 16″-wide soap compartment with sliding doors are installed under the window. The soap compartment was centered behind the sink with two bins on either side.

If you prescribe the bins in a house not yet built, you can have the builder put the insulation in place before the siding. A strip 12″ wide will be sufficient. If you install the insulation as part of a remodeling job, you probably will have to remove some of the siding temporarily.

The plate, or double 2 x 4's, customarily located under a window is dropped below the compartment base in this case, and a single 2 x 4 goes under the sill. A stool wider than usual is required since this serves as the top of the compartment.

Ten-inch lengths of 2 x 4 can be spaced vertically as desired against the insulation to frame and separate the compartments. Butt them between the compartment base, which rests on the plate, and the horizontal 2 x 4 that supports the window. Lengths of 2 x 2 stock go in front of the 2 x 4's. Vertical facing strips 1⅞″ wide are nailed to the 2 x 2's. Butt them against the 1¼″-wide apron that goes under the stool.

The metal lining for the compartment can best be made as a unit and then slipped in before the facing strips are in place. Bottom, back, and top can be bent from a single sheet of metal and the ends then soldered on. Sheet metal thinner than the gauge specified might be used here. Punch vent holes in the ends and bottom, drilling matching holes through the wood base of the compartment. If this metal work stumps you, take it to a tinsmith.

The bin itself offers no difficulties. All-wood construction is easiest, but in such a unit wood absorbs odors. Metal is a better long-range bet for sanitary reasons. Here again, if cutting and bending the metal is beyond your capabilities and equipment, a tinsmith will make quick work of the job. Punch holes in the edges for tacking the metal to the wood front and back. A keyhole saw, started by drilling a ½″ hole, can be used to cut the vents in the face of the bin. Slant the vents upward toward the inside about 45 degrees.

Careful location of the pivot and pivoting slot are essential to smooth operation of the bin. Drill ⅛″ holes in the edges of the 1⅞″ facing strips for the ⅛″ dowels that serve as pivots. Center the holes in the edge ¼″ above the compartment base. Cut slots in the lower corners of the bin face and reinforce them with metal. You then can set the bin down over the pivots and swing it back into the compartment. Bend the metal stops on the bin temporarily so they will pass the ⅛″ dowel stops that are set into the framing 2 x 2's, on a 7½″ radius.

SOAP COMPARTMENT

Uses

Designed as a companion piece to the fruit and vegetable bin just described, this soap compartment goes directly behind the sink to provide handy storage space for the washing materials used there. Like the bin, it utilizes the space within the wall. Sliding doors give access to the materials stored in it.

SOAP COMPARTMENT

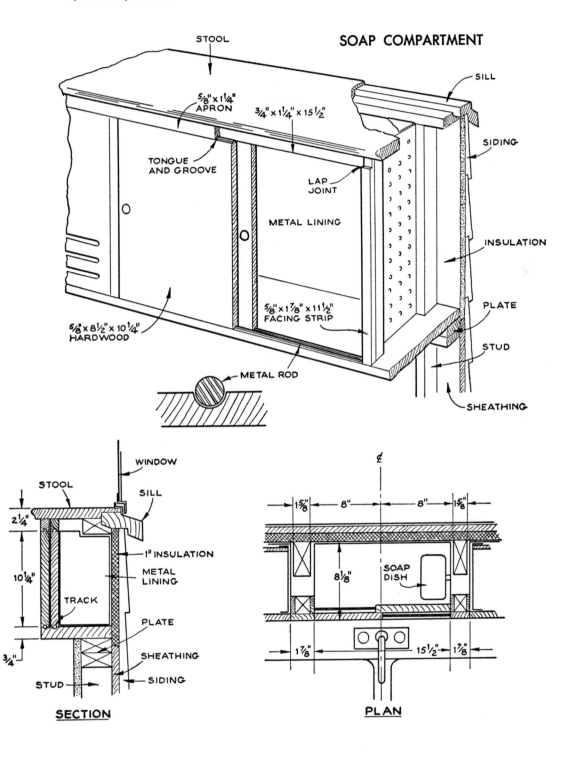

STOOL

5/8" x 1 1/4" APRON

3/4" x 1 1/4" x 15 1/2"

SILL

SIDING

TONGUE AND GROOVE

LAP JOINT

METAL LINING

INSULATION

5/8" x 1 7/8" x 11 1/2" FACING STRIP

PLATE

STUD

5/8" x 8 1/2" x 10 1/4" HARDWOOD

METAL ROD

SHEATHING

WINDOW

STOOL

SILL

2 1/4"

1" INSULATION

METAL LINING

10 1/4"

TRACK

PLATE

3/4"

SHEATHING

STUD

SIDING

SECTION

℄

1 5/8"   8"   8"   1 5/8"

8 1/8"

SOAP DISH

1 7/8"   15 1/2"   1 7/8"

PLAN

Materials

1 pc. 2″ x 4″ (nom.), length optional — window plate.

1 pc. 1″ x 10″ (nom.) , length optional — window stool.

1 pc. 1″ stock, 8⅛″ wide, length optional — compartment base.

1 sheet 1″ insulation board.

2 pc. 2″ x 4″ (nom.), 10″ long — studs in each compartment.

2 pc. 2″ x 2″ (nom.), 11½″ long — front compartment uprights.

2 pc. ¾″ x 1⅞″ x 11½″ — vertical facing strips.

1 pc. ¾″ x 1¼″, length optional — window apron.

1 pc. ¾″ x 1¼″ x 15½″ — inside top door guide.

2 pc. ⅝″ x 8½″ x 10¼″ hardwood — doors.

2 pc. ⅛″ metal rod 16″ long — door tracks.

24-gauge galvanized iron to make—

    1 pc. 15½″ x 28″⎫

    2 pc. 8⅛″ x 10″⎭ compartment lining.

NOTE: End framing members and some other parts in this cabinet are also common to the wall vegetable bin.

Pointers for Building

Build this compartment by the same procedure outlined for the wall vegetable bin. In installing the metal lining, note that the 2 x 2's at the front corners are shimmed out to give a 1⅞″ dimension. A second strip, 15½″ long, behind the apron strip is grooved to mate the tongue cut in the upper edge of the rear door. Butt this strip between the 2 x 2's. In cutting the doors, keep the grain horizontal. The ⅛″ metal rods, cut just a trifle longer than the width of the compartment, can be sprung into the holes bored in the bottom edges of the vertical facing strips (for the front door) and the 2 x 2's for the rear one. Rout grooves in the bottom board for the metal-rod door track as shown in the inset.

The doors are captive within the structure after final assembly. So make a trial assembly first to be sure they slide easily. Then put all the various parts into place.

WALL CABINET IDEAS

Crisping Cabinet

As any housewife knows, crackers, cereals, and some cookies will absorb moisture and become soggy after the container is opened. These usually can be made crisp again by heating in the oven. But why not utilize some of the available heat in the kitchen to keep such foods crisp? Sources of heat that might be utilized include the range, the room-warming outlet or fixture, and the vent of a gas refrigerator.

Any of the wall cabinets for installation over range or refrigerator already described might be adapted for crisping uses. Simply storing cereals and crackers above the range may be sufficient. The crisping procedure would be more certain, however, if an opening is provided in the bottom of the cabinet so warm air can sweep up through the stored foods and out vents in the top or upper part of the cabinet front. In the case of gas appliances, you might install a metal duct to channel heat to the cabinet from the appliance heat-exhaust vent.

End Cabinet

When a line of wall cabinets comes to an end, for instance at a door or window, you have the chance of creating a cabinet that will solve special storage problems. Install a door on the side of the final cabinet, instead of on the front, and you have a compartment suitable for storage of trays, cooky tins, and similar flat equipment. The door can be omitted if you wish and the flat articles simply shoved between vertical partitions in the cabinet. You could vary the amount of this storage space to suit the amount of equipment to be stored, and still use the front part of the cabinet for shelves accessible through a standard door on the front. The shelves might be made just wide enough (from front to back) to take a row of canned foods. Or some persons might prefer to omit the door and install open shelves to vary the appearance of the cabinets.

You could also install two banks of vertical partitions in such an end cabinet, one bank above the other, and use the compartments for storage of pan lids, pie pans, and similar equipment of this size. Adapting the cabinet to this type of storage would be most appropriate if it is located near the range or baking center.

Tool-Hanging Cabinet

Even when a drawer is compartmented, kitchen tools such as can openers, measuring spoons, and potato mashers often wind up in a jumble from which it is difficult to extract the needed item. A shallow wall cabinet with a large backboard where each tool has its own hanger—the way many home workshop enthusiasts store their tools—will keep each utensil free from the others and in plain sight for quick use. Items suitable for hanging on hooks, nails, or other supports in such a cabinet include egg beaters, large serving spoons, ladles, scissors, strainers, long-handled forks, graters, spatulas, pastry cutters, rolling pins, and cooking thermometers.

A board to accommodate the usual number of such tools found in the ordinary kitchen should have a surface area of not less than 576 square inches—a square board measuring 24″ by 24″ or a rectangular one that is longer than 24″ and less than that wide. The shape can be suited to the space available. A piece of Masonite peg board could be used as the backboard. A variety of hooks and hangers are available for insertion in the holes punched in this hardboard. An inside depth of 4″ (front to back) is enough for such a cabinet. Making it any deeper would just waste space. In some cases it might be possible to install the cabinet on a wall apart from a line of wall cabinets of conventional depth. But for greatest utility, it probably should go in the line of regular cabinets. If the kitchen-planning goal is an unbroken line of cabinets all of the same depth, you face a problem of how to do it. One way is to make the tool cabinet the front part of the end wall cabinet described elsewhere in this chapter. Here, the distance needed for storage of trays and large flat items parallel to the wall (with access from the side of the cabinet) would not be too much less than the size the tool-supporting backboard should be.

Above the range is a logical location for a tool cabinet, for it is here that many of these tools will be used most frequently.

9

Open Shelves and Wall Racks

Some authorities believe open shelves are the most practical storage device for any kitchen. And even though fashion decrees closed cabinets, it is obvious that open shelves do have advantages. First, they keep most of the stored supplies and equipment in full view and quickly accessible. Second, the housewife doesn't waste time and energy opening and closing doors. And finally, they cost less than cabinets. The same advantages hold true for wall racks.

You probably will want some open shelves even though you use closed storage units through most of your kitchen. These are easily provided. In some cases, they can be just pieces of shelving supported by metal brackets. Open shelves can be provided too as an integral part of wall cabinets. In your planning, you may find spots where you will have space for a few narrow shelves, but not for a cabinet of full depth.

On the pages that immediately follow, you'll find several examples of how shelving can be applied. But these are only a start. The ingenious builder will find many more chances to use them.

WALL SHELVES

Uses

Placed on two walls, the open shelves would supply most of the storage needs of a kitchen. Located at the end of a line of cabinets, or mounted in duplicate by a window that breaks a line of cabinets, the end shelves would provide a place for cookbooks and decorative knickknacks, if nothing else. As shown, the recessed shelves are located under a line of wall cabinets. Frequently used dishes, a radio, and many other items can be placed there within easy reach without robbing the work counter of the space needed for normal kitchen operations. In the drawing, you will notice that there still is a corner 20″ wide. The reach arc of the average woman indicates that this width will help reduce the fatigue-causing reaching that may occur with counters of conventional width. Even when the counter is wider, it often is possible to use a shelf behind it in this way.

Materials

Open shelves — 1″ stock in 12″, 10″, 8″, 6″, and 4″ (nom.) widths.
Recessed shelves — ¾″ x 6″ plywood, length to suit; 3″ cove.
End shelves — 1″ x 12″ (nom.) stock (12 linear feet) to make—

    4 pc. 24″ long — shelves.

    1 pc. 24″ long — end.

1″ x 3″ (nom.) stock (8 linear feet) to make—

    4 pc. 24″ — back pieces.

1⅝″ x 24″ dowel post.

Pointers for Building

OPEN SHELVES.   Space these shelves so the top one will be no more than 72″ above the floor, or it will be useful only for dead storage. Good workmanship will determine whether such shelves give satisfaction from an appearance standpoint. Keep them neat by using

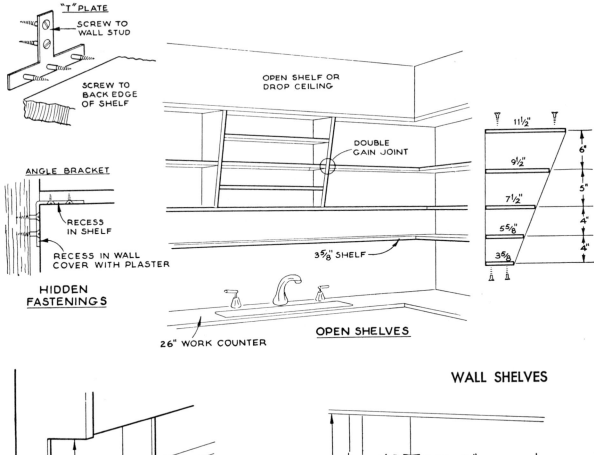

"T" PLATE

SCREW TO WALL STUD

SCREW TO BACK EDGE OF SHELF

ANGLE BRACKET

RECESS IN SHELF

RECESS IN WALL COVER WITH PLASTER

HIDDEN FASTENINGS

OPEN SHELF OR DROP CEILING

DOUBLE GAIN JOINT

$3\frac{5}{8}$" SHELF

26" WORK COUNTER

OPEN SHELVES

$11\frac{1}{2}$"

$9\frac{1}{2}$"

$7\frac{1}{2}$"

$5\frac{5}{8}$"

$3\frac{5}{8}$

6"

5"

4"

4"

WALL SHELVES

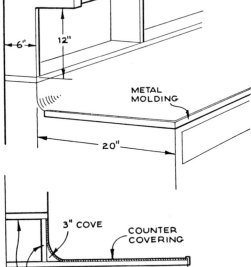

6"

12"

METAL MOLDING

20"

3" COVE

COUNTER COVERING

$\frac{3}{4}$" x 6" PLYWOOD

RECESSED SHELVES

$11\frac{1}{2}$"

24"

12" RAD.

$1\frac{5}{8}$" DIA.

36"

METAL EDGE

LINOLEUM

8"

END SHELVES

stopped dado (gain) joints when possible. However, where the end of a vertical member meets the face of a shelf, butt joints secured by screws will be best. Assemble and glue up the three middle shelves of the five-shelf sink (or range) unit to the triangular side pieces. Mount the top (11½″) and bottom (3⅝″) shelves on the wall. Then place the three-shelf unit between. Snug gain joints, cut and fitted earlier, can be used to support the outside 7½″ shelves on a line with the similar inside shelf. Conventional metal shelf brackets can be used to support the ends of the main shelves. But use only as many as absolutely needed, for they steal useful space from the shelves. The sketches suggest two ways you can hide fastenings. If a drop ceiling is used above the top shelf, it will help support the five-shelf sink or range unit.

RECESSED SHELVES.   As shown, these tie in as part of the original construction of wall cabinets above and the counter surface below. Whatever type wall cabinets you build, you can plan for the recessed shelves by extending the outer sides of the two end cabinets down far enough to serve as supports for the shelves. But vertical members 6″ x 12″ cut from ¾″ plywood also could be bracketed at intervals under the bottoms of a line of wall cabinets already in place. Attach the shelf to the verticals with screws driven from underneath. Nail the shelf to the ¾″ x 6″ strip that backs up the cove. Cement down the cove as part of the job of applying the counter covering. A set of shelves of this type might easily be installed in an existing modern kitchen. If desired, the shelf could be just a ledge, the vertical members up to the wall cabinets being omitted.

END SHELVES.   Cut gains in the 11½″ x 24″ vertical end piece for the two middle shelves. Butt the top and bottom shelves against the ends of the vertical pieces, joining them with countersunk flathead screws. Screw the back strips to the top surfaces of the shelves (from underneath), mortising the ends of the bottom three into the vertical member. Bore blind holes in the top and bottom shelves for the ends of the 1⅝″ post, with through holes in the middle two. Glue the post in place, also placing screws into the ends through the top and bottom shelves. Toenail the middle pair of shelves to the post (from underneath) after applying glue.

OPEN MIXING CENTER

Uses

This mix center would be very appropriate for the kitchen where open shelves are the rule. With space for bowls and pans, and perhaps a pull-out cutting board in a base cabinet below, it brings into one handy working area all the equipment and supplies for typical mixing and baking tasks. Two sets of adjustable racks for pie plates

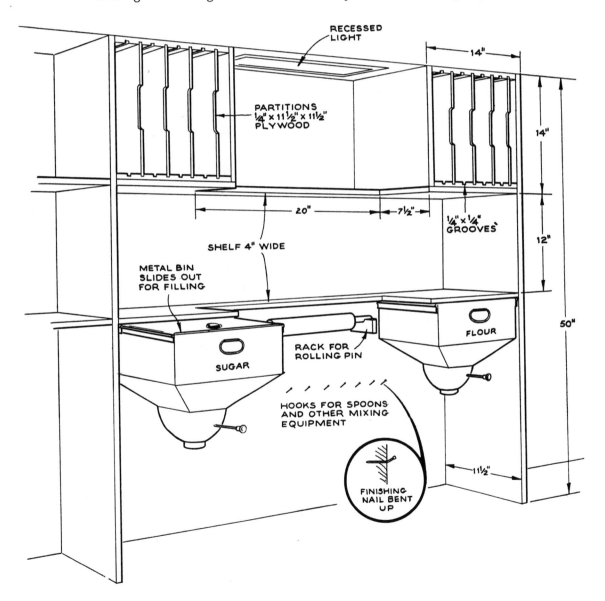

and cake tins are within easy reach of the woman of average height. Two gravity bins let sugar and sifted flour run directly into the measuring cup. These fasten to the underside of a shelf and slide out when needed. Each holds 14 pounds. The flour sifter and sugar dispenser are available from Washington Division, Ekco Building Products Co., 1250 Bedford Avenue S.W., Canton, Ohio. Ask your building supply dealer if he can order them for you.

Materials

1″ x 12″ (nom.) stock (32 linear feet) to make—

    2 pc. 50″ long — sides.

    2 pc. 47½″ long — shelves.

    2 pc. 14″ long

    2 pc. 12½″ long } pan rack.

¼″ plywood (4′ x 8′ panel) to make—

    8 pc. 11½″ x 11½″ — rack dividers.

    1 pc. 48″ x 50″ — back.

Pointers for Building

MIXING CENTER. A 50″ length of a 4′-wide panel of ¼″ plywood will provide the back. Attach this to the wall first, spacing the screws or nails to hit the wall studs. Countersink and fill the heads. Center notches 7½″ deep in the two shelves, adjusting their length to suit the dimensions of the two bins. The pan racks above can also be made to match by lengthening or shortening the four dadoed rack pieces. Match the spacing of the ¼″ x ¼″ dadoes in each pair, top and bottom, very carefully so the dividers will stand straight. For greatest strength join the two shelves to the uprights with dado or gain joints. The bottom ends of the uprights can probably be fastened by running screws through the counter from underneath. The spacing and location of hooks on the backboard will depend on individual needs and equipment.

IDEAS FOR SHELVES AND WALL RACKS

Perforated Hardboard Wall Rack

An attractive and convenient wall rack is easily made from a sheet of perforated hardboard such as Masonite Pegboard. Shim it out far enough from the wall so that there's space for the hangers to hold properly when inserted in the holes. For best appearance and holding power, insist on white plastic (Delrin) hangers similar to those in the photo. These are available in a wide variety of shapes and sizes to perform specific hanging or supporting jobs, including the support of small shelves such as the one you see in the photo. A decorative working wall like this might be placed at various locations in your kitchen. It looks good. It's useful.

Pine Paneled Display Wall

The copper bottoms of kitchen pots and pans display beautifully against a wall of knotty pine paneling that has been given a natural finish. So consider whether there's a logical place in your kitchen for such a wall. In the right circumstances the paneling can be placed on the wall horizontally instead of vertically. It's sometimes possible to find appropriate hangers for such a wall in collections of old hardware in antique shops—old meat hooks, pot holders, etc.

Remember that the more bulky kitchen items you display in this manner, the more you are reducing your cabinet storage problem.

Wall Rack for Lids

Lids for pots and pans are always a storage problem. If all are thrown helter-skelter into one large drawer, the right one's never available when wanted. Open storage in wall racks is one logical solution to the problem.

There are several ways to do this. Where space is available, you might simply put up narrow shelves with a front lip or with a recess such as you sometimes find in old corner cupboards for upright storage of plates. Perhaps you'll want to combine such shelves with a pine paneled wall.

You also might use a slot-type rack or one made with slanted openings like a wall-type magazine rack. In the former, you form a slot by nailing and gluing spacer blocks, about 1½" by 1½", at intervals between two narrow boards. Screw the rear board to the wall. Only lids with knobs can be stored in this slot rack. The knobs hook on the front board when you drop the lids into the slot. Any kind of lid, or even shallow pans, will go into magazine-type racks.

10

Sink Cabinets

Although most housewives now seem to prefer a flat-rim sink built into the counter, you should remember that you can also buy a sink integral with its cabinet. These all-in-one units come with either twin or single bowls and with or without drainboards. The cabinets may have various desirable built-in features such as towel racks.

Flat-rim sinks give a smooth, continuous work counter to the edge of the bowl or bowls. These sinks come in various sizes in three materials—steel or cast iron with porcelain enamel, also the newer stainless steel. Some of these sinks require a separate rim.

When space is available in the kitchen plan, it often makes sense to have a second sink, a small, shallow one, at a separate location. Placed near the refrigerator, the second sink will pay off as a place to wash green vegetables before they are put away. If your way of life includes considerable entertaining, you would do well to combine this second sink with a wall or base cabinet for storage of glasses and alcoholic beverages. In this connection, remember that many beverage bottles require a shelf space of not less than 14″.

SINK AND
DISHWASHER CABINET

In recent years, several kitchen designers have hit upon the idea of a V-shaped projection beyond the front edge of base cabinets. Where floor space is available, this design feature may have practical advantages. If applied to the sanitary center, it can facilitate installation of plumbing for the sink and dishwasher, as well as give more space for a waste disposer. Later servicing of the dishwasher and disposer is also made easier, for the plumbing and wiring can be kept accessible through the adjoining part of the combination cabinet.

Two possible methods of uniting the sink and dishwasher are illustrated here. In one, the sink is installed at an angle; in the other, and possibly the better way, the front of the dishwasher is swung forward 30 degrees from the general base line of the row of cabinets. In either of the proposed methods, the dishwasher might be switched to the opposite side of the sink, depending on personal preference. When sink and dishwasher fronts adjoin, sliding doors under the sink may be preferable; a swinging door could interfere with opening the dishwasher to load or unload it.

However you make use of the idea, you wind up with increased counter space. If you set the dishwasher at an angle, you might want to install a butcher-block counter in the area above it.

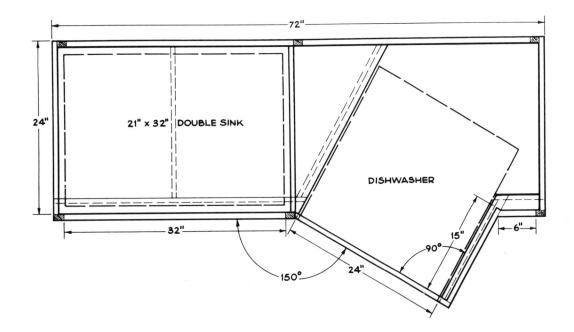

72"

24"

21" x 32" DOUBLE SINK

DISHWASHER

32"

150°

24"

90°

15"

6"

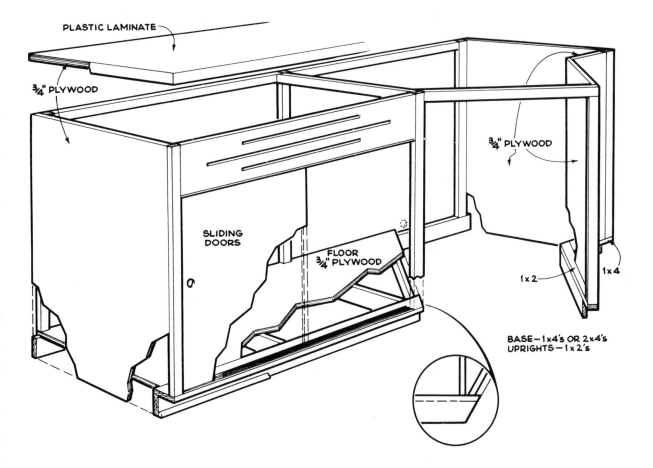

PLASTIC LAMINATE

¾" PLYWOOD

¾" PLYWOOD

SLIDING
DOORS

FLOOR
¾" PLYWOOD

1 x 2

1 x 4

BASE—1x4's OR 2x4's
UPRIGHTS—1x2's

RECESSED SINK FRONT

Uses

Most manufacturers of kitchen equipment offer sink fronts in several widths. Some are just what their name implies, fronts to hide the plumbing below the sink. Others have a floor. The front goes between two standard base cabinets, one end of each doing double duty as a wall for the sink enclosure.

If you build your own cabinets, you would do well to consider this procedure. It saves material. It simplifies the job of putting in a sink. Given two base cabinets that can be spotted on either side of where you intend to place the sink, your job is already well along. A front can be used to enclose either a roll-rim or flat-rim sink.

The lower part of the front shown is recessed. The toe board is set back a little farther than those under the cabinets on either side. The cupboard doors are farther back too. This allows the housewife an easier stance (more knee room) closer to her work. A sink front of course can also be installed flush with the adjoining cabinets if you wish.

Pointers for Building

After buying your sink and positioning the adjoining cabinets, measure and cut the 1″ x 2″ stock to fit around the sink, using corner blocks to strengthen the frame. Screw the frame to the ends of the adjoining cabinets at the proper height to bring the sink at the correct level for installing a counter.

The sink front can be built as a complete unit and then shoved into place. Cut the floor to size and notch the two front corners to allow the vertical framing members to project ¾″, the thickness of the doors. Support the floor on a base made of 1″ x 4″ nominal stock. Set back the toe board a distance equal to that used under the adjacent cabinets.

Sink Cabinets

RECESSED SINK FRONT

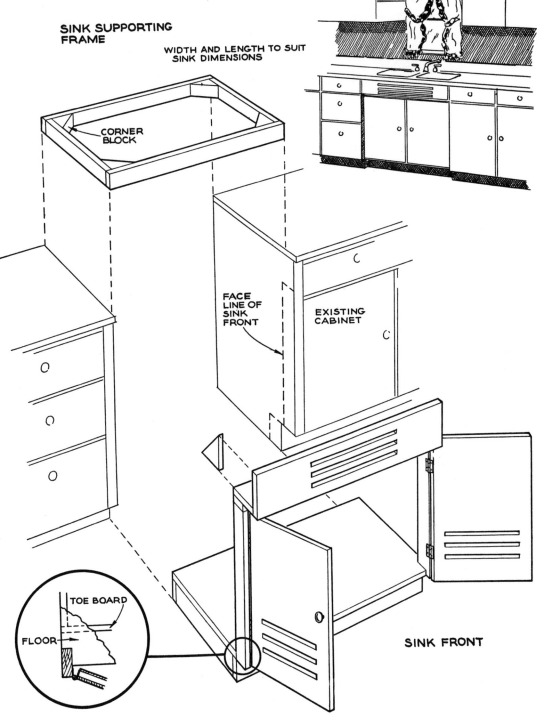

SINK SUPPORTING
FRAME

WIDTH AND LENGTH TO SUIT
SINK DIMENSIONS

CORNER
BLOCK

FACE
LINE OF
SINK
FRONT

EXISTING
CABINET

TOE BOARD

FLOOR

SINK FRONT

Cap the two vertical framing members with another piece of 1" x 2" stock placed edgewise. On top of this align a piece of 1" x 4" stock to bring the vent board flush with the fronts of the adjoining cabinets. Support the vent board with corner blocks or corner irons. The ventilating louvers in the doors and vent board can be started by drilling a hole at each end and then sawing out the slot. The front edge of the sink-front floor acts as a stop for the doors. Push the sink front between its companion cabinets and fasten it with screws driven through the vertical framing members.

SIMPLE SINK CABINET

Uses

Like the sink front previously described, this unit becomes an integral part of two adjoining base cabinets, and it is built as such. Ends of the adjoining cabinets serve as its side walls. The base, including the recessed toe board, is common to all three cabinets.

It is designed for a single-bowl sink, one large enough to hold two dishpans or a dishpan and a drainer. The cabinet is left without shelves or other obstructions, so that two dishpans and a drainer can be stored in it. Additionally there still is room for a bucket or basket of fruit or vegetables for daily use. Soap flakes and scouring powder can be kept in the rack on the left door. A garbage pail placed on the holder mounted on the other door is always easy to reach.

Materials

CABINET:

¾" plywood (4' x 4' panel) to make—

1 pc. 23" x 30" — bottom.

2 pc. 15" x 23⅞" — doors.

1 pc. 25" x 30" — counter. (This can be continuous with adjoining cabinets.)

2″ x 2″ (nom.) stock to make—

  2 pc. 35″ long — rear posts.

1″ x 6″ (nom.) stock to make—

  1 pc. 30″ long — apron.

  2 pc. 3″ x 5″ — apron cleats.

1″ x 2″ (nom.) stock to make—

  1 pc. 30″ long — horizontal face strip. (This can be continuous with the adjoining cabinets.)

$\frac{1}{4}$″ plywood to make—

  1 pc. 30″ x 35″ — cabinet back.

RACK:

1″ (nom.) stock to make—

  2 pc. $4\frac{1}{2}$″ x 8″

  1 pc. $3\frac{1}{2}$″ x $10\frac{1}{2}$″

2 pc. $\frac{1}{4}$″ x $1\frac{1}{2}$″ x 12″ plywood.

GARBAGE PAIL HOLDER:

1″ (nom.) stock or $\frac{3}{4}$″ plywood to make parts to suit the size of the pail used.

Pointers for Building

The cabinet is built as part of the two adjoining ones. The base is common to all. The sink cabinet itself has no framing other than the two sink-supporting posts at the rear corners. The plywood bottom is notched to allow these to continue to the kitchen floor. They are set forward enough to allow the $\frac{1}{4}$″ plywood back to be recessed as shown in the detail drawing. The horizontal facing strip at the top is a continuation of the one used on the adjoining cabinets. The doors are attached to the vertical facing strips at the ends of the other cabinets.

Cleats hold the apron in position between these vertical strips. Louvers can be cut in this board to ventilate the cabinet. As suggested alternatively in the drawing, you might also want to use a metal grille here for ventilation and to add a decorative note. A grille

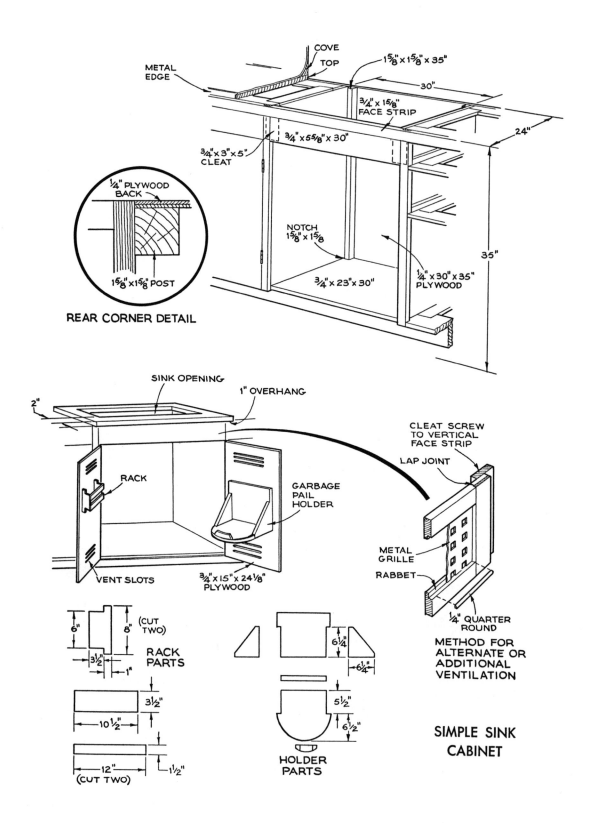

COVE

METAL
EDGE

TOP

$1\frac{5}{8}" \times 1\frac{5}{8}" \times 35"$

30"

$\frac{3}{4}" \times 1\frac{5}{8}"$ FACE STRIP

$\frac{3}{4}" \times 5\frac{5}{8}" \times 30"$

$\frac{3}{4}" \times 3" \times 5"$ CLEAT

24"

$\frac{1}{4}"$ PLYWOOD BACK

NOTCH
$1\frac{5}{8}" \times 1\frac{5}{8}$

35"

$1\frac{5}{8}" \times 1\frac{5}{8}"$ POST

$\frac{3}{4}" \times 23" \times 30"$

$\frac{1}{4}" \times 30" \times 35"$ PLYWOOD

REAR CORNER DETAIL

SINK OPENING

1" OVERHANG

2"

CLEAT SCREW TO VERTICAL FACE STRIP

LAP JOINT

RACK

GARBAGE PAIL HOLDER

METAL GRILLE

RABBET

VENT SLOTS

$\frac{3}{4}" \times 15" \times 24\frac{1}{8}"$ PLYWOOD

$\frac{1}{4}"$ QUARTER ROUND

6"

8" (CUT TWO)

$3\frac{1}{2}"$

1"

RACK PARTS

$6\frac{1}{4}"$

$6\frac{1}{4}"$

METHOD FOR ALTERNATE OR ADDITIONAL VENTILATION

$3\frac{1}{2}"$

$10\frac{1}{2}"$

$5\frac{1}{2}"$

$6\frac{1}{2}"$

12"

$1\frac{1}{2}"$

(CUT TWO)

HOLDER PARTS

SIMPLE SINK CABINET

such as the type designed for radiator enclosures is one possibility.

Building the rack and holder is simply a matter of sawing your stock as shown and assembling the parts with screws. Adjust the size of the holder base to fit the garbage pail you will use.

SINK STOOL AND SOAP TRAY

Uses

Dead storage wall cabinets too high for easy reach usually require a step-stool for access. What better place could you store this bulky piece of equipment than under the kitchen sink? The back of the stool shown here serves also as the cabinet front, disguising the fact that it actually is a stool. Pulled out, the stool can have a secondary use as a work seat beside a pull-out board located adjoining the sink. The stool need not be any wider than 18″. But it can be adapted to a sink recess of any width by projecting the front board and toe-recess members equally on either side to make a full enclosure.

Besides soap, the hinged tray will hold boxes of cleanser, polish, and similar materials. The keyhole openings make it possible to lift the tray off its retaining screws for cleaning.

Materials

(FOR A SINK RECESS 24″ WIDE)

¾″ plywood (4′ x 4′ panel) to make—

   1 pc. 19⅝″ x 24″ — front.

   2 pc. 19½″ x 22½″ — stool sides.

   1 pc. 8½″ x 24″ (or 1″ x 9″ (nom.) stock) — soap tray front.

1″ x 8″ (nom.) stock (10 linear feet) to make—

   6 pc. 18″ long — treads and risers.

1″ x 4″ (nom.) stock (4 linear feet) to make—

   2 pc. 24″ long — toe recess.

1″ x 2″ (nom.) stock (4 linear feet) to make—

   2 pc. 24″ long — horizontal framing.

1 pc. 11″ x 18″ sheet metal.

Pointers for Building

Before you set out to build this stool and soap tray, be sure your sink installation allows space for them. If the sink is too far forward, you may not be able to put in the tray. If the plumbing comes down too far, you will find it impossible to slide a stool of this height into the recess. The sink itself can be supported on the counter spanning the two adjoining base cabinets. No framing or additional support should be needed if you use a steel sink or can place the adjoining cabinets close enough together so they help bear the weight of the sink. The adjoining cabinets should have full ends to the floor, and the kitchen floor covering should be laid back into the recess.

For a work counter 36″ high, the indicated dimensions allow for a horizontal facing strip of 1″ x 2″ just under the counter and a similar strip below to which the soap tray can be hinged.

After cutting the stool parts to size, assemble them with flat-head wood screws. If you use enough screws and set them well, no interior bracing should be required to make the stool fully safe. Triangular openings cut in each side of the stool will lighten it a bit without detracting materially from the strength. At the same time, these openings will provide passage for ventilating air that enters through two or three louvers cut in the face board. Two vertical lines of $\frac{1}{2}$″ holes bored in the soap-tray facing board will help do the ventilating job above.

Strips of $\frac{3}{4}$″ half round attached to the bottom edges of the stool sides with finishing nails should make the stool easier to slide in and out. Set the nails and sand the strips smooth. The strips will serve as runners if you leave a clearance of about $\frac{1}{32}$″ between the floor and the bottom edges of the first riser and the toe board. After the finish coat has been applied, coat the runners with wax.

Plywood scraps left over from the stool can be used as end pieces for the soap tray. If available, a piece of sheet stainless steel would be ideal for the tray itself. Otherwise, use galvanized sheet, or sheet aluminum. Bend the metal to fit the wood ends, cut two keyhole openings for mounting, and tack the metal to the wood ends. After the tray facing board has been hinged to its crosspiece, adjust a metal elbow stop or a light chain so the tray won't open far enough to spill its contents on the floor.

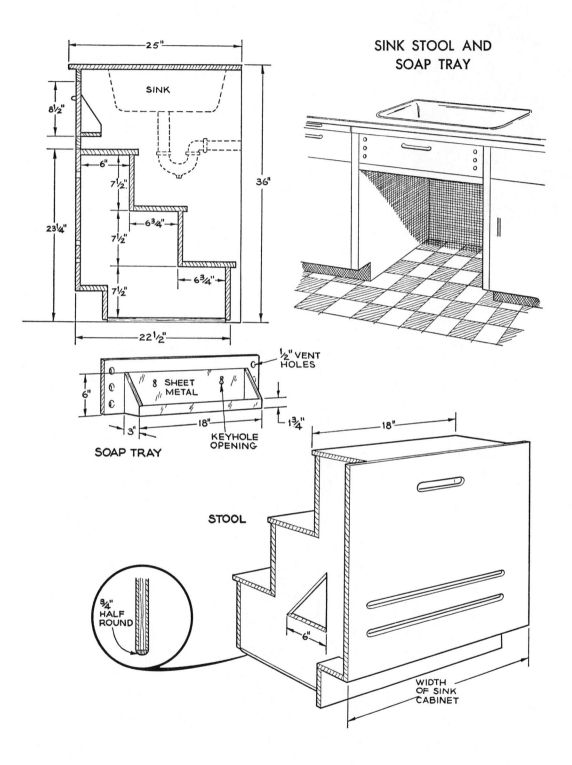

25"

SINK

8½"

6"

7½"

6¾"

7½"

6¾"

7½"

36"

23¼"

22½"

SINK STOOL AND
SOAP TRAY

½" VENT
HOLES

8 SHEET
METAL

6"

3"

18"

1¾"

KEYHOLE
OPENING

SOAP TRAY

STOOL

18"

6"

¾"
HALF
ROUND

WIDTH
OF SINK
CABINET

SINK CABINET WITH TOWEL RACK

A slide-out towel rack is convenient at the sink—and that's one of the features of this sink cabinet. Your local building-supply dealer should be able to order the rack for you—or you can check the chapter on kitchen hardware later in this book. Note that ¾″ vent holes are drilled on the ceiling of the toe space, and that vent slots are located at the upper edge of the 8″-wide facing board above the doors. Photo and drawing by American Plywood Association.

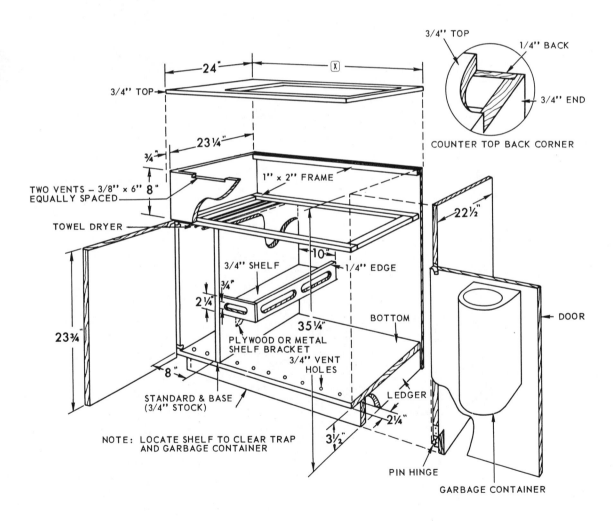

DIAGONAL CORNER SINK

A sink placed across a corner will sometimes improve kitchen working arrangement, besides creating a novel effect. Located at 45 degrees across the inside of the corner formed by the line of base
cabinets, the front of the sink cabinet tends to round and smooth
the flow of the cabinet fronts, as you see in the above Caloric kitchen
installation. A deep corner cabinet is required for the sink. For its
shape, see the sketch of the diagonal corner cabinet, in the chapter on
corner cabinets.

In general, a single bowl is most suitable for corner sink installation. Most double bowls would increase the length of the sink front
so much, at the same time boosting depth, that it would become impossible to utilize the space at the far back corner inside the cabinet.
If the sink front is limited to about 24″, the housewife will be able
to use most of the cabinet space—with a little reaching, of course.
Installation of one or two sliding shelves will improve the utility
of such a cabinet. These can be mounted between hardwood guides
or on metal slides as suggested for the sliding shelf cabinet in the chapter on base cabinets. In the case of the corner sink cabinet, the
shelves could be given a 90-degree point at the rear to fit into the
corner. Stationary shelves could fill the cabinet space on either side
of the sliding shelves—at the same level. A lip an inch or two high
on the rear edges of the sliding shelves would keep stored articles
from falling off to the rear when the shelves are pulled out.

PENINSULA SINK

A kitchen sink doesn't always have to be backed up by a wall. For a more efficient working layout, it sometimes is located in a "peninsula" of cabinets jutting from the wall or in an "island" in the middle of the room—with walking space all around. Your basic kitchen plan will help you determine whether such a location is desirable. Any against-the-wall type of sink cabinet can be used. It will of course need its own back. But before placing a sink in such a location, be sure that piping the water there and installing the drain will present no difficulty or costly plumbing problems.

A good idea worth copying in more kitchens is pictured in this Tappan photo. A single sink was installed on each side of the corner with a swing faucet between.

11

Special-Purpose Base Cabinets

Base cabinets are the work horses of the kitchen. Their tops provide a convenient work space for the many activities that go on in a kitchen. Their drawers and shelves store the bulk of the equipment required for these activities.

Modern base cabinets should not be confused, however, with old-fashioned cupboards. Inside the modern cabinets you will find far more than mere shelves and drawers. A shelf, strangely enough, no longer means just a fixed board in a fixed position between two uprights. Not only may today's shelf adjust up and down; it may in some base cabinets slide forward and out to display its stored wares for the housewife's ready selection. Shelves sometimes stand on end, too, sliding out of the cabinet (on rollers perhaps) and bringing into the light an array of kitchen tools and pots and pans supported on hooks.

Drawers also are in step with the times. They no longer are just catch-all boxes. Instead, some drawers lead an extremely specialized life, designed and fitted to do only one job. But they do this one job well.

Examples will be found on the following pages for your selection.

SLIDING SHELF CABINET

Uses

If you have known the annoyance of sorting through a cluttered bottom cupboard shelf and finally, perhaps, removing the contents to reach an article stored at the rear, you must have wished for a better method of storage. You can have it by installing shelves that slide forward and out. You then can see and reach anything, anywhere on the shelf.

Sliding shelves have become an important feature of modern kitchens. They serve a variety of purposes. With egg-crate divisions they store bottles nicely. Most commercial pull-out shelves have a surrounding lip to keep the contents from sliding off. These can be kept low, an inch or so above the shelf surface if you wish. How high you make the lip depends on what you plan to store on the shelf.

The simplest form of pull-out shelf is sketched at the bottom right on the accompanying page of drawings. This is simply a board with a rear ledge. The sliding shelf rests on the bottom shelf of an existing cabinet. Whatever the base cupboards you have, adding pull-out shelves like this one would make a big hit with the housewife. In some cases a breadboard of the right size might be used.

Materials

1″ x 2″ (nom.) stock (45 linear feet) — framing.

1″ x 3″ (nom.) stock (30 linear feet) — framing.

1″ x 4″ (nom.) stock (8 linear feet) — base.

⅝″ plywood (2′ x 4′ panel) to make—

    1 pc. 21⅛″ x 23″ — shelf.   1 pc. 21″ x 23″ — shelf.

    Strips of desired width around shelves, drawer sides, and back.

¾″ plywood (3′ x 4′ panel) to make—

    1 pc. 21¾″ x 25″ — door.   1 pc. 24¾″ x 25″ — counter.

    1 pc. 5″ x 21½″ — drawer front.

¼″ x 21½″ x 23″ plywood — drawer bottom.

Ball-bearing pull-out slides if available or desired.

⅛″ material for egg-crate construction for bottle tray.

SLIDING SHELF CABINET

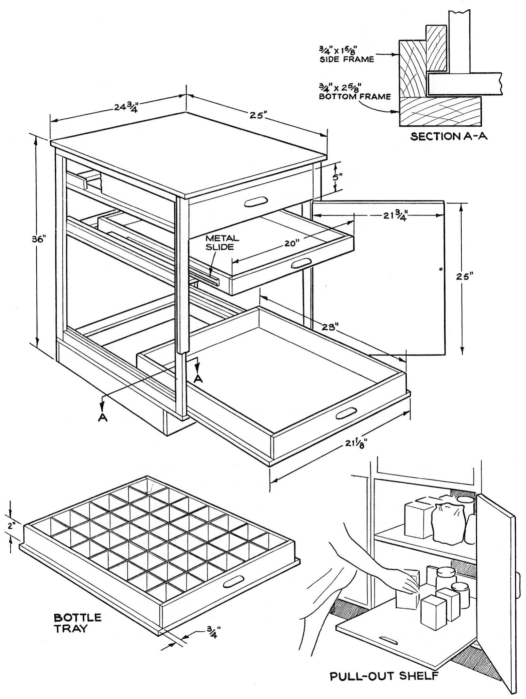

3/4" x 1 5/8" SIDE FRAME

3/4" x 2 5/8" BOTTOM FRAME

SECTION A-A

24 3/4"

25"

5"

21 3/4"

36"

METAL SLIDE

20"

25"

23"

A

A

21 1/8"

2"

BOTTLE TRAY

3/4"

PULL-OUT SHELF

Pointers for Building

Because of the variations suggested in the project, a hard-and-fast construction procedure is impossible. However, the cabinet itself can be built about the same in any case.

Make three 24″ x 24″ frames of 1″ x 3″ (nom.) material—for use under the two pull-out shelves and the drawer. Make another frame of 1″ x 2″ (nom.) stock for use just under the counter. Notch the front corners of this frame ¾″ x ¾″ to inset the vertical facing strips. Attach these horizontal frames between vertical side frames made of 1″ x 2″ (nom.) stock. Install 1″ x 2″ (nom.) strips on the side frames as guides for the drawer and the sliding shelves.

As shown, the cabinet sides can be enclosed with ¾″ material. The counter and vertical facing strips overhang for that reason. However, the cabinet probably will be located between others. In that case no partitions will be needed.

Two slide possibilities are shown. The bottom tray has a protruding lip on each side that rides in a suitable recess (see Section A-A) in the framing. The upper tray is mounted on metal drawer slides, which are available at hardware stores.

WIRE VEGETABLE BIN

This makes use of a ready-made wire basket—an accessory storage container such as sold by Sears Roebuck and others for home freezers. The mesh is small enough to hold all except the smallest fruits and vegetables. An overall length of 22¾″ makes the basket exactly right for installation behind a door in cabinets that have a 25″ work counter with a 1″ overhang. Close fitting would also put the basket into a cabinet that is 1″ less from front to back. A 12″ opening in the cabinet front will take the basket and a suitable mounting frame. Since the basket is 9″ deep, you can easily stack in two plus a conventional drawer. Three would go into a standard cabinet 36″ high, if your household needs this much vegetable and fruit storage.

The drawing suggests one way of mounting the baskets so they

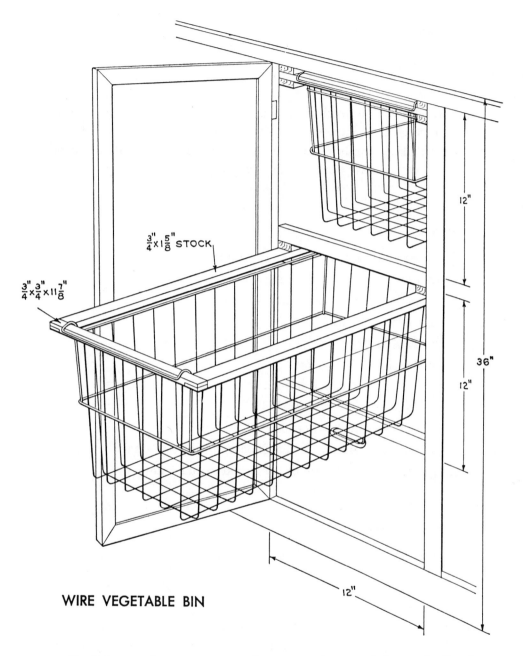

$\frac{3}{4}"\times 1\frac{5}{8}"$ STOCK

$\frac{3}{4}"\times\frac{3}{4}"\times 11\frac{7}{8}"$

12"

36"

12"

12"

WIRE VEGETABLE BIN

will slide out for easy access. A rectangular wood frame is fitted around the basket and the frame slides in parallel guides screwed to the sides of the cabinet or cabinet frame. Hardwood is best for this.

SWINGING BIN CABINET

Uses

You'll never find a much easier way of keeping vegetables and fruit within reach than these swinging bins. You can buy such bins from some building supply dealers or, if they are hard to find, you can make them or have them made. Despite the space the bins take, there's still room at the back of the shelves for other supplies.

Materials

1″ x 2″ (nom.) stock (26 linear feet) — framing.

1″ x 4″ (nom.) stock (8 linear feet)— base.

¾″ plywood (4′ x 5′ panel) to make—

   1 pc. 20″ x 25″ — top.

   2 pc. 23¼″ x 31¼″ — sides.

   2 pc. 14 1/16″ x 17″ — doors.

⅜″ plywood (2′ x 4′ panel) to make—

   1 pc. 18½″ x 24″ — middle shelf.

   1 pc. 18½″ x 23¼″ — bottom shelf.

¼″ x 20″ x 31⅝″ plywood or hardboard — back (optional).

1 16 11/16″ x 22″ breadboard, or hardwood to make same.

Pointers for Building

Make the top frame of 1″ x 2″ stock placed flat as shown in the detail. Below this, spacing to allow clearance for the pull-out board, mount a second frame, this one with the side members each moved inward 1⅝″—the width of the stock—to support the pull-out board.

   If you can't buy suitable bins, you can make each one from two pieces of easily worked sheet metal as suggested in the drawing. Solder the seams. The bottom of the bins might be made from wood.

SWINGING BIN CABINET

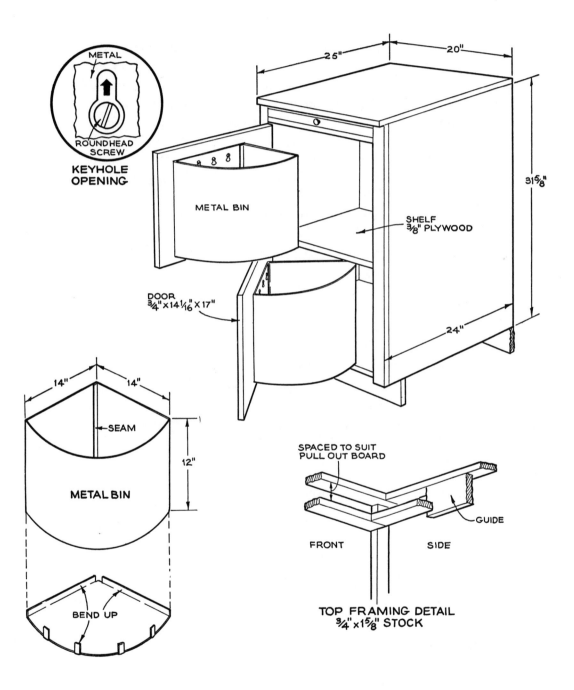

KEYHOLE
OPENING

METAL

ROUNDHEAD
SCREW

25"

20"

31⅝"

METAL BIN

SHELF
⅜" PLYWOOD

DOOR
¾"x14¹⁄₁₆"x17"

24"

14"   14"

SEAM

12"

METAL BIN

BEND UP

SPACED TO SUIT
PULL OUT BOARD

GUIDE

FRONT   SIDE

TOP FRAMING DETAIL
¾"x1⅝" STOCK

TRAY AND BREAD CABINET

Uses

This combination unit could of course be separated and the two parts used in different parts of the kitchen. It is economical of material and effort, however, to put two such units into one. The stand-up rack holds trays neatly on end, making it easy to select the one you want. Keeping bread and pastries fresh no longer requires a container out in the open. The sketches suggest three things you can do to hide them. Building supply dealers, hardware stores, and mail-order houses can furnish insertable metal boxes to fit drawers of various depths, some with sliding tops, others with lift-up lids. Two sketches show how to use these types. A third indicates how you can adapt a deep drawer to a conventional shelf-type bread box. Cutting out or leaving off one side of the drawer will let the housewife keep the box endwise and open it from the side of the drawer. Such a box could also be kept on just a simple pull-out shelf.

Materials

1″ x 4″ (nom.) stock (12 linear feet) — base.

1″ x 2″ (nom.) stock (24 linear feet) — framing.

¾″ plywood (4′ x 8′ and 3′ x 4′ panels) to make—

    1 pc. 25″ x 33½″ — top.   2 pc. 23″ x 35¼″ — sides.

    1 pc. 14⅞″ x 30″ — door.

    2 pc. 15¾″ x 23″ — rack top and floor.

    2 pc. 13¾″ x 14¼″ — drawer fronts (or to suit).

¼″ plywood (4′ x 8′ and 3′ x 4′ panels) to make—

    1 pc. 33½″ x 35¼″ — back (optional).

    4 pc. 23″ x 30⅜″ — dividers.

    2 pc. 13″ x 22″ — drawer bottoms.

    2 pc. 13¾″ x 14¼″ — drawer backs.

2 pc. ⅝″ plywood 14¼″ x 22″ — drawer sides.

Insertable metal bread boxes.

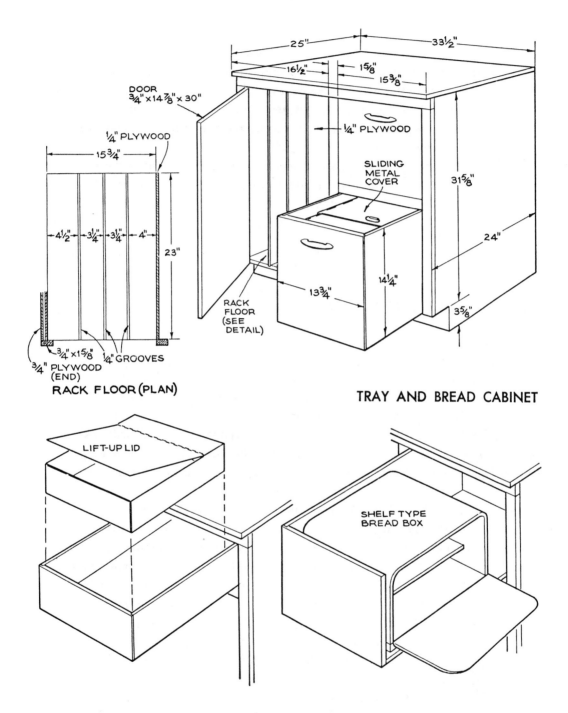

DOOR
$\frac{3}{4}$" × 14$\frac{7}{8}$" × 30"

$\frac{1}{4}$" PLYWOOD

$\frac{1}{4}$" PLYWOOD

SLIDING
METAL
COVER

25"

33$\frac{1}{2}$"

16$\frac{1}{2}$"

1$\frac{5}{8}$"

15$\frac{3}{8}$"

15$\frac{3}{4}$"

23"

4$\frac{1}{2}$" 3$\frac{1}{4}$" 3$\frac{1}{4}$" 4"

31$\frac{5}{8}$"

24"

14$\frac{1}{4}$"

13$\frac{3}{4}$"

3$\frac{5}{8}$"

RACK
FLOOR
(SEE
DETAIL)

$\frac{3}{4}$" × 1$\frac{5}{8}$"

$\frac{1}{4}$" GROOVES

$\frac{3}{4}$" PLYWOOD
(END)

RACK FLOOR (PLAN)

TRAY AND BREAD CABINET

LIFT-UP LID

SHELF TYPE
BREAD BOX

Pointers for Building

Cut three ¼″ x ¼″ grooves lengthwise in the two 15¾″ x 23″ pieces of ¾″ plywood that will support the tray rack partitions. Install one as the base of the cabinet. Attach the other under the counter with the dadoes facing downward. Glue the ¼″ partitions in place. One goes against the edge to separate the tray rack from the bread cabinet.

Adjust the size of the drawers you build to the bread box or boxes you intend to use. Make the boxes an easy fit so they can be removed from the drawers for cleaning.

PULL-OUT BOARD CABINET

The original of this base cabinet forms part of a food preparation and clearing center designed and tested by kitchen specialists in the U.S. Department of Agriculture.

A handy feature of the cabinet is the pull-out board with self-locking stop that provides a surface slightly lower than the 36-inch counter for rolling, kneading, or mixing. The food grinder can also be clamped here.

Rather than make the pull-out board, the builder may prefer to buy one ready-made. Either the board itself can be cut down to the dimensions indicated or the recess in the counter top framing altered to suit. In either case, keep the 1⁄16″ difference (clearance) between the thickness of the board (1¹⁄₁₆″) and the depth of the recess (¾″) to assure proper operation. The stops under the board must work easily so that gravity will cause them to drop. As the drawing shows, the rear stop limits the position to which the board can be pulled out. The front one, pressed into its slot while the board is being withdrawn, automatically drops and locks the board. Pressing up this stop releases the board so it can be shoved in.

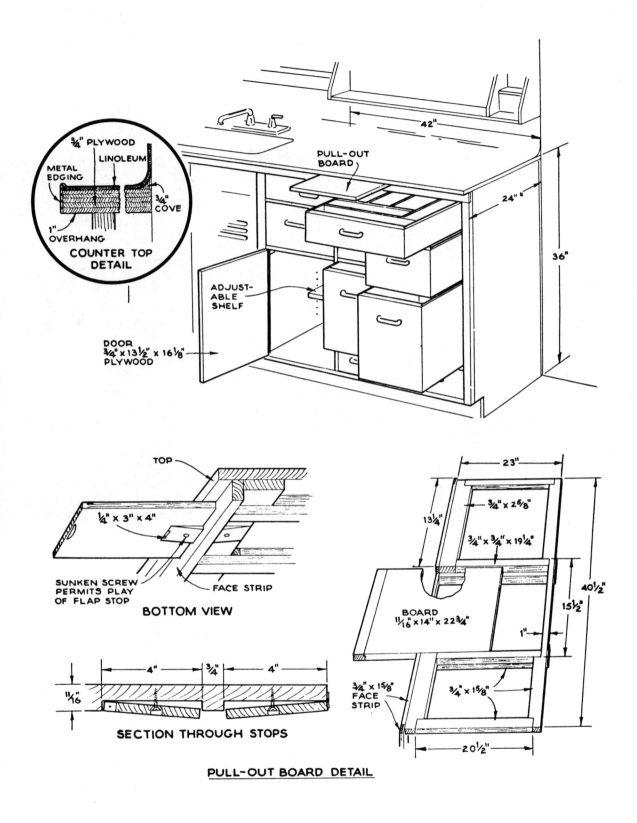

COUNTER TOP DETAIL

¾" PLYWOOD

LINOLEUM

METAL EDGING

¾" COVE

1" OVERHANG

PULL-OUT BOARD

42"

24"

36"

ADJUST-ABLE SHELF

DOOR
¾" × 13½" × 16⅛"
PLYWOOD

TOP

¼" × 3" × 4"

SUNKEN SCREW
PERMITS PLAY
OF FLAP STOP

FACE STRIP

BOTTOM VIEW

4"   ¾"   4"

11/16"

SECTION THROUGH STOPS

23"

¾" × 2⅝"

¾" × ¾" × 19¼"

13¼"

40½"

15½"

1"

BOARD
11/16" × 14" × 22¾"

¾" × 1⅝"
FACE STRIP

¾" × 1⅝"

20½"

PULL-OUT BOARD DETAIL

POP-UP MIXER CABINET

A spring-actuated shelf raises the mixer to working height from its storage space within the cabinet, a convenience that any housewife will enjoy. At least two types of such hardware are available. One permits use of drawer under the countertop above the mixer storage compartment. The other elevates the mixer from immediately below the countertop.

With all the features shown, this cabinet becomes a complete center for all kitchen mixing operations. The lapboard offers a restful place to work. The slide-out shelves bring stored equipment out for easy access. Drawing and photos by American Plywood Association.

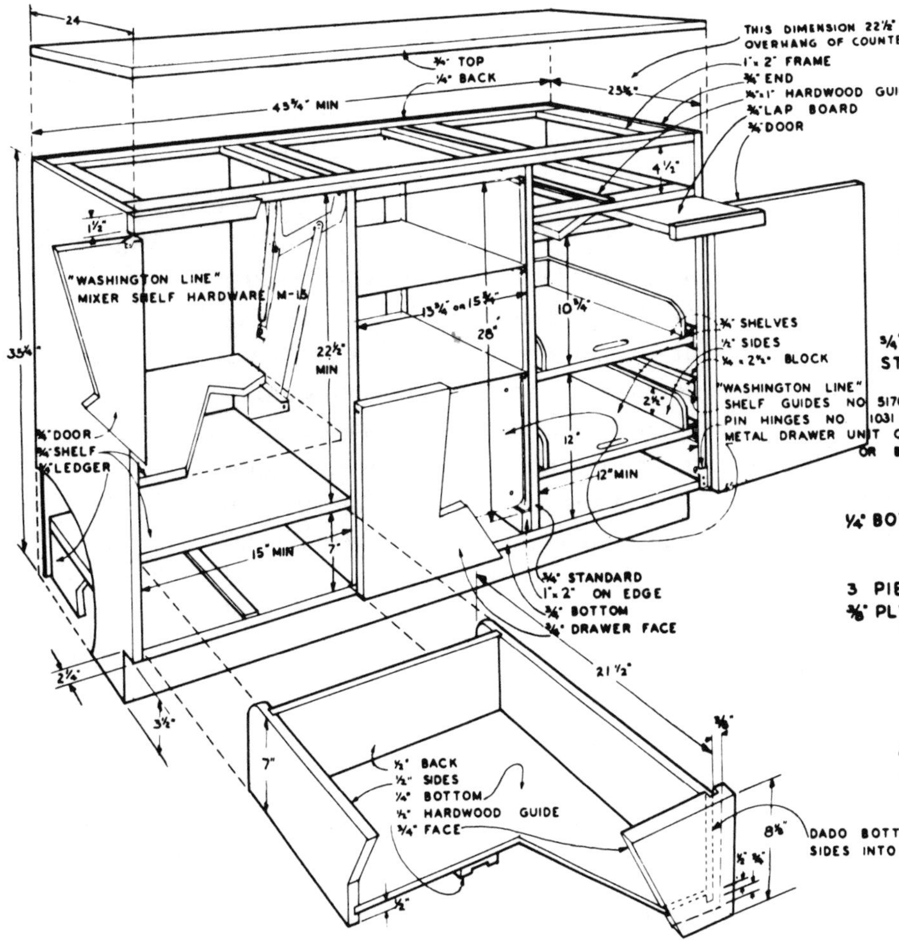
24
THIS DIMENSION 22½" FOR ¾" OVERHANG OF COUNTER EDGE
¾" TOP
¼" BACK
1" x 2" FRAME
¾" END
¾" x 1" HARDWOOD GUIDE
¾" LAP BOARD
¾" DOOR
43¾" MIN
23⅝"
4½"
1½"
"WASHINGTON LINE" MIXER SHELF HARDWARE M-15
35¾"
22½" MIN
13¾" OR 15¾"
28"
10¾"
¾" SHELVES
½" SIDES
¾ x 2½" BLOCK
2½"
"WASHINGTON LINE" SHELF GUIDES NO 5170
PIN HINGES NO 1031
METAL DRAWER UNIT C2CD 15¾" WIDE OR B2BE 13¾" WIDE
12"
12" MIN
¾" DOOR
¾" SHELF
¾" LEDGER
15" MIN
7"
¾" STANDARD
1" x 2" ON EDGE
¾" BOTTOM
¾" DRAWER FACE
2⅛"
3½"
21½"
7"
½" BACK
½" SIDES
¼" BOTTOM
½" HARDWOOD GUIDE
3/4" FACE
8⅛"
DADO BOTTOM AND SIDES INTO FACE
½"

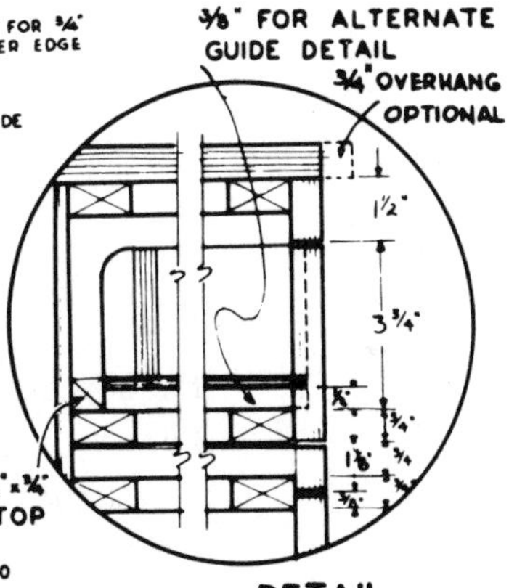
⅜" FOR ALTERNATE GUIDE DETAIL
¾" OVERHANG OPTIONAL
1½"
3¾"
3/4" x 3/4" STOP

DETAIL

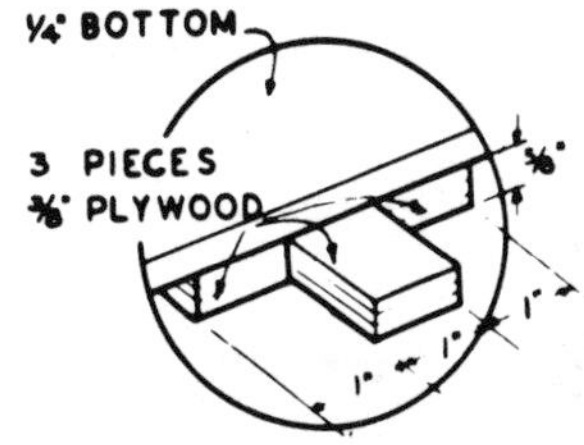
¼" BOTTOM
3 PIECES
⅜" PLYWOOD
⅝"
1"
1"
1"

ALTERNATE DRAWER GUIDE DETAIL

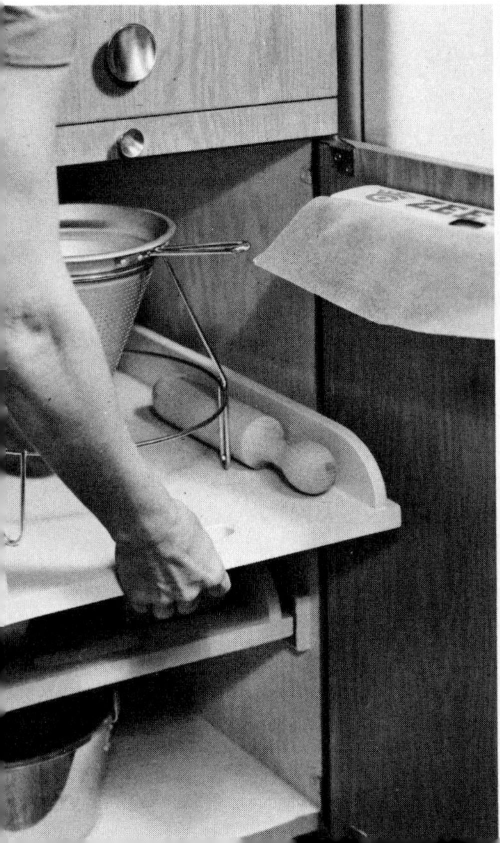

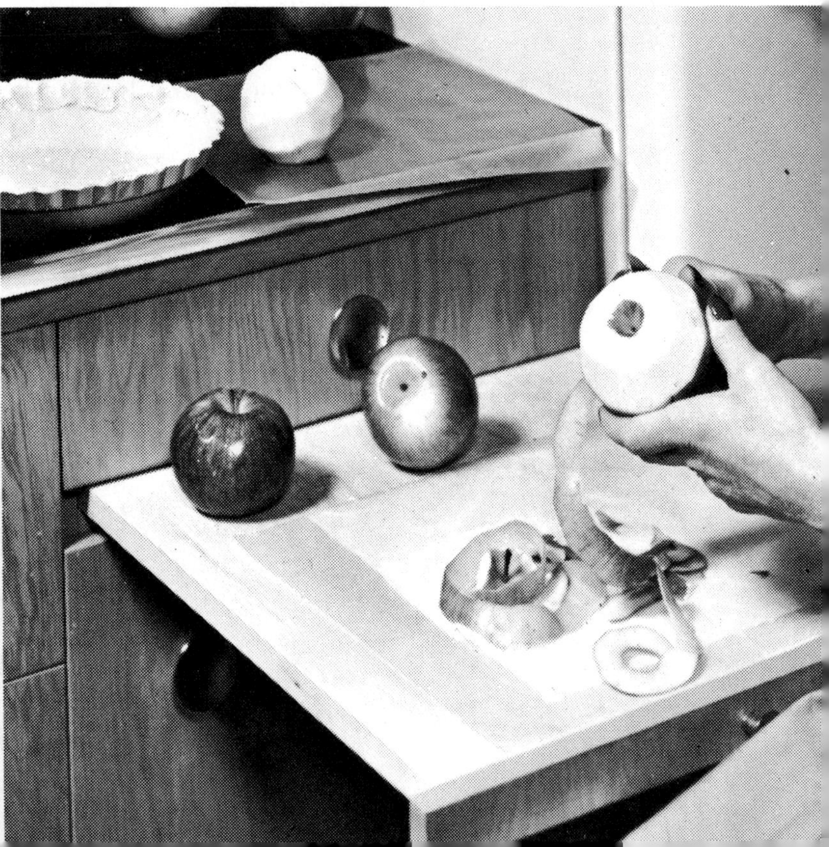

UTENSIL CABINET

Uses

The space behind the two doors will hold the largest cooking utensils. The adjustable shelf, only 18″ wide, makes it possible to use the space to best advantage. The fact that the shelf is narrow enables the house-wife to see and reach articles stored on the bottom of the cupboard.

Kitchen textiles, place mats, and the like can be kept in the shallow bottom drawer. Silver, serving spoons, and dish towels and cloths can go in the upper drawers. The plans show four possible arrangements of dividers for these drawers. One or more of these divider plans can also be used in the corresponding drawers of the food preparation cabinet.

Materials

FRAMING:

1″ x 2″ (nom.) stock (46 linear feet).

1″ x 3″ (nom.) stock (12 linear feet).

1″ x 4″ (nom.) stock (12 linear feet).

1″ x 5″ (nom.) stock (6 linear feet).

¾″ plywood (4′ x 8′ panel, 2′ x 4′ panel) to make—

2 pc. 23″ x 35″ — ends.

1 pc. 23¾″ x 40½″ — fixed shelf.

1 pc. 18″ x 40½″ — adjustable shelf.

2 pc. 19⅛″ x 19⅜″ — doors.

1 pc. 25″ x 42″ — counter top.

2 pc. 4⅜″ x 19″ — drawer fronts.

1 pc. 4″ x 38¾″ — drawer front.

½″ plywood (4′ x 4′ panel) — drawer sides and back.

¼″ plywood (4′ x 4′ panel) to make—

1 pc. 22½″ x 38¼″ ⎤
2 pc. 18½″ x 22½″ ⎦ drawer bottoms.

Drawer partitions as desired.

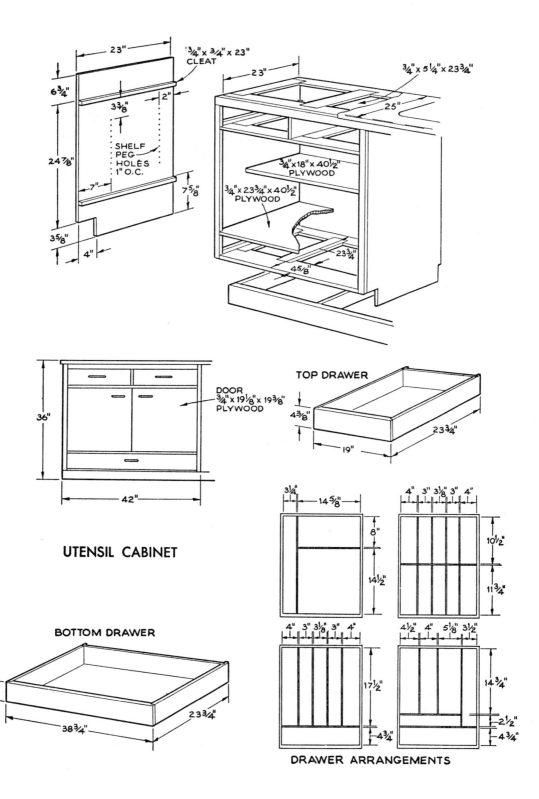

UTENSIL CABINET

TOP DRAWER

BOTTOM DRAWER

DRAWER ARRANGEMENTS

SERVING CABINET

Uses

Located beside the range, this cabinet offers counter space for dishing up a meal, and the drawer and shelves below provide storage for utensils and equipment used in the job of cooking it. The shelves are adjustable to permit best use of the space.

Materials

1" x 2" (nom.) stock (14 linear feet)
1" x 4" (nom.) stock (12 linear feet) } framing.

¾" plywood (4' x 8' panel) to make—

   2 pc. 23" x 35" — ends.
   2 pc. 10⅜" x 24¼" — doors.
   1 pc. 24" x 25" — counter.
   1 pc. 18" x 22½" — shelf.
   1 pc. 20" x 22½" — shelf.
   1 pc. 22½" x 23" — bottom.
   1 pc. 5" x 20¾" — drawer front.

½" plywood (16" x 24" sheet) — drawer sides and back.

¼" plywood (3' x 4' panel) to make—

   1 pc. 24" x 35¼" — back.
   1 pc. 20½" x 23¼" — drawer bottom.

8 pc. ¼" x 1¼" dowels — shelf pegs.
2 pr. 1½" x 1½" hinges.
2 door pulls.
1 drawer pull.
2 cabinet catches.
½ lb. 4d finishing nails.
1½ lb. 6d finishing nails.
1 doz. 1½" No. 8 wood screws.
1 doz. 1¼" No. 4 wood screws.

SERVING CABINET

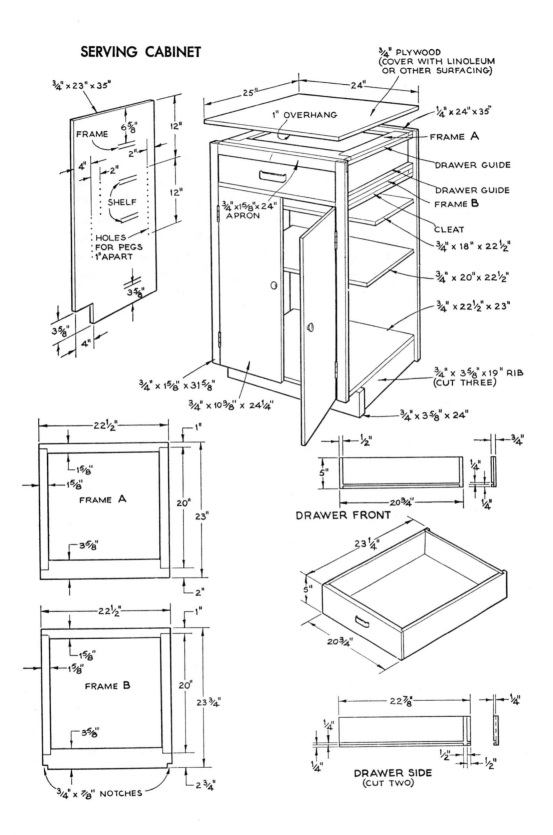

3/4" x 23" x 35"

FRAME

6 5/8"

12"

2"

4"

2"

SHELF

12"

HOLES
FOR PEGS
1" APART

3 5/8"

3 5/8"

4"

3/4" PLYWOOD
(COVER WITH LINOLEUM
OR OTHER SURFACING)

25"

24"

1" OVERHANG

1/4" x 24" x 35"

FRAME A

DRAWER GUIDE

DRAWER GUIDE

FRAME B

CLEAT

3/4" x 18" x 22 1/2"

3/4" x 20" x 22 1/2"

3/4" x 22 1/2" x 23"

3/4" x 1 5/8" x 24"
APRON

3/4" x 1 5/8" x 31 5/8"

3/4" x 10 3/8" x 24 1/4"

3/4" x 3 5/8" x 19" RIB
(CUT THREE)

3/4" x 3 5/8" x 24"

22 1/2"

1"

1 5/8"

1 5/8"

FRAME A

20"

23"

3 5/8"

2"

22 1/2"

1"

1 5/8"

1 5/8"

FRAME B

20"

23 3/4"

3 5/8"

2 3/4"

3/4" x 7/8" NOTCHES

1/2"

5"

20 3/4"

3/4"

1/4"

1/4"

DRAWER FRONT

23 1/4"

5"

20 3/4"

22 7/8"

1/4"

1/4"

1/4"

1/2"

1/2"

DRAWER SIDE
(CUT TWO)

PLATTER CABINET

Uses

In the step-saving U-kitchen designed by the Bureau of Human Nutrition and Home Economics, this cabinet adjoins the pull-out towel rack described in a later chapter and is located under the serving counter. (Sliding doors at the rear of the counter provide a pass-through opening to the dining room.) From top to bottom, the base cabinet includes a large breadboard, a drawer for small utensils used at the range (meat forks, basting spoons, potato masher, and other pieces), a metal-lined bread box big enough for four loaves and a pan or two of rolls, and a vertical file cupboard for trays, cooling racks, a turkey platter, and other large items most conveniently stored upright. The cabinet of course can be built as a separate unit and used at any desired location in the kitchen.

Materials

1″ x 2″ (nom.) stock (44 linear feet) — framing.

1″ x 4″ (nom.) stock (10 linear feet) — base.

16½″ x 22″ breadboard (or hardwood to make).

¾″ plywood (4′ x 6′ panel) to make—

    2 pc. 8¼″ x 16⅜″ — doors.

    1 pc. 7⅝″ x 16½″ (or 1″ x 8″ (nom.) stock) — drawer front.

    1 pc. 4⅝″ x 16½″ (or 1″ x 5″ (nom.) stock) — drawer front.

    2 pc. 23″ x 35″ — cabinet ends.

    1 pc. 20″ x 25″ — counter.

    1 pc. 17¼″ x 23″ — cabinet bottom.

    1 pc. 8″ x 17¼″ — backing for dividers.

½″ plywood (2′ x 4′ panel) to make—

    1 pc. 18¾″ x 35″ — cabinet back.

    7 pc. 12″ x 20½″ — dividers.

    2 pc. 16″ x 24″ — drawer bottoms.

⅛″ x 1¼″ plywood or hardboard strips (7 linear feet) — drawer dividers.

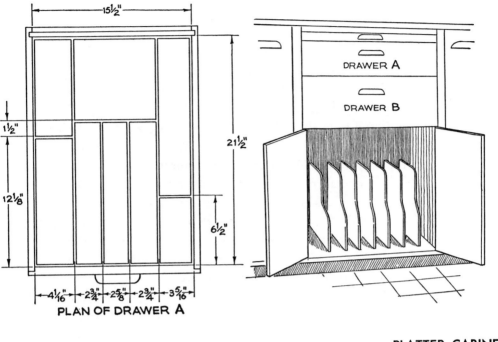

15½"

1½"

12⅛"

21½"

6½"

4 1/16" 2¾" 2⅝" 2¾" 3 5/16"

PLAN OF DRAWER A

DRAWER A

DRAWER B

PLATTER CABINET

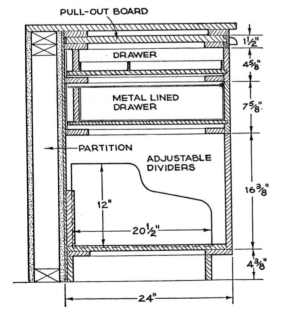

PULL-OUT BOARD

DRAWER

1½"

4⅝"

METAL LINED
DRAWER

7⅝"

PARTITION

ADJUSTABLE
DIVIDERS

12"

16⅜"

20½"

4⅜"

24"

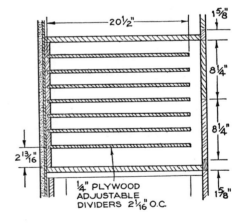

20½"

1⅝"

8¼"

8¼"

2 13/16"

¼" PLYWOOD
ADJUSTABLE
DIVIDERS 2 1/16" O.C.

1⅞"

Pointers for Building

Cut the two ¾″ plywood sides for the cabinet and lay out on each the positions for the frames that will support the two drawers, the pull-out board, and the bottom of the cabinet. Cut and assemble these frames, using 1″ x 2″ stock or 1″ x 3″ if desired. Note, however, that a piece of 1″ x 4″ stock is required for the front piece of the bottom frame to enclose the toe space. Cut ¾″ x 1⅝″ notches in the front corners of this frame, as well as the counter-supporting frame at the top, to take the two 1″ x 2″ (nominal) vertical facing strips. Make the overall length of both of these frames 23¾″. Those that support the drawers and pull-out board are only 23″ long.

Build the two drawers by conventional methods, using the materials indicated. Install dividing strips ⅛″ thick in drawer A according to the plan given. The other deeper drawer (B) can be lined with metal according to procedures previously described. Or you may wish to change the dimensions to suit a box that you are able to buy ready-made. As suggested for other cabinets, you may find it most satisfactory to install a ready-made breadboard instead of assembling your own. A 1½″ strip screwed, glued or otherwise fastened to the forward edge as indicated in the drawings will provide a lip to butt against the frame in which the board slides. Install a locking stop in the board as described in previous projects. For the file compartment below, cut ¼″ grooves ¼″ deep in the bottom and backing pieces for the ¼″ plywood dividers. Space these grooves as shown in the plan.

BASE CABINET IDEAS

Cabinet End Storage

Where a line of base cabinets comes to an end, perhaps at a door, you can set aside a narrow space adjoining the wall in the end cabinet for storage of large baking sheets, trays, and similar flat utensils. The depth of the drawers or cupboard shelves at the front of this cabinet of course will have to be reduced by the width devoted to the end recess. Fit a narrow door to the recess.

Curved shelves at the corner would provide a freer passageway past the end of the cabinet. The shelves might be utilized either for decorative knickknacks or such practical items as a toaster or mixer. Triangular shelves could be used too.

Laundry Hamper

The kitchen-cabinet builder can make provision in various ways for storage of soiled laundry.

A metal-lined chute behind a base-cabinet door is a big time saver if laundry is done in the basement. An entire base cabinet can also be devoted to temporary storage by hinging its door to swing downward. If a 6″ or 8″ strip of the upper end is separately hinged to the door itself, opening the strip will allow laundry to be stuffed into the cabinet. The entire door need be opened only when the laundry is to be removed on wash day.

A tilt-out hamper installed in a cabinet is one of the most favored storage devices. For a bin occupying the full base-cabinet height, curve the upper edges to a radius slightly less than the height of the front, with the bottom hinge as the pivot point. Make the front-to-back dimension about 1″ less than the cabinet depth. If the bin is made removable, the load can be carried direct to the washer. One way of doing this: Cut key-hole slots in the bin face, with the large ends down, and suspend it on roundhead screws driven part way into the rear surface of the door. A limit chain or other stop device can be used to keep the door from swinging down too far when opened.

Screen-Bottom Vegetable Drawers

Stored fruits and vegetables should be well ventilated. Drawers with wire screen bottoms in a base cabinet offer one convenient way of providing ventilation. Frame and build the cabinet in the usual way. On the face just below the counter, leave an opening about 3″ wide and almost as long as the cabinet is wide. Fill this with a metal grill, or perhaps wood lattice work. Also screen a narrow opening in the ceiling of the cabinet toe space. Air entering there will sweep up through the screen bottoms of the drawers and out the upper vent. You could have either two or three drawers. Heavy, rust-resistant mesh would be best for the drawer bottoms, but ordinary copper or aluminum window screening could be used if supported by wood strips spaced at intervals across the drawer bottom.

Heated Towel Dryer

There are several ways an ingenious builder might speed the drying of kitchen towels stored on rods inside a base cabinet.

For instance, why not make use of the heat source that warms the kitchen? If this is a steam or hot-water radiator, simply locating the cabinet beside it, or perhaps above, could be considered. If an unsightly old-fashioned radiator is to be hidden behind a perforated enclosure, it may be possible to combine a towel storage unit with it. If a warm-air system sends heat into the kitchen through a wall or floor register, the drying cabinet might go in front of or above the register, with a decorative grill in the cabinet door to pass the stream of heat on into the kitchen after it has passed around the towels. All such heating-source methods, of course, have a major drawback. They'll only help dry towels during the house-heating season. For all-year use, they might be combined with electrical heat that the housewife could switch on and off as desired. Such a combination would help hold down the electric bill.

Electrical units suitable for installation in a towel cabinet—a fan-heater, a hair dryer, a glass panel heater—all are likely to cost too much if devoted to towel drying alone. But this can be avoided by retaining the unit *for its original use* and merely *storing* it in the towel cabinet in a way that it can be used there, but withdrawn when desired. An ordinary cooling fan might also be put to use the same way. A pilot light mounted outside the towel cabinet will guard against forgetting that the dryer is on.

Aluminum-Foil Bread Box

Using household aluminum foil, you can convert a base-cabinet drawer into a bread box that offers storage protection equal to a metal box. Use the heavy foil designed for wrapping frozen foods.

If you build the drawer from scratch, you could use a separate piece of foil on the inside surface of each piece of the drawer, cutting the foil slightly larger than the drawer part and then wedging the edges into the joints when you assemble the drawer. Tape designed for use on foil will seal the joints. In the case of a finished drawer, you can cut and fold the foil to line the interior. Again seal the foil joints with tape.

Install a hinged cover on the drawer. Brad small cleats to the inner surfaces of the sides, front and back, locating them ½" below the upper edges. Cut a cover from ⅜" stock to fit down snugly on the cleats. Then saw the cover crosswise at a point about two-thirds of the way to the rear. Face the cover pieces with foil flapped over the edges. After hinging the two parts together, brad the rear piece permanently down on the cleats. Punch several ventilation holes through the cover and install a flat knob or other finger pull for opening the lid when the drawer has been withdrawn from the cabinet part way.

Sliding-Shelf Mixer Cabinet

A narrow-base cabinet designed just for storage of the mixer may be preferred by some home owners, the mixer being removed and used on the counter top. A compartment with an inside width of about 14" is sufficient for such storage. Since the mixer does not require the full cabinet depth (front to back), a sliding shelf to carry it to the rear and bring it out again easily will make it possible to install shelves on the inside of the door—and thus utilize some of the space that would be lost at the rear if the mixer were stored at the front of a stationary shelf. Locate the sliding shelf at the height where the top of the mixer will just clear the top of the door opening. Use the area below this shelf for storage of mixing bowls and related equipment.

12

Vertical Pull-Out Racks

Vertical pull-out racks in base cabinets are a comparatively new type of kitchen storage device. They take a variety of forms, each designed for a special job. They are divided into two general classes—those that slide on a raised floor in the cabinet (perhaps on rollers or special bearings) and those that have their own rubber-tired casters to roll out from under the work counter on the kitchen floor.

Sliding racks generally are of greatest value for storage of bulky lightweight materials. If heavy articles are introduced, slides with roller bearings become necessary. In this respect, it is interesting to note that some home cabinet builders have put skate wheels to excellent use. Mounted on large rubber-tired caster wheels (about 2″ diameter) the roll-out racks will move easily even with quite a heavy load.

Home economics research workers at the Oregon State College, Corvallis, Oregon, have made an extensive exploration of the possibilities of pull-out racks. They make these recommendations about designing racks for specific purposes:

"Use the following method of determining the height of the available storage space: Determine the construction allowances for: (1) distance from top of cabinet to bottom of apron, (2) top of base to floor. Add these two figures and subtract the sum from the overall height of the cabinet. This gives you the overall height of the pull-out rack. To determine the width of the available storage space, add the widths of the facing strips and subtract the sum from the overall width of the cabinet.

"Draw a sketch of the face of the cabinet and draw lines to indicate the construction allowances. After you have decided how to utilize the available storage space enter the measurements on your sketch.

"If you are planning a rack with shelves, cut pieces of paper the width and depth of the available space. Arrange your utensils and supplies and determine the number of shelves, the distances between them and the minimum overall width of the rack. Remember to allow clearances for handling contents, also thickness of materials used in the rack itself.

"If you are planning a rack for hanging utensils, cut pieces of paper the height and depth of this space and arrange the utensils with handle holes in a row at the top. After you have decided how to utilize the storage space, complete your sketch, entering dimensions and proposed use."

BESIDE-THE-RANGE TOWEL RACK

Uses

This pull-out towel rack draws heat from the range to dry tea towels placed on the four $1/2''$ rods staggered across its width at varying heights. This is probably the best location in the kitchen for such a rack. Safety requirements are met by placing a sheet of asbestos board on the side next to the range, and holes bored in the asbestos and toe board and near the top of the front panel provide a flow of warm air to dry the towels. The rack slides out on the mating parts of a hardwood slide. A stop limits its travel, yet turns to allow the rack to be removed from the cabinet and placed beside a register or other source of heat to dry the towels faster.

Materials

1″ x 2″ (nom.) stock (18 linear feet) — framing.

1″ x 4″ (nom.) stock (4 linear feet) — base.

¾″ plywood (4′ x 4′ panel) to make—

    1 pc. 8½″ x 33½″ (or 1″ x 9″ (nom.) stock) — rack front.

    1 pc. 7⅝″ x 33½″ (or 1″ x 8″ (nom.) stock) — rack back.

    1 pc. 7⅝″ x 20¾″ (or 1″ x 8″ (nom.) stock) — rack base.

    1 pc. 24″ x 35¼″ — cabinet side.

    1 pc. 9½″ x 23″ (or 1″ x 10″ (nom.) stock) — cabinet bottom.

1 sheet ⅛″ asbestos 24″ x 35¼″.

2 pc. ¾″ x ¾″ x 19¼″ hardwood — bottom rack guides.

1 pc. ⅜″ x ⅜″ x 19″ hardwood — center rack track.

2 pc. ¾″ x 1³⁄₁₆″ x 23″ hardwood — rack slide.

4 rods ½″ x 20¾″.

2 corner blocks 1⅝″ x 1⅝″ x 7¾″.

1 pc. ½″ x ⅝″ x 2½″ — stop.

1 pc. ⅛″ x 3″ x 9¼″.

Pointers for Building

As shown, this cabinet is framed as part of the vertical filing cabinet described in the base cabinet chapter and the builder would conserve material and effort by building the two as a unit.

The top frame consists of pieces of 1″ x 2″ stock placed flat. The same material is used to form a framework on the range side to support the sheet of ⅛″ asbestos. The other side of the cabinet can be a piece of ¾″ plywood. Two vertical facing strips of 1″ x 2″ stock also are needed at the front.

If the rack is to have a smooth, trouble-free action, you must give close attention to the guides and side slide. One ¾″ x ¾″ guide goes behind the framing members on the range side. The other fills the bottom corner at the right and the rack face board butts against its end when the rack is closed. The bottom of the rack has a ⅜″ x ⅜″ groove centered through its full length underneath. By means of this groove, the rack then rides on a ⅜″ x ⅜″ hardwood single track glued to the bottom of the cabinet. One member of the side guide

BESIDE-THE-RANGE TOWEL RACK

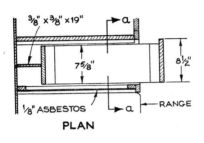

3/8" x 3/8" x 19"

7 5/8"

8 1/2"

1/8" ASBESTOS

RANGE

PLAN

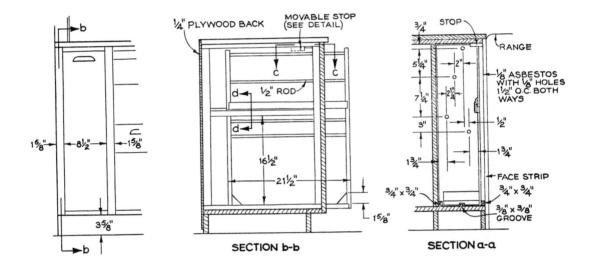

b

1 5/8"   8 1/2"   1 5/8"

3 5/8"

b

1/4" PLYWOOD BACK

MOVABLE STOP
(SEE DETAIL)

C

C

1/2" ROD

d

d

16 1/2"

21 1/2"

1 5/8"

SECTION b-b

3/4"   STOP

RANGE

5 1/4"   2"

1/8" ASBESTOS
WITH 1/8" HOLES
1 1/2" O.C. BOTH
WAYS

7 1/4"   2 1/4"

3"   1/2"

1 3/4"   1 3/4"

FACE STRIP

3/4" x 3/4"

3/4" x 3/4"

3/8" x 3/8"
GROOVE

SECTION a-a

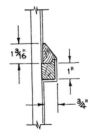

1 3/16"   1"

3/4"

DETAIL d-d

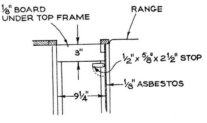

1/8" BOARD
UNDER TOP FRAME

RANGE

3"

1/2" x 5/8" x 2 1/2" STOP

1/8" ASBESTOS

9 1/4"

DETAIL c-c

must overlap the other as shown in the detail sketch. If shaping this slide is beyond your capabilities or shop equipment, a shop specializing in such work can do it for you. Sand all the guide members glass smooth, apply a coating of wax, and rub it hard.

The drawings show where to locate the towel rods in the front and rear of the rack. Bore ½″ blind holes at the points indicated and make the assembly with glue. If desired, metal or plastic rods could be used, the rack ends holding them captive when the assembly is complete. Pivot the stop so it will allow the rack to be drawn out when pushed back against the cabinet side.

RANGE RACK

Uses

The range rack is designed for storage of part of the equipment and supplies needed at the range. Lids for sauce pans can go in the slots on the bottom shelf. Frying pans, skillets, ladles, and other bulky but flat equipment go on hooks turned into the vertical storage board. Salt, pepper, sugar, and cereals that require cooking are among the staples that can be kept on the shelves.

Materials

¼″ plywood (2′ x 4′ panel) to make—
   3 pc. 12″ x 12″ — shelf dividers.
   3 pc. 1½″ x 22¼″ — shelf edging.
¾″ plywood (4′ x 6′ panel) to make—
   1 pc. 17″ x 30″ — front.
   1 pc. 12¼″ x 29¼″ — back.
   1 pc. 17″ x 23″ — base.
   2 pc. 12¼″ x 23″ — shelves.
   1 pc. 23″ x 29¼″ — partition.
1″ x 4″ (nom.) stock 17″ long — toe board.
Casters.

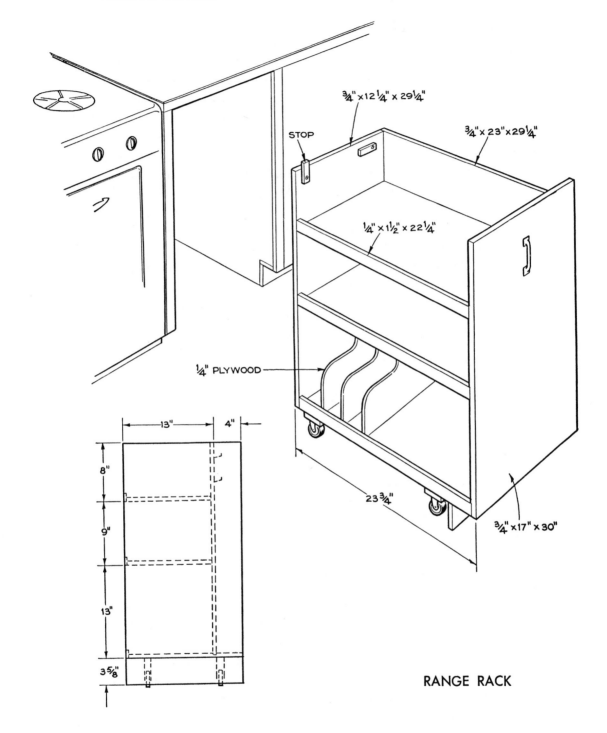

¾" ×12¼" × 29¼"

¾" × 23" ×29¼"

STOP

¼" × 1½" × 22¼"

¼" PLYWOOD

23¾"

¾" ×17" × 30"

13"   4"

8"

9"

13"

3⅝"

RANGE RACK

Pointers for Building

The counter part of a unit like the range rack is best approached as part of the job of building the adjoining cabinet or cabinets. Ends of adjoining cabinets can be enclosed with $3/4''$ plywood or by building frames of 1" x 2" stock and covering with $1/4''$ plywood or hardboard. Adjoining the range, a sheet of asbestos board may also be advisable. Build a 1" x 2" frame at the rear of the counter opening and surface this too with $1/4''$ material—plywood or composition board. The kitchen floor covering is carried back into the recess.

For strength, use dadoes and glue in joining the rack shelves to the ends. Butt joints secured with countersink screws and glue should do elsewhere.

Glue the $1/4''$ dividers into grooves cut in the base and the dividing boards. Install as many dividers as you have pan lids to store. The casters should project just far enough so there is about $1/32''$ clearance between the $3 5/8''$ toeboard and the floor. Shim the casters with wood blocks to achieve this clearance. Pivoted stops on the top of the rear upright will restrict normal outward movement of the racks by striking on the cabinet apron, yet these can be quickly turned to free the racks when this is desired.

ROLLING VEGETABLE BIN

(Drawing on page 159)

Uses

The vegetable bin has enough compartments to store current supplies of vegetables and fruit. Wire mesh bottoms in all compartments and mesh in the front provide necessary ventilation.

Rolling easily on the four large casters, the bin can be moved anywhere in the kitchen where the worker may prefer—to the sink, perhaps, or to the unloading counter where the grocery order is sorted and distributed.

Materials

1″ x 12″ (nom.) stock (10 linear feet) to make—
  2 pc. 22¾″ long — sides.
  6 pc. 10″ long — bottom bin partitions.
1″ x 5″ (nom.) stock 36″ long — top bin at front.
1″ x 4″ (nom.) stock (6 linear feet) to make—
  2 pc. 16½″ long — sides of top rear bin.
  1 pc. 8″ long — end of top rear bin.
  1 pc. 24″ long — toe board.
¾″ plywood (3′ x 4′ panel) to make—
  1 pc. 24″ x 30″ — front.
  1 pc. 22¾″ x 29″ — center partition.
Heavy wire mesh.
½″ half round or other molding.
4 ball-bearing casters (3″ wheels).

Pointers for Building

Cut a 4⅝″ x 5″ piece out of the upper corner of the 22¾″ x 29″ center partition to accommodate the shallow bin at the top front. The double rear bin is built around this center partition. Strengthen the assembly with corner blocks or corner irons. Corner blocks used in all four corners of the base will provide places to mount the casters. Staple the mesh across the bottom of all bins.

CANNED GOODS SHELVES

(Drawing on page 159)

Uses

Cans and jars of food can be placed on both sides of the centered partition of the canned goods shelves. The shelves are wide enough for the average can or jar without wasting space.

Materials

1″ x 9″ (nom.) stock (8 linear feet) to make—
   2 pc. 30″ long — front and back.
   1 pc. 21″ long — bottom.
1″ x 4″ (nom.) stock (12 linear feet) to make—
   6 pc. 21″ long — shelves.
¾″ x 21″ x 29¼″ plywood — middle partition.

Pointers for Building

There's nothing special to watch out for here. Follow the suggestions given for building similar cabinets.

PULL-OUT BOARD AND SLIDING RACK

Uses

These two units would serve practically the same purposes. Both are intended for the orderly hanging of long-handled utensils—ladles, stirring spoons, and such. In the width shown, they would also handle pans with an overall depth of less than 3″.

Materials (Pull-out Board)

1 pc. ¾″ x 22″ x 28¼″ plywood.   ½″ quarter round.

Materials (Rack)

1 pc. ¾″ x 21″ x 27″ plywood — center partition.
1″ x 8″ (nom.) stock (8 linear feet) to make—
   2 pc. 29¼″ long — front and back.   1 pc. 21″ long — bottom.

Pointers for Building

Smooth the quarter round and the bottom and top edges of the pull-out board thoroughly with sandpaper and then apply paste wax. Screw down the quarter round to the compartment floor and the top of the compartment with clearance for the board to slide smoothly.

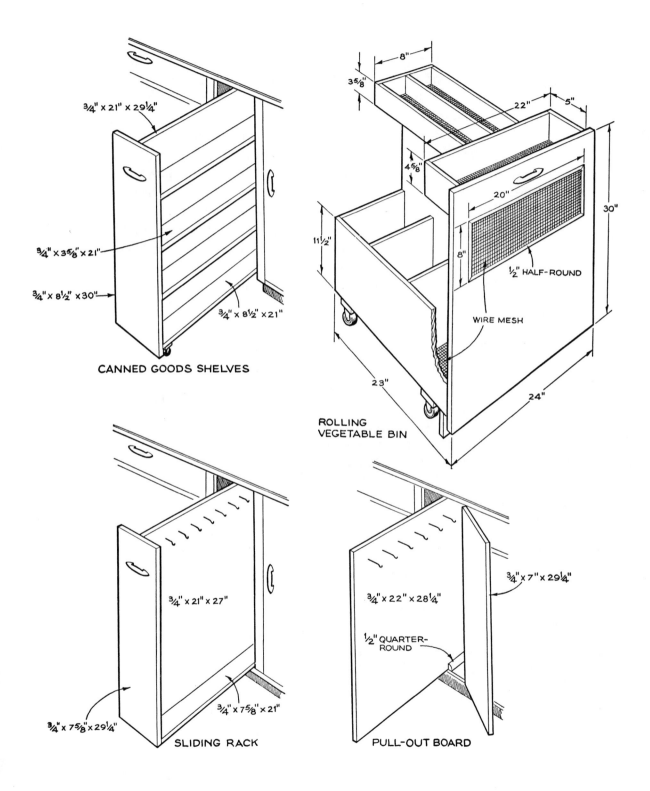

3/4" x 21" x 29¼"

3/4" x 35/8" x 21"

3/4" x 8½" x 30"

3/4" x 8½" x 21"

CANNED GOODS SHELVES

8"

35/8"

22"

5"

4 5/8"

20"

30"

11½"

8"

½" HALF-ROUND

WIRE MESH

23"

24"

ROLLING
VEGETABLE BIN

3/4" x 21" x 27"

3/4" x 7 5/8" x 29¼"

3/4" x 7 5/8" x 21"

SLIDING RACK

3/4" x 22" x 28¼"

3/4" x 7" x 29¼"

½" QUARTER-
ROUND

PULL-OUT BOARD

SINK PULL-OUT RACKS

Uses

These two racks provide convenient and out-of-sight storage for dish towels, soaps, and washing powders. Potatoes and vegetables might also be stored in the five-inch-deep bins at the bottom of the racks. Ventilation openings help wet towels to dry.

The back ends of the racks are curved to avoid striking the pipes coming down from the sink. If you should choose to build the entire unit wider, an electric garbage-disposal unit might be mounted between the racks. The 18″ x 22″ opening in the counter can be adjusted to suit the sink you wish to use. The original installation, designed by the makers of Malarkey plywoods, has a recessed shelf built above the rear six inches or so of the counter. That explains why the cabinet is deeper (from front to back) than most others. In many cases it might be better to reduce this dimension to the usual 25″ and shorten the racks accordingly.

Materials

¾″ plywood (4′ x 8′ panel, 2′ x 4′ panel) to make—
   1 pc. 24″ x 31⅝″ — cabinet front.
   1 pc. 24″ x 31½″ — counter.
   2 pc. 29¾″ x 35¼″ — cabinet ends.
   1 pc. 22½″ x 29¾″ — cabinet floor.
⅜″ plywood (4′ x 4′ panel) to make—
   2 pc. 7¼″ x 28⅞″ — rack bottoms.
   2 pc. 23¼″ x 29¼″ — rack sides.
   2 pc. 5″ x 29¼″ — rack sides.
   2 pc. 8″ x 23¼″ — rack backs.
   1 pc. 5″ x 28⅞″ ⎫
   1 pc. 4″ x 28⅞″ ⎬ rack shelf.
   2 pc. 4″ x 5″ ⎭
1″ x 2″ (nom.) stock (34 linear feet) — frame.
1″ x 4″ (nom.) pine stock (10 linear feet) — base.
4 pc. ¾″ quarter round 22¾″ long.
4 pc. ¾″ quarter round 4½″ long.
3 towel rods.

SINK PULL-OUT RACKS

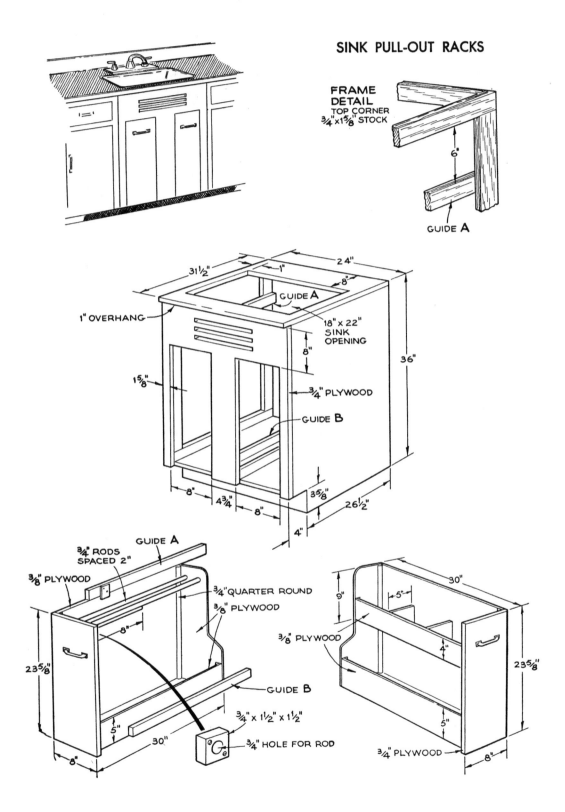

FRAME DETAIL
TOP CORNER
¾"x1⅝" STOCK

6"

GUIDE **A**

31½"
1"
24"
8"
GUIDE **A**
1" OVERHANG
18" x 22" SINK OPENING
8"
36"
1⅝"
¾" PLYWOOD
GUIDE **B**
8"
4¾"
8"
3⅝"
26½"
4"

GUIDE **A**
¾" RODS SPACED 2"
⅜" PLYWOOD
¾"QUARTER ROUND
⅜" PLYWOOD
8"
23⅝"
GUIDE **B**
¾" x 1½" x 1½"
5"
30"
¾" HOLE FOR ROD
8"

30"
9"
5"
⅜" PLYWOOD
4"
23⅝"
5"
¾" PLYWOOD
8"

Pointers for Building

Assemble the base first and put down the cabinet floor. Then cut the framing members from nominal 1" x 2" stock. Assemble these with lap or other joints. Notice that the frame length should be enough less than 24" to allow the thickness of the two ¾" plywood ends to make up the total 24" dimension.

Careful use of the saw will yield fronts for the two racks and the cabinet itself from one 24" x 32" piece of ¾" plywood. The cutouts become the rack fronts. Use a piece of vertical grain plywood for this. Install the cabinet front so that the horizontal frame member at the bottom of each end becomes a guide for its neighboring pull-out rack.

For greatest cabinet strength, use ¾" plywood on the ends. The ends could, however, be of lesser thickness, especially if you take pains with the framing. Or they could be dispensed with entirely to save material if you don't mind side openings in the adjoining cabinets. A ¼" back, of plywood, hardboard, or composition material, on the cabinet also is optional.

Curve the inside edges of the back ends of the racks so they do not strike the sink plumbing. Rabbet the rack sides to the front, but butt joints will do at the rear. Nailed, or perhaps screwed, in place, the pieces of ¾" quarter round will help make the racks rigid. Either ¾" dowel stock or metal rods might be used in the towel rack. Bored holes in blocks offer the easiest way to mount these, although the rods also could go into blind holes in the rack ends before the rack is assembled.

When the racks are complete, use them to position the four guides A and B in the cabinet. For these pieces, you might do better to use hardwood than the pine stock suggested. Highly polished before installation, the hardwood will allow the racks to slide with greater ease. In any case, treat all the guides, as well as the rubbing rack surfaces, with a hard wax.

13

Built-in Ovens and Cooking Tops

Streamlining of modern kitchens extends even to the range. Divided into two major units (oven and cooking top), each part can be installed for maximum efficiency and good looks. Raised to chest height, the oven typically is built into a floor-to-ceiling structure and there's no more stooping to see what's baking. Placed on or slipped into the top of a base cabinet, the cooking top becomes an integral part of its row of cabinets. Variations include built-in warming drawers (for keeping cooked foods hot), separate griddles, and complete ranges designed especially for blending into a line of base cabinets. Built-in units are available for both electricity and gas.

Anyone who can build other cabinets in this book can also build cabinets to house range built-ins. A cabinet for a sink would also suit a drop-in cooking top. The cabinets described in the sink chapter, therefore, are all possibilities for cooking tops that slip into work-counter openings. In contrast to drop-ins, some range tops are designed to rest on a cabinet just high enough to bring the cooking surface level with the kitchen work counter. Range tops are available

NOTE: These are typical rough-in drawings provided by manufacturers for specific models. Buy your cooking equipment before you build any of your kitchen cabinets. You'll then get drawings suited specifically to what you buy.

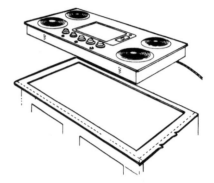

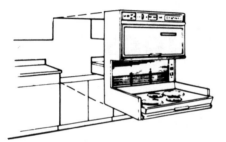

HIGH LEVEL OVEN
AND COOKING TOP

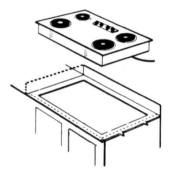

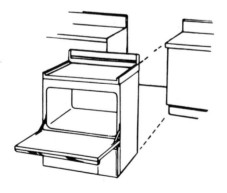

SLIDE-IN RANGE

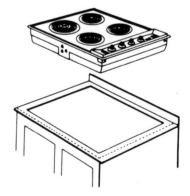

DROP-IN COOKING TOP

COUNTER-HUNG RANGE

DOUBLE WALL OVEN

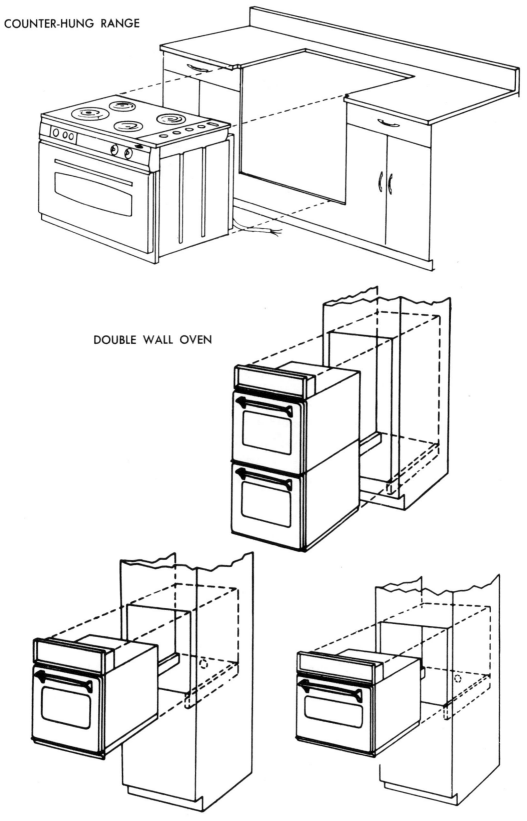

SINGLE WALL OVEN

with varying numbers of cooking units. Some include griddles.

Built-in ovens are sometimes bricked into a chimney-like structure. But this usually is for appearance only. Ovens designed for wall installation are so well insulated that no special fireproofing treatment is needed in a supporting structure. An oven can go into a simple wood cabinet fitted with a pair of horizontal 2 x 4's to provide support and serve as slides for shoving it into place.

A floor-to-ceiling cabinet as deep as the base cabinets is often used to house an oven. But the part above the oven could be omitted. A cabinet this deep (from front to back) presents awkward storage space at or above head height when utilized in conventional cupboard fashion. If oven venting is required, a vent pipe might occupy the rear of this upper part of the cabinet and a wall cabinet of standard depth the front. In certain situations, it might also be possible to use the rear space for a duct leading to a kitchen exhaust fan.

Some builders have found it convenient to stop the oven enclosure immediately above the raised oven, topping it off with a surface that can be used for open storage or display. Others have set the base low enough in the row of base cabinets so that the oven top slips under the bottom of the wall cabinets above. Some ovens need no side or top enclosure.

The drawings on the two preceding pages show cabinet construction suggested by major manufacturers of built-ins. If you buy a built-in, you will receive cabinet instructions to suit it. Be sure to buy your built-ins before you build any of your cabinets. This applies to automatic dishwashers and refrigerators as well as to the cooking units. You then can make any necessary adjustments in cabinet plans you have chosen.

Here's cooking convenience in a setting of handsome provincial-style cabinets—a cooking top in the counter and a combination wall oven and broiler. Photo by Kelvinator.

A range hood carries away cooking odors, greasy vapors, and excess moisture from the kitchen. You can buy both ducted and non-ducted types. The latter have easily-replaced charcoal filters. Photo by Caloric.

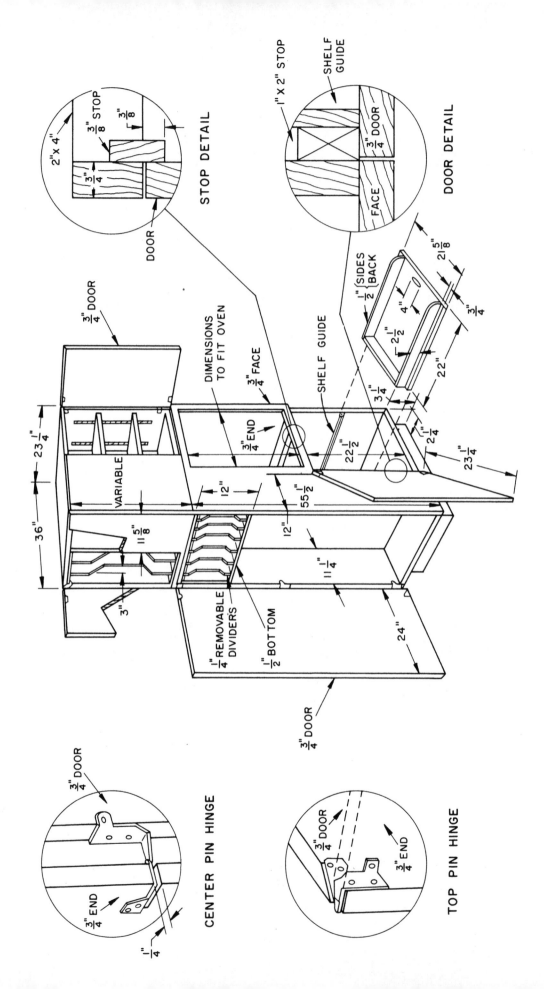

STOP DETAIL

$\frac{3}{8}$" STOP

$\frac{3}{8}$"

2" x 4"

$\frac{3}{4}$"

DOOR

DOOR DETAIL

1" x 2" STOP

SHELF GUIDE

SHELF GUIDE

$\frac{3}{4}$" DOOR

FACE

$\frac{3}{4}$" DOOR

DIMENSIONS TO FIT OVEN

$\frac{3}{4}$" FACE

$\frac{3}{4}$" END

SHELF GUIDE

$\frac{1}{2}$" {SIDES BACK

21$\frac{5}{8}$"

$2\frac{1}{2}$"

4"

$\frac{3}{4}$"

22"

$3\frac{1}{4}$"

$2\frac{1}{4}$"

$22\frac{1}{2}$"

$55\frac{1}{2}$"

$1\frac{1}{2}$"

$23\frac{1}{4}$"

$23\frac{1}{4}$"

36"

VARIABLE

12"

12"

$11\frac{5}{8}$"

$11\frac{1}{4}$"

3"

$\frac{1}{4}$" REMOVABLE DIVIDERS

$\frac{1}{2}$" BOTTOM

24"

$\frac{3}{4}$" DOOR

CENTER PIN HINGE

$\frac{3}{4}$" DOOR

$\frac{3}{4}$" END

$\frac{1}{4}$"

TOP PIN HINGE

$\frac{3}{4}$" DOOR

$\frac{3}{4}$" END

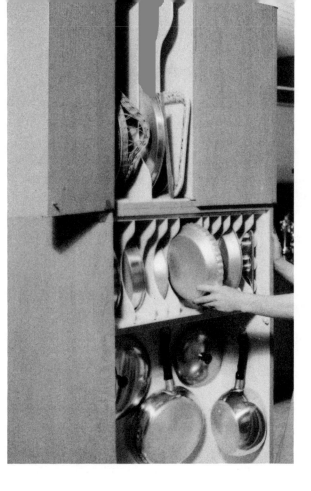

WALL-OVEN UTENSIL CABINET

The bulky structure into which wall ovens must go doesn't always make the best use of available space. Here's one that does. Since it's designed to stand at the left end of a line of wall and base cabinets, you can also make use of the side around the corner from the face of the oven. As you see in the accompanying photo this side of the cabinet is fitted out to receive pots and pans, pie plates, trays and other items that are so often awkward to store.

Be sure you have roughing-in dimensions for your specific oven before you start to build. Support the oven on horizontal 2 x 4's. Reverse the construction if your kitchen plan calls for the oven structure at the right end of a line of cabinets. If you'd rather have base cabinets and a counter on each side of the oven, you may want to abandon the side storage and change the plan accordingly. Or you may want to keep the side storage that falls above the counter.

A list of materials is omitted because of the variations suggested.

COOKING-TOP CABINET

Adjust the dimensions of this cabinet as necessary to suit the cooking-top you buy. The possible adjustments include the 8¼″ width of the ¾″ plywood face strip just under the counter edge. You may be able to make this area shallower and gain storage below.

Three types of slide-out features are indicated in the lower part of the cabinet. A metal slide-out rack hangs pots and pans in the compartment at the left. At the center, a vertical slide-out shelf provides other hanging storage. Leave a minimum of 8″ spacing between the two plywood standards on either side of it. At the right, you see a handy slide-out shelf. Mount it on metal shelf guides screwed to the end of the cabinet and one of the vertical standards at the center.

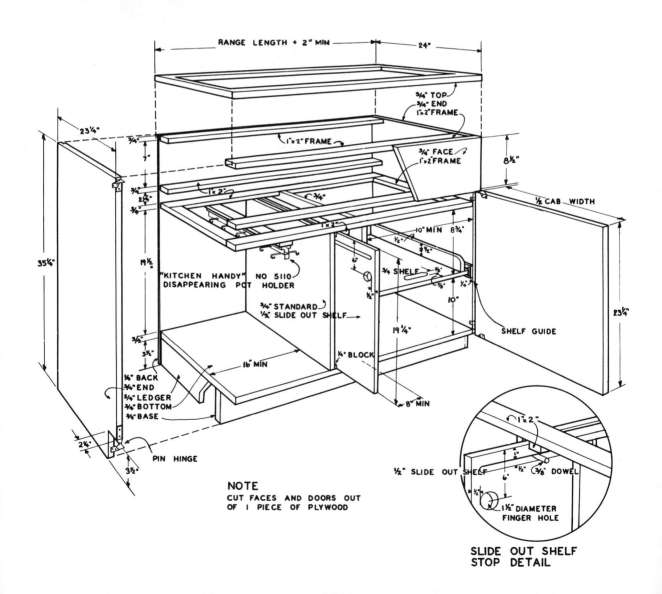

NOTE
CUT FACES AND DOORS OUT
OF 1 PIECE OF PLYWOOD

SLIDE OUT SHELF
STOP DETAIL

14

Corner Cabinets

When rows of cabinets along adjacent walls meet in a corner, the question arises of how to use the corner space most efficiently. Wall cabinets offer no difficulty. But base cabinets do. The diagonal depth, from the point where the cabinet fronts form a right angle back to the far corner, no longer is an easy reach. The corner storage space in effect is blocked off. Access is sometimes gained by opening the door of the adjoining cabinet and reaching sideways into the corner. This, however, tends to make the space a dead storage catch-all, which it needn't be.

Various ways have been worked out to make corner space just as accessible and useful as the space in other base cabinets. Some of these ways are presented in the following pages for your selection. Merry-go-round corner shelves are a common way of using the space. But there are others too. When you consider that approximately 11 cubic feet of useful storage space is available in the standard base-cabinet corner, it is readily apparent that here at least is one corner you should not attempt to cut.

SLIDING-SHELF CABINET

Uses

This cabinet might serve its best purpose as the storage space for bulky utensils—roasters, large baking pans, perhaps an electric mixer. Seldom-used items could go on the floor, others that are needed more frequently on the sliding shelf. Opening the cabinet door not only brings the contents of the two swing shelves out into the open; it clears the way for the sliding shelf to be drawn to the left, making its contents more easily reached. The lip at the end keeps items from sliding off the pull shelf. Nearly 8″ of cabinet space available back of the swing shelves when the door is closed might be devoted to sacked supplies, especially the floor area up to the level of the sliding shelf. A pan or two could also be placed on hooks on the upper part of the back wall. But anything stored in the area might have to be removed before the sliding shelf could be drawn out.

Materials

FRAMING:

2″ x 2″ (nom.) stock 30⅛″ long — corner post.

1″ x 2″ (nom.) stock (32 linear feet).

1″ x 4″ (nom.) stock (14 linear feet) — base.

¾″ plywood (4′ x 8′ panel) to make—

    1 pc. 23″ x 31⅝″ — end.   1 pc. 23″ x 42½″ — floor.

    1 pc. 23″ x 25⅝″ — shelf.   1 pc. 16″ x 30″ — door.

    1 pc. 25″ x 43¼″ — counter.

½″ plywood to make—

    2 pc. 15″ x 15″ — swing shelves.

    1 pc. ¾″ x 16″ — swing shelf separator.

¼″ plywood (4′ x 6′ panel) to make—

    1 pc. 31⅝″ x 43¼″ — back.   1 pc. 24″ x 31⅝″ — end.

    1 pc. ¾″ x 20½″ — sliding shelf lip.

⅛″ plywood or hardboard ¾″ wide — shelf edging.

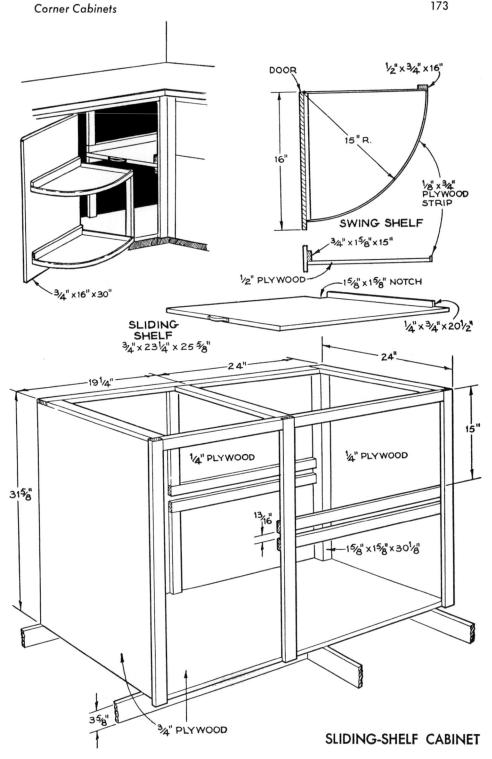

DOOR

½" × ¾" × 16"

15" R.

16"

SWING SHELF

⅛" × ¾" PLYWOOD STRIP

¾" × 1⅝" × 15"

½" PLYWOOD

1⅝" × 1⅝" NOTCH

SLIDING SHELF
¾" × 23¼" × 25⅝"

¼" × ¾" × 20½"

¾" × 16" × 30"

24"

24"

19¼"

15"

¼" PLYWOOD

¼" PLYWOOD

31⅝"

13/16"

1⅝" × 1⅝" × 30⅛"

3⅝"

¾" PLYWOOD

SLIDING-SHELF CABINET

Pointers for Building

Cut four pieces of the 1″ x 2″ stock 31⅝″ long for vertical framing members. Cut three pieces 24″ long to go across the top, front to back, and two 43¼″ pieces for the longitudinals. Four pieces 25⅛″ long are needed as the sliding shelf guides.

Put on the ¼″ plywood back and end after the frame and ¾″ plywood end and floor are in place atop the sub-framing. No enclosure is needed over the section at the right of the cabinet door since the end of the adjoining base cabinet will butt here. Install the two bottom guides first for the sliding shelf. Then slip the shelf into the cabinet framework and rest it on these two guides while fastening the upper ones with screws. You can provide for proper sliding clearance by inserting thin cardboard between the guides and shelf while positioning and attaching the upper ones. A drawer pull on the end of the shelf will make it easier to draw.

The swing shelves are quarters of a full circle, having a 15″ radius. Glue and screw each of these on the narrow edge of a 15″ length of 1″ x 2″ stock and screw the latter to the door. Locate the bottom shelf so it will just clear the cabinet floor when the door closes. Locating the other 16″ above probably will give best use of both shelves. A supporting strip of ½″ plywood located as shown in the drawing will make the assembly more rigid. Put this on after ⅛″ plywood or hardboard strips have been curved around the edges of the two shelves and nailed in place.

REVOLVING SHELF CORNER BASE CABINET 1

Uses

Shelves that revolve in Lazy Susan fashion make use of most of the space that otherwise is lost when two rows of cabinets come together in a corner. This one was designed for the U.S. Department of Agriculture's model U-kitchen, and plans were drawn by J. Robert Dodge, architect. Two are used in this kitchen—one in the left corner of the

U, one in the right. Mounted level with the revolving shelves, fixed shelves keep stored goods from falling down behind the revolving unit. But the toe board is made removable, in case items do fall. This also makes it possible to clean the unit easily. If used for seldom-needed supplies, the fixed shelves offer a tremendous expansion of available storage space.

Materials

1″ x 2″ (nom.) stock (8 linear feet) — facing strips, cleats.

1″ x 3″ (nom.) stock (18 linear feet) — top frame.

1″ x 4″ (nom.) stock (14 linear feet) — base.

1″ x 8″ (nom.) stock (6 linear feet) — bottom frame.

2″ x 2″ (nom.) stock 34½″ long — corner post.

2″ x 2″ (nom.) stock 27½″ long — center post.

¾″ plywood (two 4′ x 8′ panels) to make—

    2 pc. 23″ x 35¼″ — ends (optional).

    1 pc. 38″ x 38″ — counter.

    1 pc. 12⅜″ x 29⅞″ — door.

    1 pc. 13⅛″ x 29⅞″ — door.

    2 pc. 37″ x 37″ — circular and fill-in shelves.

    1 pc. 20″ x 20″ — circular shelf.

¼″ plywood or hardboard (4′ x 6′ panel) to make—

    2 pc. 35½″ x 38″ — back.

    1 pc.   9½″ x 36″ — bottom shelf reinforcing.

Pointers for Building

Find the center of the two 37″ x 37″ squares of ¾″ plywood by crossing lines from the corners. Then lay out on these centers circles of an 18⅛″ radius. Just outside, lay out other circles with a radius of 18¼″. Then saw out the larger circles, cutting outside the line and keeping the outer area intact. As the plan details show, this area becomes the fixed fill-in shelves that are placed inside the cabinet on the same level as the two large revolving shelves. Now reduce the

REVOLVING SHELF CORNER BASE CABINET 1 (A)

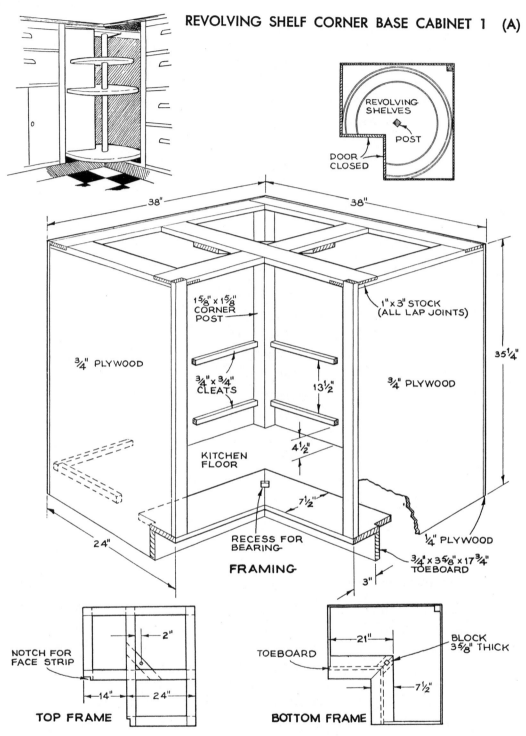

REVOLVING SHELVES

POST

DOOR CLOSED

38"

38"

1" x 3" STOCK
(ALL LAP JOINTS)

1⅝" x 1⅝"
CORNER
POST

35¼"

¾" PLYWOOD

¾" x ¾"
CLEATS

13½"

¾" PLYWOOD

4½"

KITCHEN
FLOOR

7½"

¼" PLYWOOD

RECESS FOR
BEARING

24"

FRAMING

3"

¾" x 3⅝" x 17¾"
TOEBOARD

NOTCH FOR
FACE STRIP

2"

14"   24"

TOP FRAME

TOEBOARD

21"

BLOCK
3⅝" THICK

7½"

BOTTOM FRAME

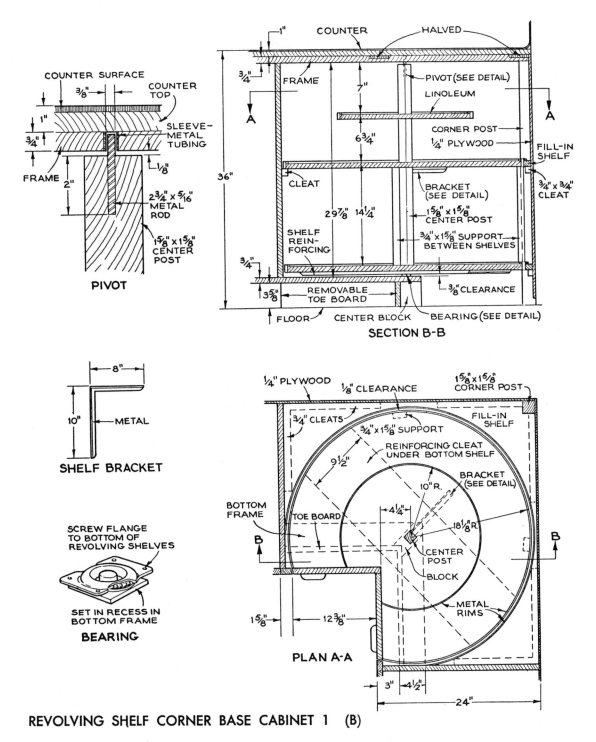

COUNTER SURFACE
⅜"
COUNTER TOP
1"
¾"
SLEEVE-METAL TUBING
FRAME
2"
⅛"
2¾" x 5/16" METAL ROD
1⅝" x 1⅝" CENTER POST

PIVOT

1"
COUNTER
HALVED
¾"
FRAME
7"
PIVOT (SEE DETAIL)
LINOLEUM
CORNER POST
¼" PLYWOOD
FILL-IN SHELF
¾" x ¾" CLEAT
CLEAT
6¾"
BRACKET (SEE DETAIL)
1⅝" x 1⅝" CENTER POST
¾" x 1⅝" SUPPORT BETWEEN SHELVES
36"
29⅞" 14¼"
SHELF REIN-FORCING
¾"
⅜" CLEARANCE
3⅝"
REMOVABLE TOE BOARD
FLOOR
CENTER BLOCK
BEARING (SEE DETAIL)

SECTION B-B

8"
10"
METAL

SHELF BRACKET

SCREW FLANGE TO BOTTOM OF REVOLVING SHELVES
SET IN RECESS IN BOTTOM FRAME

BEARING

¼" PLYWOOD
⅛" CLEARANCE
1⅝" x 1⅝" CORNER POST
¾" CLEATS
¾" x 1⅝" SUPPORT
FILL-IN SHELF
REINFORCING CLEAT UNDER BOTTOM SHELF
9½"
10" R.
BRACKET (SEE DETAIL)
BOTTOM FRAME
TOE BOARD
4¼"
18⅛" R.
CENTER POST
BLOCK
METAL RIMS
1⅝"
12⅜"
3"
4½"
24"

PLAN A-A

REVOLVING SHELF CORNER BASE CABINET 1   (B)

diameter of each disk by cutting on the inner lines. Smooth the edges of each disk and apply copper or aluminum edging around it. Also apply edging on the fill-in shelves. This will then allow the two larger shelves to revolve without spilling their contents. The fill-in shelves are held by $\frac{3}{4}''$ x $\frac{3}{4}''$ cleats.

Cut openings in the two upper circular shelves for the center post. Make the openings a drive fit if possible. Mount the shelves to the post with metal brackets and glue. Two 1" x 2" posts between the two larger shelves also help keep the assembly rigid.

Form the bottom bearing from a furniture caster as shown by the sketch. Screw it to the $\frac{1}{4}''$ reinforcement piece under the bottom shelf. The bottom of the bearing simply slips snugly in a recess cut for it on the upper face of the bottom frame. After the cabinet framing has been built around the revolving assembly, keep the latter captive by slipping down the triangular framing piece on top that contains the metal sleeve for the upper pivot.

Note About Lazy Susan Hardware

In the years since the accompanying plans were drawn for revolving corner cabinets, manufacturers have made available a variety of suitable hardware that makes building such cabinets much easier. It is suggested that you substitute such hardware for the fittings listed in the plans given here. You'll find descriptions of the new items in the chapter on hardware later in the book.

REVOLVING SHELF CORNER BASE CABINET 2

Uses

This example has two shallow drawers at the top. In the original, a design by the makers of Malarkey plywoods, one of these drawers is devoted to sharp knives and the counter above has a hardwood chopping block. Details of these are given in the chapter on kitchen accessories.

Materials

1″ x 4″ (nom.) stock (22 linear feet) — base.

1″ x 2″ (nom.) stock (50 linear feet) — framing.

1 pc. 2″ x 2″ (nom.) stock 12″ long — top flange mount.

2 pc. 2″ x 2″ (nom.) stock 14″ long — shelf separators.

5/8″ or 3/4″ plywood (two 4′ x 8′ panels) to make—

    2 pc. 23″ x 35¼″ — ends (optional).

    1 pc. 18″ x 25″ — door.

    1 pc. 18¾″ x 25″ — door.

    2 pc. 38″ x 38″ — circular shelves.

    1 pc. 43⅝″ x 43⅝″ — counter.

¼″ plywood or ⅛″ hardboard (4′ x 8′ panel) to make—

    2 pc. 35¼″ x 42⅝″ — back.

    2″-wide bands around shelves.

1 pc. 3/4″ pipe 34″ long — stanchion.

2 flanges for 3/4″ pipe.

1 ball-bearing race.

2 flanges with setscrews.

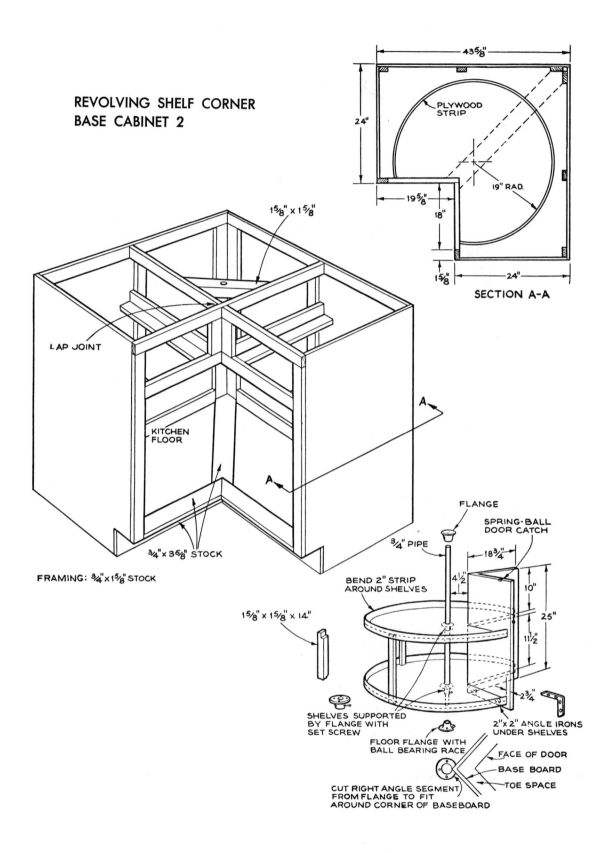

REVOLVING SHELF CORNER
BASE CABINET 2

$43\frac{5}{8}$"

PLYWOOD
STRIP

24"

$19\frac{5}{8}$"

19" RAD.

18"

$1\frac{5}{8}$"

24"

SECTION A-A

$1\frac{5}{8}$" x $1\frac{5}{8}$"

LAP JOINT

KITCHEN
FLOOR

A

A

$\frac{3}{4}$" x $3\frac{5}{8}$" STOCK

FRAMING: $\frac{3}{4}$" x $1\frac{5}{8}$" STOCK

$1\frac{5}{8}$" x $1\frac{5}{8}$" x 14"

FLANGE

SPRING-BALL
DOOR CATCH

$18\frac{3}{4}$"

$\frac{3}{4}$" PIPE

$4\frac{1}{2}$"

10"

25"

BEND 2" STRIP
AROUND SHELVES

$11\frac{1}{2}$"

$2\frac{3}{4}$"

2" x 2" ANGLE IRONS
UNDER SHELVES

SHELVES SUPPORTED
BY FLANGE WITH
SET SCREW

FLOOR FLANGE WITH
BALL BEARING RACE

FACE OF DOOR

BASE BOARD

TOE SPACE

CUT RIGHT ANGLE SEGMENT
FROM FLANGE TO FIT
AROUND CORNER OF BASEBOARD

Pointers for Building

Since its dimensions make the revolving assembly a captive within the cabinet, this is a project you should build, or at least assemble, from the inside out.

If you are working by hand, the two circular shelves might be cut with a compass saw. Smooth the edges and apply the 2″ strips of ¼″ plywood by bending it gradually while progressively drawing it in with screws. If this gives you trouble, strips of ⅛″ hardboard will be easier and just as satisfactory. Two posts of 2″ x 2″ stock support the shelves at one edge, the doors do the job at the other. Drive nails through the doors into the edges of the shelves. Angle irons also help keep the assembly rigid. You will save time and energy by having the pipe stanchion cut to the correct length when you buy it. A hacksaw will cut the pie segment from the bottom flange.

Cut all parts of the cabinet and make a trial assembly before enclosing the revolving unit.

REVOLVING WALL CABINET

Uses

Two of these wall units are used in the Step-Saving U-Kitchen developed by the Bureau of Human Nutrition and Home Economics, one at each rear corner of the U. The one shown in the drawing is located at the immediate left of the mixing counter. Its small shelf is designed especially for spices. This cabinet is big enough so that staples in daily use can occupy the outer part of the shelves and yet leave room at the rear for reserves. The shelves extend down to the counter, providing storage at working level for the heaviest and most often used staples.

In the twin Lazy Susan on the wall of the opposite corner, heavy dishes and those most often used are on the lowest shelves. Ready-to-eat cereals are kept on the top shelf. Steps are saved when cereals and bowls are in the same cupboard. Shelves in this cabinet are all the same size.

Many wall Lazy Susans are cut off at the bottom even with adjoining flat wall cabinets. Where that would be preferred, the accompanying plans could be altered to suit and the shelves spaced accordingly.

Materials

1″ x 2″ (nom.) stock (8 linear feet) to make—

    2 pc. 51¾″ long — vertical facing strips.

    1 pc. 10½″ long — horizontal facing strip.

    1 pc. 11¼″ long — horizontal facing strip.

2 pc. 1″ x 12″ (nom.) stock 51″ long — cabinet sides.

2 pc. ¼″ plywood 22½″ x 51″ — back.

¾″ plywood (4′ x 6′ and 4′ x 5′ panels) to make—

    2 pc. 21½″ x 21½″ — base and top of cabinet.

    5 pc. 21″ x 21″ — large shelves.

    1 pc. 16″ x 16″ — small shelf.

    1 pc. 9″ x 49⅜″ (or 1″ x 10″ (nom.) stock) — door.

    1 pc. 9¾″ x 49⅜″ (or 1″ x 10″ (nom.) stock) — door.

2 4″ x 6″ shelf angles.

6 6″ x 6″ shelf angles.

Pointers for Building

Saw a 10″ x 10″ segment from one corner of each of the two 21½″ x 21½″ pieces of ¾″ plywood, cut the 1″ x 2″ stock to length, and you have all the parts for the cabinet frame. One notched square of plywood goes on the counter to form the cabinet base; the other can be placed under a drop ceiling in place of a soffit board. The 12″ pine stock connects these pieces on the sides while the two 51″ strips of 1″ x 2″ (nom.) form the vertical facing strips. Depending on the construction, the short horizontal facing strips might be dispensed with.

REVOLVING WALL CABINET

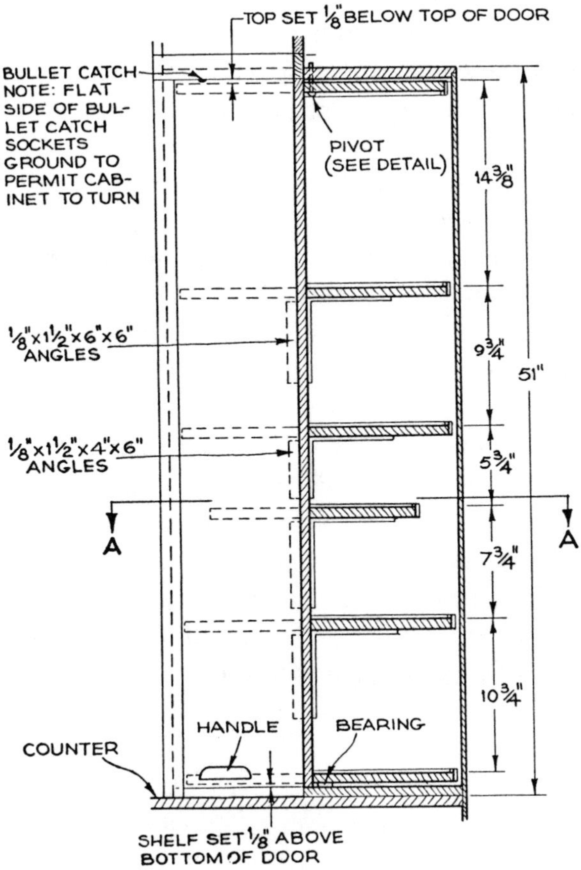
TOP SET 1/8" BELOW TOP OF DOOR
BULLET CATCH
NOTE: FLAT SIDE OF BULLET CATCH SOCKETS GROUND TO PERMIT CABINET TO TURN
PIVOT (SEE DETAIL)
14 3/8"
9 3/4"
51"
5 3/4"
7 3/4"
10 3/4"
1/8" x 1 1/2" x 6" x 6" ANGLES
1/8" x 1 1/2" x 4" x 6" ANGLES
A
A
HANDLE
BEARING
COUNTER
SHELF SET 1/8" ABOVE BOTTOM OF DOOR

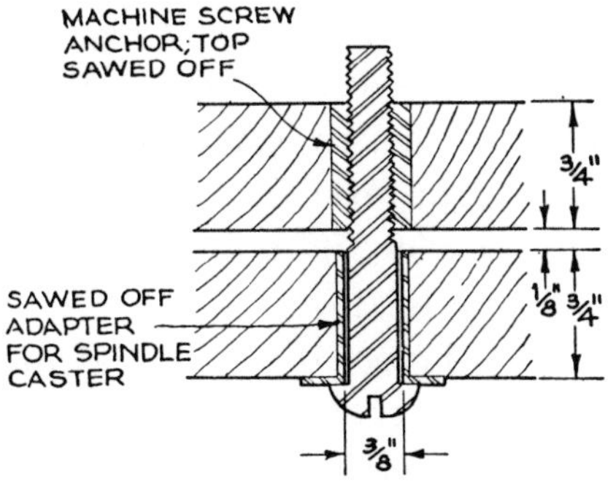
MACHINE SCREW ANCHOR; TOP SAWED OFF
3/4"
SAWED OFF ADAPTER FOR SPINDLE CASTER
1/8"
3/4"
3/8"

PIVOT DETAIL

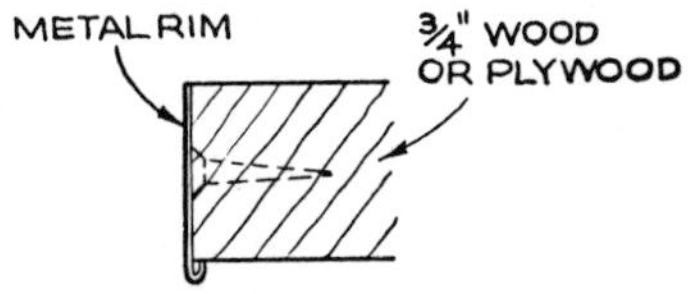
METAL RIM
3/4" WOOD OR PLYWOOD

TOP OF CABINET DETAIL

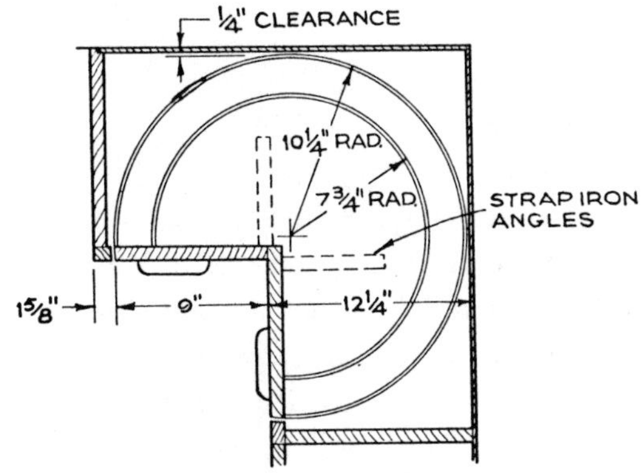
1/4" CLEARANCE
10 1/4" RAD.
7 3/4" RAD.
STRAP IRON ANGLES
1 5/8"
9"
12 1/4"

PLAN A-A

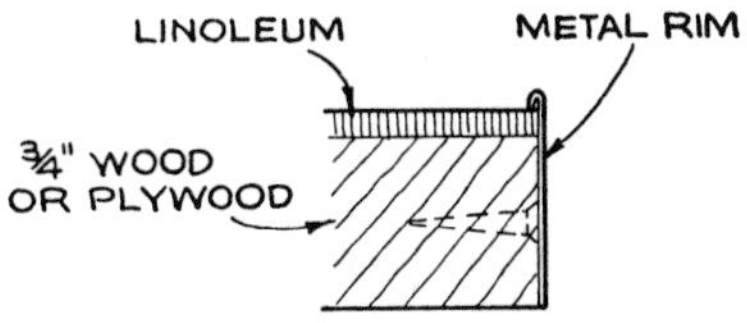
LINOLEUM
METAL RIM
3/4" WOOD OR PLYWOOD

SHELF DETAIL

If power equipment is available, you would do well to clamp or tack the five 21″ x 21″ shelf blanks together and saw the 20½″ diameter shelves in a single operation. If a ⅜″ center hole is bored through all the blanks, the assembly might be revolved in a jig while the cut is made. Also saw out the segments where the doors go before taking the finished shelves apart.

A cut-off ball-bearing furniture caster can be used as the bearing. This should be recessed in the top of the horizontal frame member that is fastened to the top of the counter and in a mating recess in the bottom surface of the first revolving shelf. Make the bearing a tight press fit. A hacksaw will enable you to cut the machine-screw anchor and the adapter for the spindle caster that are specified for the top pivot.

Locate the shelves as indicated along the doors, attaching them with countersunk wood screws run through the doors. Then apply the shelf brackets. Locate the top and bottom shelves so there will be revolving clearance. Sand the top and bottom edges of the doors until the unit revolves freely. For appearance, the metal rim is placed upside down on the top shelf as the detail sketch shows. Position the bullet catch so that the revolving shelves will stop with the doors in their closed position.

DIAGONAL-FRONT CABINET

Uses

Diagonal-front cabinets can utilize corner space in a variety of ways. The shape is excellent for full-circle revolving shelves, either in a wall or base unit. As outlined in the sink chapter, a diagonal-front base cabinet will make a sink the conversation piece of a modern kitchen. If a trap door is installed in the back corner of the counter, space behind the sink may be utilized for a trash chute to the basement, or for a garbage compartment—with access to the container from outside the house through a small door in the wall.

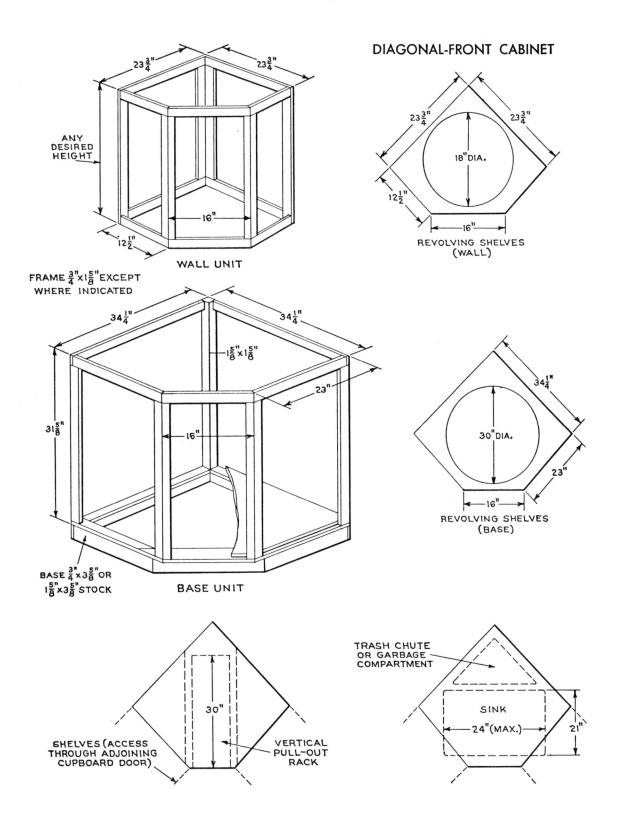

DIAGONAL-FRONT CABINET

WALL UNIT

$23\frac{3}{4}"$ $23\frac{3}{4}"$

ANY DESIRED HEIGHT

16"

$12\frac{1}{2}"$

FRAME $\frac{3}{4}" \times 1\frac{5}{8}"$ EXCEPT WHERE INDICATED

REVOLVING SHELVES (WALL)

$23\frac{3}{4}"$ $23\frac{3}{4}"$

18" DIA.

$12\frac{1}{2}"$

16"

BASE UNIT

$34\frac{1}{4}"$ $34\frac{1}{4}"$

$1\frac{5}{8}" \times 1\frac{5}{8}"$

23"

16"

$31\frac{5}{8}"$

BASE $\frac{3}{4}" \times 3\frac{5}{8}"$ OR $1\frac{5}{8}" \times 3\frac{5}{8}"$ STOCK

REVOLVING SHELVES (BASE)

$34\frac{1}{4}"$

30" DIA.

23"

16"

30"

SHELVES (ACCESS THROUGH ADJOINING CUPBOARD DOOR)

VERTICAL PULL-OUT RACK

TRASH CHUTE OR GARBAGE COMPARTMENT

SINK

24" (MAX.)

21"

Shelves, of course, are the most common storage device in these cabinets. In a wall unit, shelves offer easy access to the stored items. But in the base cabinet, the shelf depth and the comparatively narrow door lower the cabinet's efficiency.

A base cabinet is another possible location for one of the vertical pull-out racks described in the chapter devoted to these handy storage devices. In this case, the rack might have a 90-degree pointed end to fit fully into the cabinet corner. The head-on area directly behind the door could also be partitioned vertically for on-edge storage of large trays, etc. For this, a door might be omitted from the cabinet. Alternatively, a bank of drawers could go into the space.

Pull-out racks, partitions, and drawers, however, all have one drawback in common when used in a diagonal-front cabinet. They shut off the space remaining at the right and left. But this can be overcome in many cases by installing shelves in the space and providing access to them through the doors of cupboards on the right and left of the corner unit. The shelves actually would be extensions of those in the adjoining base units. Triangular shelves within the cabinet could be devoted to dead storage if a roll-out rack is used. The space offers many possibilities, too, for a secret compartment—accessible, perhaps, by removing a drawer from the corner cabinet or one of its neighbors.

Materials

A list is omitted because of the variations suggested.

Pointers for Building

Before starting work, the builder should consider whether the dimensions shown in the drawings will yield a cabinet to suit his needs and fit the adjoining cabinets, either wall or base. To illustrate, the 12½″ dimension of the wall cabinet may have to be adjusted to a different depth dimension that has been chosen for the other wall cabinets. If this must be increased, say to 14″, the width of the door will automatically decrease. The builder will then want to consider whether the lesser door width is acceptable. If not, the 23¾″ dimension along each wall should be increased to bring the door to the desired width.

The same principle applies of course to a base unit. If it is desirable to increase the door width, as might be the case when a sink is being installed, it will be necessary to increase the $34\frac{1}{4}''$ dimensions at the back. But such increases, it should be noted, produce a corresponding increase of the cabinet's diagonal depth from door to back corner.

Assemble the framing as for other cabinets, using the joint procedure you prefer, and make and install the door. The floor of the wall cabinet can be cut to fit on the top edges of the lower frame members. In the case of a wall unit, a door could be omitted and the shelves used for display or open storage. Another possibility is a door with one or two glass panels. Set the glass in rabbets cut in a glued-up wood frame.

Full-circle revolving shelves can be built like the revolving units shown previously. However, since the present ones lack the support that the doors provide the former, vertical supporting strips between the shelves probably will be needed at intervals around the rim of the unit, especially the base cabinet. Install an additional frame member across the top of the cabinet to take the bearing for the revolving unit.

A trash chute or garbage compartment and a work-counter access door can be built as described in the chapter on base cabinets. If a vertical pull-out rack is used, parallel guide strips will be required inside the cabinet.

CORNER CABINET IDEAS

Adjoining Room Cabinet

Straight-line access into a corner base cabinet can sometimes be provided through what normally would be one of the rear faces. This possibility may occur in two ways. First, one arm of the L formed by the cabinets may serve as a peninsula instead of being backed against the wall. Second, one arm may back against a wall separating the kitchen from another room. In either case, the corner cabinet can be fully utilized by providing access into it in the opposite direction from its companions in the peninsula or along the partition.

In a peninsula, the switch is simple. Just install drawers or doors on the side facing away from the kitchen. If the peninsula separates kitchen and dining area, this rear-facing cabinet might be used for table linen, mats, silver, dishes, and other items.

When the cabinet backs against a partitioning wall, a hole must be cut through the wall at the proper spot and a frame of 2 x 4's installed to substitute for the wall studs that are cut. Again, either doors or drawers can be installed. The useful depth of the cabinet in this case will be increased by the thickness of the wall. If the cabinet opens into the dining room, it can be put to use as previously suggested. If it opens into the living room, a television set could be hidden inside or the space could be used for phonograph records.

Corner Mixer Cabinet

An electric mixer can be stored in a triangular corner cabinet installed between the counter and bottom of the wall cabinets. From ¾″ plywood cut a triangular base large enough so that no part of the mixer will protrude beyond its edges. Mount this base with brackets to the bottom edge of a door hinged to a simple frame mounted diagonally across the kitchen counter. When the door is opened, swung back against the wall and latched, the mixer rides into the open on the triangular base, ready for use. A matching diagonal-front corner unit can be located in the line of wall cabinets above.

If one end of the work counter butts against a floor-to-ceiling cabinet, a swing-out door shelf also might be located in the cabinet to carry the mixer to working position over the counter.

Corner Wall Shelves

Instead of joining two right-angle lines of wall cabinets with a corner cabinet, you might prefer simple open shelves in the corner. Stop the cupboard-type cabinets at equal distances from the corner—at a point equal to about one and one-half times their depth (front to back dimension). Then cut shelves with a diagonal front edge to fill the corner. Or, cut the front edges to a concave curve to improve the appearance.

15

Peninsula Cabinets

A line of cabinets jutting out from the wall in a peninsula arrangement frequently improves the utility of a modern kitchen. Some peninsulas extend only a few feet. Others reach most of the way across the room. Base cabinets in a peninsula may or may not have wall-type cabinets suspended from the ceiling above them. Both base and wall cabinets may be accessible from either one or two sides.

Peninsulas take many forms and serve many functions. One of the simplest to build is just a counter, without cabinets under it, extending at right angles to the end of a line of base cabinets backed against the wall. A pipe or curtain-pole leg, or perhaps a tier of shelves, supports the free end of the counter, which is usually rounded. Because of its knee space, a counter peninsula is a convenient breakfast bar if stools are kept under it. It also may double as a serving counter between the range and dining table.

A peninsula has its major use, however, as one arm of a U-shaped kitchen plan. If a large kitchen is being remodeled, the peninsula is often chosen as a means of keeping the work area compact. In new construction a peninsula may serve as a divider between kitchen and dining areas, or perhaps between kitchen and laundry. This saves the cost of a full wall. Also, it gives the open construction that many modern homeworkers prefer.

Either sink or range may go into the peninsula against a low backing wall. A narrow counter on top of or against the opposite side of the wall will then serve as a handy breakfast bar or as a stacking area for dishes being taken to the sink. A breakfast bar of this type will be found in the chapter devoted to kitchen tables. A dish washer or a home food freezer of the horizontal type might also go into a peninsula that bounds a kitchen.

Peninsula cabinets, both floor and ceiling-suspended types, may be exactly like those built for use against a wall. However, the builder has the opportunity of making the storage space accessible from either side. With the kitchen on one side and the dining area on the other, this double accessibility has obvious advantages. If a hanging cabinet has doors on both sides, dishes can be reached or stored from either the kitchen or dining area. Double-faced drawers put silverware, table mats, etc., at your fingertips no matter which area you are in. Peninsula cabinets usually are the same depth as standard base and wall types. But this can sometimes be varied if circumstances call for it. You should note that where a counter 24″ wide is used, with a 1″ overhang on each side, the depth (face-to-face) dimension of the base cabinet will be only 22″ instead of the usual 23″.

When a peninsula separates kitchen and dining areas, the space between upper and lower cabinets makes a convenient pass-through. Sliding doors are sometimes used here to close off the kitchen from the dining area. Rather than mount wall-type cabinets above a peninsula, however, some home owners have used open shelves, lattice work, bamboo curtains, and the like. Lattice work above a peninsula-located range might serve as a place to hang pots and pans, especially those with copper bottoms.

Island arrangement of cabinets is another possibility that the kitchen planner may want to consider. In this case, the range, sink, or several base cabinets are placed in the open, with walking space all around. Construction features would be similar to those required for a peninsula plan.

Peninsula Cabinets

A peninsula is just the place to keep a portable dishwasher. Roll it to the sink for loading. Let its top serve as a handy extension of the peninsula counter at other times. Photo by Tappan.

An easily-built peninsula breakfast bar is a logical divider for kitchen and dining areas in an open modern home. Marlite woodgrain paneling was used on the end of the counter and on the walls of the hall at the right. Get free plans for building this peninsula counter. Mail a post card with your name and address to Handyman Plans, P.O. Box 250, Dover, Ohio 44622. Ask for plan No. 106.

CURVED-DOOR END CABINET

Uses

Here is the cabinet to place at the end of a peninsula if the builder wants all enclosed storage space. Shelves on the curved door have a usable length of a little more than 12″ and a depth of about 3″. A 1″ retaining strip rising above the shelf edges will keep stored items from sliding off. The two middle door shelves meet the middle cabinet shelves when the door is closed. The bottom shelf enters the cabinet above the rounded bottom shelf; the top one slips under the top cabinet framing. Articles stored in the main cabinet are all accessible through the one door, but a similar door could be placed on the opposite side if desired.

Built without a door and enclosing wall, the cabinet offers convenient open shelving. In that case, the middle shelves should be cut to a full 11″ radius instead of being sliced off as indicated for the door version.

Pointers for Building

The top framing of the cabinet can be two or more pieces of stock cut and assembled as suggested in the sketch of the base frame. However, the builder may find it simpler to cut a full semicircle of ¾″ plywood to the same radius as the bottom shelf. In laying out these parts, be careful to allow a ⅞″ extension beyond the radius base line to reach the back piece. Notches are required in the corners of these pieces for the one-by-two vertical frame members, also another athwart the center line for the door mullion. After laying out the radius for the two middle shelves, draw a straight line between the points where the arc bisects the base and center lines. Saw along this to form the straight edges that face the door. Set these shelves in notches cut in the middle frame members. Assemble the cabinet with glue and screws. The shelves can be set in dadoes cut in the back piece if desired.

To lay out the door shelves, strike a quarter-circle arc on a 11″ radius. Measure in ¾″ on both the right angle lines. Connect these points with a straight line. This gives the shape for the top and bottom shelves since they are butted against the ends of the end frame

CURVED-DOOR END CABINET

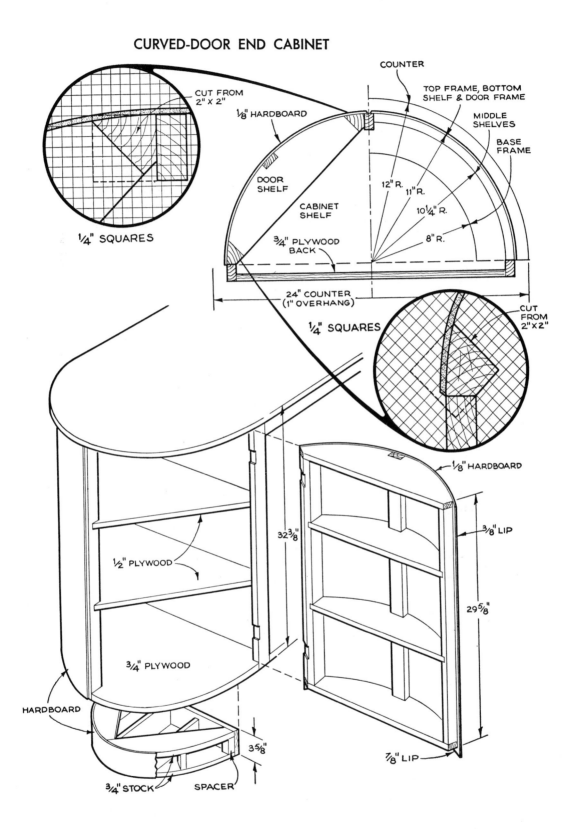

¼" SQUARES

CUT FROM 2" X 2"

COUNTER

TOP FRAME, BOTTOM SHELF & DOOR FRAME

MIDDLE SHELVES

BASE FRAME

⅛" HARDBOARD

DOOR SHELF

CABINET SHELF

12" R. 11"R.

10¼" R.

8" R.

¾" PLYWOOD BACK

24" COUNTER (1" OVERHANG)

¼" SQUARES

CUT FROM 2"X2"

⅛" HARDBOARD

3/8" LIP

32⅜"

½" PLYWOOD

29⅝"

¾" PLYWOOD

HARDBOARD

3⅝"

¾" STOCK

SPACER

7/8" LIP

pieces. Center notches in all four pieces for the middle frame piece. The ends of the middle shelves are shaped as shown in the drawing. Make allowance in the length of each so they will extend into dadoes cut in the end frame pieces. Starting with the 2″ x 2″ stock, shape the two frame pieces to the sections shown in the sketch. Sand the outer edges to conform to the shelf radius. The middle frame piece also must be rounded off. Glue and screw the door parts together into a rigid framework, being careful that you get it true with all matching parts in exactly the same plane. Cut the parts and assemble the base frame in the same way.

Cut the hardboard into three sheets approximately the size required. Hardboard of this thickness can be bent without difficulty to the radius of the door and cabinet. For the 8″ radius required for the base, however, it will be necessary to moisten the panel thoroughly by leaving it in water for several hours. With the smooth side out, fasten each panel at one end and then gradually bend it into position, driving finishing nails about $1\frac{1}{8}$″ long every 4″ or less as you go. The nailheads can be countersunk slightly and filled with putty before the finish is applied.

CURVED-DOOR QUARTER-CIRCLE CABINET

A curved-door cabinet of quarter-circle section may be desirable in some kitchen layouts in place of the half-circle one just described. To match base cabinets with a 25″ counter and a 1″ overhang, this should have two flat outer surfaces—the back and side—at right angles to each other, joined by a door (or perhaps two) bent to a 24″ radius.

A cabinet like this could be used at the end of a peninsula backed against a low divider wall—in the same manner as the square end cabinet that is illustrated immediately following. It could also be located at various other spots in the kitchen—at the end of a bank of base cabinets along a wall, in a corner by itself, adjoining a refrigerator or range, anywhere in fact where you need the clearance and added appearance that the curved surface gives. When a line of cabinets ends at a door, it would increase walking clearance and eliminate the hazard of sharp corners. Four quarter units, of course, will form a circular island. Three placed together, with the open segment as the work area, would give an island unit that could be a big work saver.

Construction of a quarter-circle unit would roughly parallel the half-circle type. Two doors could be used across the arc—or a single wide one. Here, as well as in the semicircular cabinet, the builder might like to install a curved hardboard door without a supporting framework. For the 24″ radius of the quarter-circle, ¼″ material, or perhaps ⁵⁄₁₆″, would be the best bet. Soak the panel for several hours and then leave it between wet cloths or newspapers for 48 hours. To form the panel to a permanent curvature, it must be fastened to a curved form until it has dried thoroughly. The temporary form must have a radius slightly less than the desired curvature to allow for a slight springback.

END CABINET

Uses

This cabinet was designed for a particular spot—the end of a peninsula unit dividing the kitchen and dining areas. Handy to both areas, it stores equipment needed in each. Recipes on standard 3″ x 5″ index cards can be filed in the top drawer, which also has space for several cookbooks within easy reach of the range. Lower drawers hold silver, linen, and place mats used in the dining area just around the corner. Located beside the range, the top of the cabinet serves as a convenient serving counter.

The same cabinet might also be used to advantage in some cases at the end of a line of base cabinets backed against a full wall. Your own kitchen floor plan will suggest whether you should use this one or a cabinet with normal front openings. The drawing for the cabinet was adapted from a design of the makers of Malarkey plywoods.

Materials

1″ x 2″ (nom.) stock (64 linear feet) — framing.

1″ x 4″ (nom.) stock (8 linear feet) — base.

¾″ plywood (4′ x 6′ panel) to make—

   1 pc. 17¼″ x 31⅝″ — side.

   1 pc. 24″ x 35¼″ — back.

   1 pc. 19″ x 25″ — top.

   1 pc. 16½″ x 21¼″ — bottom.

   4 pc. 4″ x 20¾″ — drawer fronts.

   1 pc. 9⅜″ x 20¾″ — drawer front.

⅝″ plywood (3′ x 4′ panel) to make—

   8 pc. 4″ x 17″ — drawer sides.

   4 pc. 4″ x 20¾″ — drawer backs.

   2 pc. 9⅜″ x 17″ — drawer sides.

   1 pc. 9⅜″ x 20¾″ — drawer back.

¼″ plywood (4′ x 6′ panel) to make—

   5 pc. 17″ x 20¾″ — drawer bottoms.

   1 pc. 4″ x 17″ — recipe file partition.

   Drawer partitions as desired.

Pointers for Building

Cut and assemble the base first, using the 1″ x 4″ stock. Dimension it to allow a 3″ toe recess on two sides. Then put down the 16½″ x 21¼″ cabinet floor, allowing it to project 2¼″ on the two sides where the toe recess is to be. Cut and fit the ¾″ plywood back (the side next to the range in the drawing) and then position the assembly thus far completed and attach it to the wall. Attach the front piece of ¾″ plywood and finish the main framing at the top and front as shown in the sketches. Pieces of 1″ x 2″ stock, placed flat, serve as runners for the drawers. Others mounted on edge are guides.

A partition placed 5⅛″ from the edge of the top drawer will provide a space for 3″ x 5″ index cards. Partitions of ¼″ plywood can be added to the silver drawer as indicated—or ready-made trays can be used if you prefer.

END CABINET

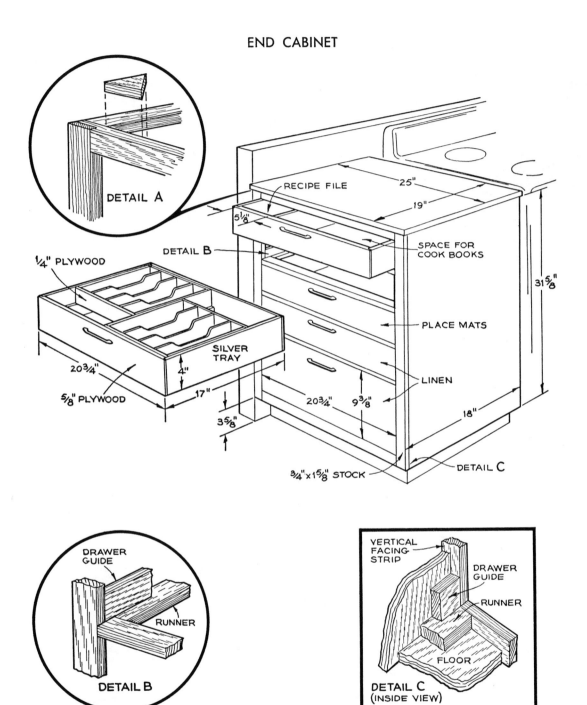

DETAIL A

1/4" PLYWOOD

DETAIL B

RECIPE FILE

25"

19"

5 1/8"

SPACE FOR
COOK BOOKS

31 5/8"

SILVER
TRAY

20 3/4"

5/8" PLYWOOD

4"

17"

PLACE MATS

LINEN

20 3/4"

9 3/8"

18"

3 5/8"

3/4" x 1 5/8" STOCK

DETAIL C

DRAWER
GUIDE

RUNNER

DETAIL B

VERTICAL
FACING
STRIP

DRAWER
GUIDE

RUNNER

FLOOR

DETAIL C
(INSIDE VIEW)

HANGING PENINSULA CABINET

The hanging cabinet for which plans are given on this page and the base cabinet on the facing page together form the peninsula arrangement shown in the photo. Note that the hanging cabinet has sliding doors on both sides. This makes dishes stored there accessible from either the kitchen or dining-room side of the peninsula divider. This cabinet is very easy to build. It becomes more so if you buy and use readymade sliding door grooves instead of cutting them yourself. Make the ends, top, and bottom from ¾″ plywood. Use hardboard for the doors. Install the cabinet by driving wood screws through the top board into the ceiling. This project is used through courtesy of the American Plywood Association.

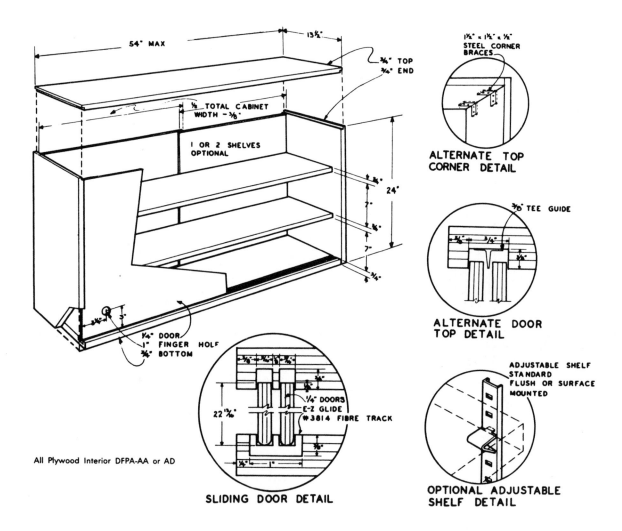

54″ MAX
13½″
¾″ TOP
¾″ END

⅛ TOTAL CABINET WIDTH − ⅜″

1 OR 2 SHELVES OPTIONAL

1½″ x 1½″ x ½″ STEEL CORNER BRACES

ALTERNATE TOP CORNER DETAIL

24″

7″

7″

¾″

⅜″ TEE GUIDE

¾″   ¾″

ALTERNATE DOOR TOP DETAIL

¼″ DOOR
1″ FINGER HOLE
¾″ BOTTOM

All Plywood Interior DFPA-AA or AD

22¹³⁄₁₆″

¼″ DOORS E-Z GLIDE #3814 FIBRE TRACK

SLIDING DOOR DETAIL

ADJUSTABLE SHELF STANDARD FLUSH OR SURFACE MOUNTED

OPTIONAL ADJUSTABLE SHELF DETAIL

PENINSULA SERVING CENTER

The wide counter atop this peninsula base cabinet makes it ideal for serving breakfast and other light meals. Note that the cabinet is designed to butt against the end of a standard-width base cabinet placed at right angles to it. Revolving shelves on the door are used to make items stored in the back corner of the cabinet more readily accessible. The door, a piece of ¾″ plywood 24″ high and 35″ long, is mounted on pivot hinge at its mid point. Thus, when its left end is swung outward, items on the shelves are brought within reach. The drawing suggests mounting knife-holding hardwood blocks in the drawer.

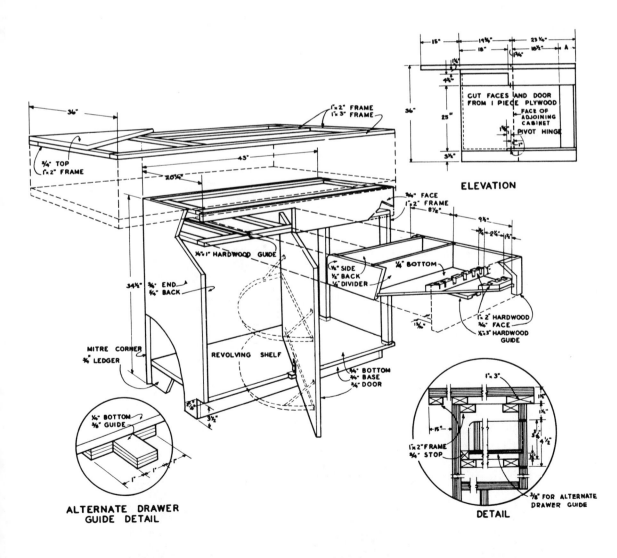

ELEVATION

ALTERNATE DRAWER
GUIDE DETAIL

DETAIL

An electric range built into the countertop of a cantilevered peninsula divider is a feature of this handsome modern kitchen. Note that the range counter is several inches lower than the normal-height counter at the left. Most kitchen designers now agree that cooking operations are carried on more comfortably at a lower level. Cooking supplies are right at hand on the predecorated Marlite Peg-Board paneling behind the range. Marlite paneling with a permanent plastic finish also was used for the sliding cabinet doors.

An island with a free-form breakfast bar is a noteworthy feature of this Hotpoint kitchen. The cooking top is located in the island cabinet, with plenty of storage below. Note also the convenient laundry area in the background.

Breakfasts and lunches are served quickly at this bar, adjoining an island that contains a cooking top. Both island and bar were angled to give free passage to the room beyond. Accented natural birch was used for the cabinets. The Weather-Seal Division of the Louisiana-Pacific Corporation provided the photo.

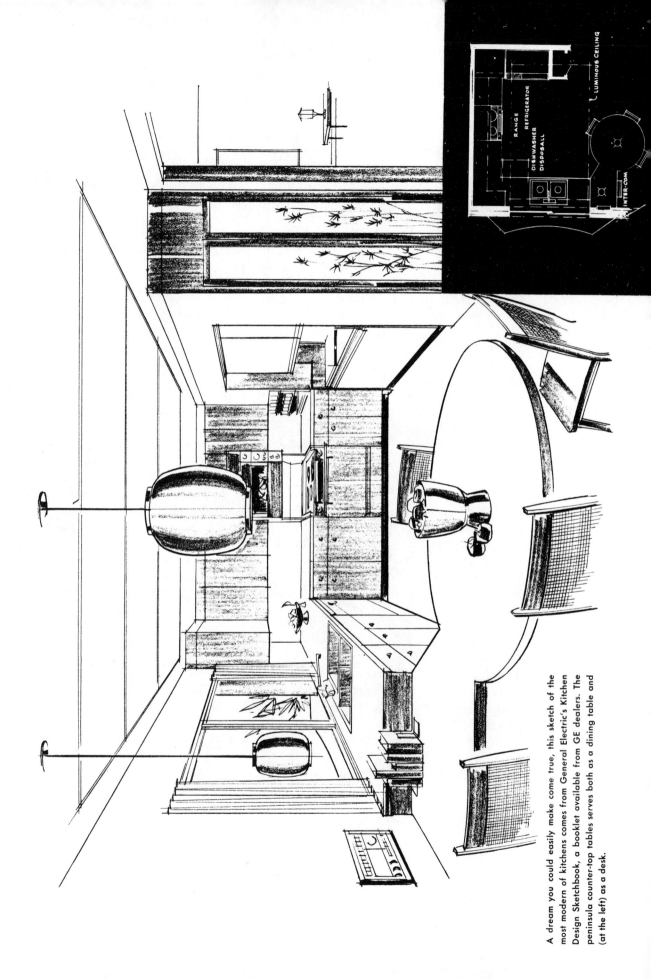

A dream you could easily make come true, this sketch of the most modern of kitchens comes from General Electric's Kitchen Design Sketchbook, a booklet available from GE dealers. The peninsula counter-top tables serves both as a dining table and (at the left) as a desk.

16

Space-Saving Dining Areas

If a modern home has dining space in the living room, or even if there is a separate dining room, the housewife usually finds it most convenient to serve at least breakfast and luncheon in the kitchen. If economy has dictated a compact kitchen, and all space must be carefully utilized, a dual-purpose unit will furnish eating facilities.

For instance, a counter that increases the kitchen work surface can do double duty as a dining table. If the kitchen floor plan includes a base-cabinet peninsula, extending the work counter about 30″ beyond the cabinets and supporting it on one or two wood or pipe posts will furnish eating space for two, and possibly three, persons. Stools can be pushed under the counter while not in use. Or, perhaps folding camp-style stools can be used and hung on hooks under the counter or on a wall. (Ordinary chairs are unsuitable at a work counter 36″ high. They can be used, however, if this section of the counter is lowered to conventional table height.) A similar arrangement might be worked out at the end of a line of base cabinets along a wall, although two persons would not be able to sit opposite each other as they would at a peninsula extension.

203

WINDOW-BOX TABLE

Uses

This unit adds both utility and a decorative note to the kitchen without detracting from the light-giving function of the windows. The shelves offer additional kitchen storage. The fold-down table can be used for the children's lunch or breakfast or as extra counter space.

Materials

1″ x 8″ (nom.) stock (24 linear feet) to make—

   3 pc. 69½″ long (or width of your window) — shelves.

   2 pc. 26″ long — ends.

   1 pc. 69½″ long (width of this member will depend on height of lower edge of windows from floor and width of baseboard) — flower recess side.

1″ x 4″ (nom.) stock (12 linear feet) to make—

   3 pc. 25¼″ long — hinging strips.

   2 pc. 17⁹⁄₁₆″ long — folding support for table.

1″ x 2″ (nom.) stock to make—

   1 pc. 19″ long — door stop.

¾″ plywood (4′ x 8′ panel) to make—

   2 pc. 15″ x 25¼″ — doors.

   1 pc. 25¼″ x 30″ — table.

Pointers for Building

Since lumber is used in its actual width, sawing to length is mostly all that is required. However, it will be best to have the bottom of the flower recess level with the window sill. This may require ripping or planing away some of the width of the piece of 1″ x 8″ (nom.) stock indicated for the front of the recess, if the 30″ height of the table is to be retained. When you determine the width needed, by trial, it may be possible to use nominal stock of a lesser width and avoid ripping. Chisel out notches in the middle shelf for the folding leg and door stop after sawing to depth. Adjust the length of the two parts of the folding table leg by trial to be sure it brings the table

WINDOW-BOX TABLE

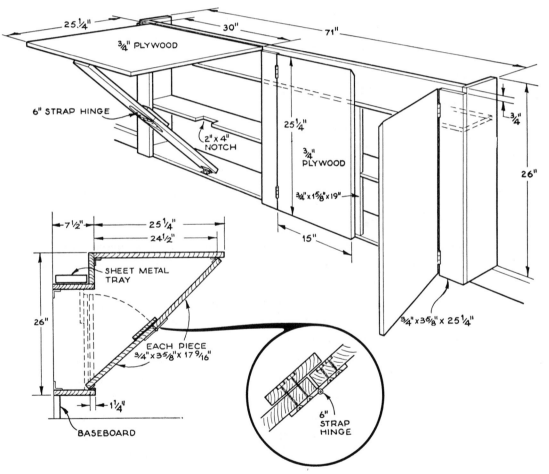

level. As the circled detail shows, a block bolted to the rear of the lower shelf keeps the leg from collapsing.

Shallow trays for the flower pots can be soldered together from galvanized sheet metal. However, if you do not want to attempt this job, hardware stores, dime stores and florist shops sell plastic watering coasters that will serve just as well.

FOLDING WALL TABLE

Uses

A unit like this can go where the space must be used for other purposes during most of the time, as in a hallway, for instance. However, it also makes an attractive and useful table as the major kitchen dining installation for a small family. The linoleum-covered table top is large enough for three place-settings. Necessary dishes can be stored on the shelves so as to be quickly available for use. A screen-door hook is positioned under one shelf to hold up the bending leg when the unit is closed. Decorative knickknacks might be kept on the open shelves at the bottom. A unit like this might also find uses in other rooms of the home.

Pointers for Building

If you have a power saw and if you are content to rest the shelves on cleats instead of cutting more professional dadoes, this project could be ready for painting an hour after you set to work.

Shelves set back about an inch above the table top allow the closed top to go in flush with the edges of the sides. Locate the upper stop carefully so that the top comes to rest evenly. If desired, a piece of quarter-round could be used for this strip. Position the folding leg parts by trial to be sure they hold the table level and function smoothly. Cut out the rear edges of the two side pieces as required to fit over the kitchen baseboard. Don't worry too much if you have a bad cut. Putty will fill in, and paint will hide the defect. Find the position for the screen-door hook under the hinge shelf while holding the table top up—that is, closed.

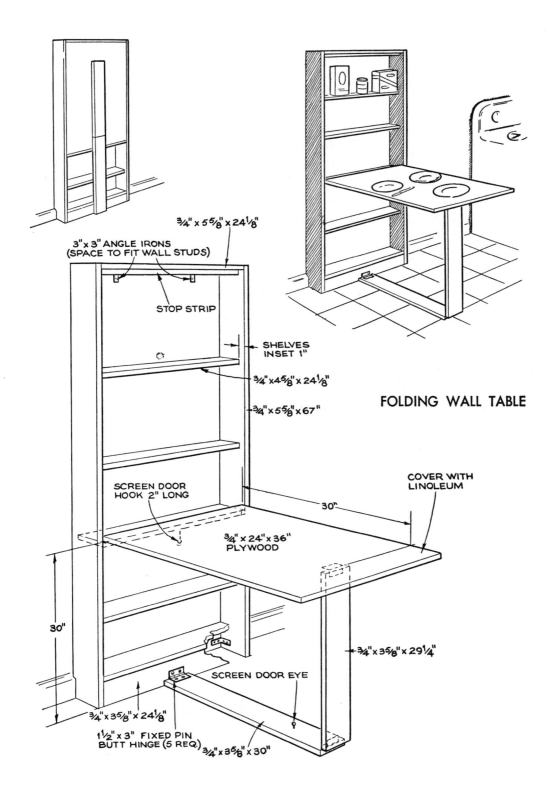

3/4" x 5 5/8" x 24 1/8"

3"x 3" ANGLE IRONS
(SPACE TO FIT WALL STUDS)

STOP STRIP

SHELVES
INSET 1"

3/4" x 4 5/8" x 24 1/8"

3/4" x 5 5/8" x 67"

FOLDING WALL TABLE

SCREEN DOOR
HOOK 2" LONG

COVER WITH
LINOLEUM

30"

3/4" x 24"x 36"
PLYWOOD

30"

3/4" x 3 5/8" x 29 1/4"

SCREEN DOOR EYE

3/4" x 3 5/8" x 24 1/8"

1 1/2" x 3" FIXED PIN
BUTT HINGE (5 REQ.) 3/4" x 3 5/8" x 30"

UNDER-THE-COUNTER TABLE

Uses

While not in use, this kitchen eating center packs away snugly under the counter surface. The chairs fit on either side of the centered leg that supports the sliding table in its outward position. Their backs form a line with the fronts of the adjoining base cabinets.

The second page of drawings shows variations in the general plans —how a shallow drawer may be located above the table and space below the chair seats put to use for a drawer or bottle storage. A table unit like this would find a practical place in a very small kitchen or in one where base cabinets fill all available wall space. It is dimensioned to fit under a counter surface 36″ high.

Materials

⅝″ plywood (4′ x 8′ panel) to make—

    1 pc. 22¼″ x 29″ — table.

    2 pc. 12″ x 13″ — chair seats.

    4 pc. 12½″ x 16¼″ — chair sides.

    2 pc. 14½″ x 31⅞″ — chair backs (if preferred).

1″ x 4″ (nom.) stock (30 linear feet) to make—

    8 pc. 31⅞″ long — chair backs.

    5 pc. 14½″ long — toe recess, battens, chair brace.

1″ x 2″ (nom.) stock (4 linear feet) to make—

    1 pc. 26¾″ long — table leg.

    1 pc. 13″ long — chair brace.

5 pc. 1″ x 1″ x 21½″ hardwood.

UNDER-THE-COUNTER TABLE (A)

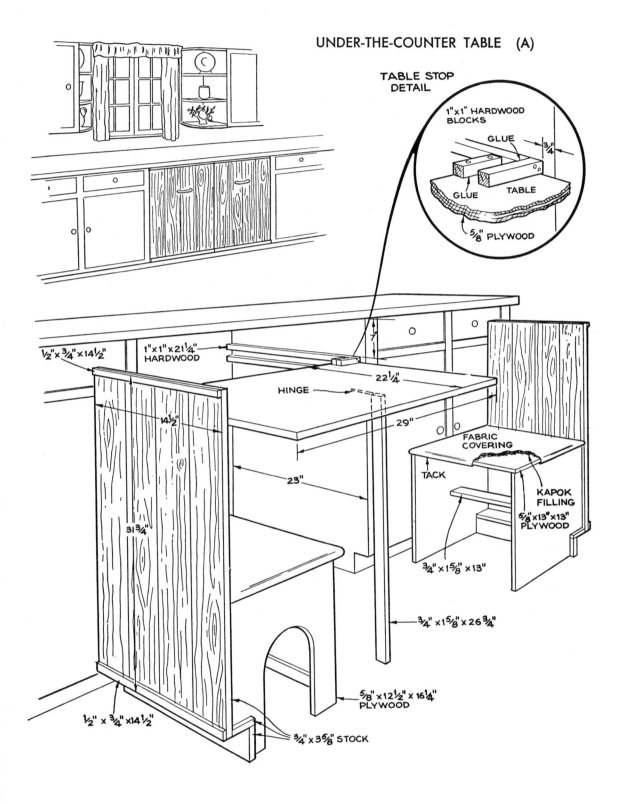

TABLE STOP DETAIL

1"x1" HARDWOOD BLOCKS

GLUE

3/4"

GLUE

TABLE

5/8" PLYWOOD

1/2" x 3/4" x 14 1/2"

1"x1" x 21 1/4" HARDWOOD

7"

22 1/4"

HINGE

14 1/2"

29"

23"

FABRIC COVERING

TACK

KAPOK FILLING

5/8" x13" x13" PLYWOOD

31 3/4"

3/4" x 1 5/8" x 13"

3/4" x 1 5/8" x 26 3/4"

1/2" x 3/4" x14 1/2"

3/4" x 3 5/8" STOCK

5/8" x 12 1/2" x 16 1/4" PLYWOOD

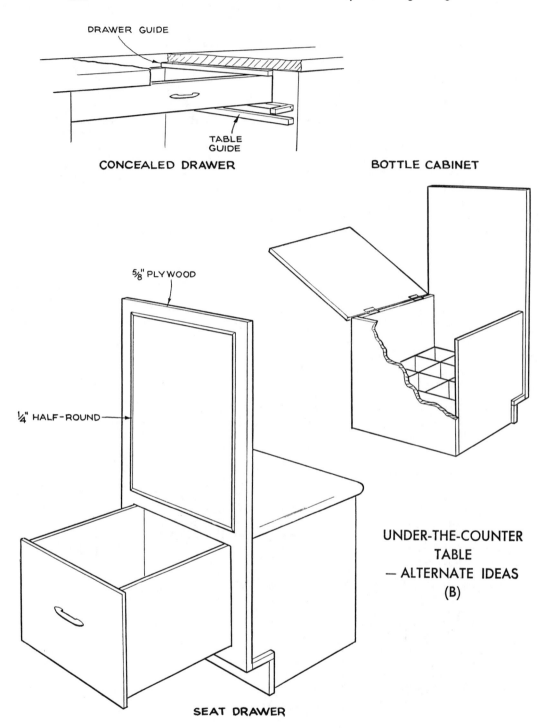

DRAWER GUIDE

TABLE
GUIDE

CONCEALED DRAWER

BOTTLE CABINET

⅝" PLYWOOD

¼" HALF-ROUND

**UNDER-THE-COUNTER
TABLE
— ALTERNATE IDEAS
(B)**

SEAT DRAWER

Pointers for Building

Prepare the counter recess as part of the construction of the adjoining base cabinets, applying finished ends to each one and spanning them with the counter. Make the opening 29⅛" wide, the extra ⅛" to allow clearance for the chairs when you slide them into place. Chairs of the height shown fit under a counter 36" high, with the counter made of ¾" material.

Cut four table-stop blocks from the fifth piece of 1" x 1" hardwood in the materials list. Sand each of the other four 21¼" pieces to a polished smoothness and wax them. Then screw one of them to the side of one base cabinet in the recess, carefully leveling it with the upper edge 8¹¹⁄₁₆" below the counter. Mount a second one at exactly the same level on the opposite cabinet. Sink the screw heads below the surface of the strips. Then rest the table board on these strips. To assure sliding clearance, rest thin strips of cardboard on the table and push them up against the cabinets on either side. Install the upper 1" x 1" strips on top of the cardboard. Remove the cardboard after the strips are secure.

Mark a middle position near the outer edge of the 29" dimension of the table and attach the 26⅜" leg there, using a small hinge. To avoid marks on the kitchen floor, you might cement a piece of rubber on the bottom end of the leg. Screw the stops to the rear edge of the table a shade over ¾" from the edges, slide the table between the parallel strips and screw the second pair of stops to the end of the upper strips.

The width of the chairs permits use of four pieces of 1" x 4" (nom.) stock to make the back of each one. After sawing the two 14½" pieces of 1" x 4" needed for the toe recess, rip a strip ½" wide from the edge of one. Use this strip as the bottom batten to hold the back pieces together, the remainder for the top part of the toe recess. Rip two other ½" strips from the fifth 14½" piece of 1" x 2" and use them as the top battens on the two chairs, and shorten the remainder to make a crosswise brace if desired, under one of the chairs.

Two styles are shown for the chair sides. The open style reduces the overall weight and makes a better appearance, but you may prefer the solid type for its simplicity of construction.

CURVED-SEAT BREAKFAST NOOK

Uses

Built-in booths for serving breakfast and other light meals are
favored by many persons. Here is a nook with seats curved for more
comfort. You could install it in front of a window or in a corner.

This drawing was adapted from a design made by John Macsai
for the Masonite Corporation. The nook utilizes the easy bending
properties of this firm's tempered hardboard. A sheet of this material
in black covers the table. The size of the seat and the placing of the
table are based on average body measurements. The nook will seat
four without crowding.

Materials

2″ x 4″ (nom.) stock (90 linear feet) to make—

    20 pc. 48″ long.

    4 pc. 18″ long.

    4 pc. 9″ long.

2″ x 6″ (nom.) stock (8 linear feet) to make—

    4 pc. 40″ long.

2″ x 8″ (nom.) stock (8 linear feet) to make—

    4 pc. 22″ long.

1 pc. ¾″ x 30″ x 50″ plywood.

1 pc. ⅛″ x 30″ x 50″ black tempered hardboard.

¼″ tempered hardboard (two 4′ x 7′ panels, one 4′ x 5′ panel) to
    make—

    2 pc. 40″ x 48¼″ — seat backs.

    2 pc. 18″ x 48¼″ — seat fronts.

    2 pc. 25″ x 40″ — seat ends.

3⁄16″ tempered hardboard (two 4′ x 5′ panels) to make—

    2 pc. 30″ x 48¼″ — back rests.

    2 pc. 18″ x 48¼″ — seats.

1 pc. 1″ pipe 29″ long.   2 floor flanges.   2 angle brackets.

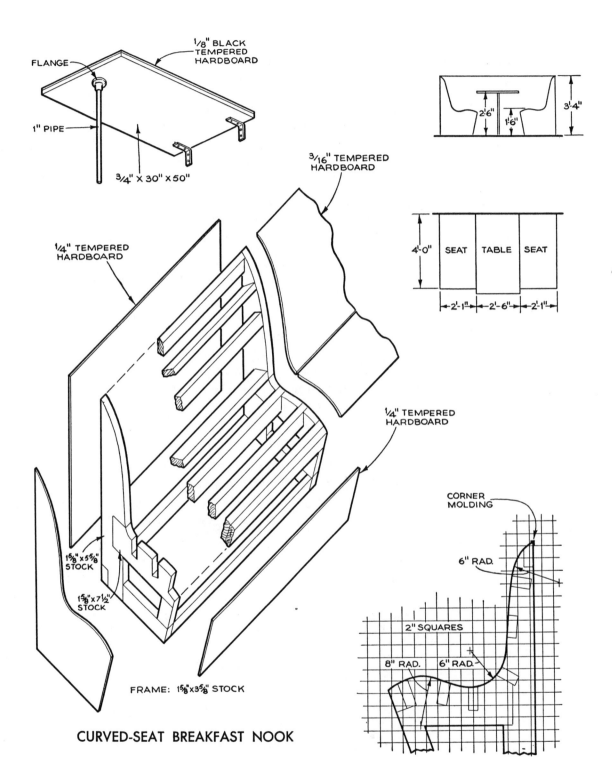

FLANGE

1/8" BLACK
TEMPERED
HARDBOARD

1" PIPE

3/4" X 30" X 50"

1/4" TEMPERED
HARDBOARD

3/16" TEMPERED
HARDBOARD

1/4" TEMPERED
HARDBOARD

2'-6"

1'-6"

3'-4"

4'-0"

SEAT   TABLE   SEAT

2'-1"   2'-6"   2'-1"

1⁵⁄₈" x 5⁵⁄₈"
STOCK

1⁵⁄₈" x 7½"
STOCK

FRAME: 1⁵⁄₈" x 3⁵⁄₈" STOCK

CORNER
MOLDING

6" RAD.

2" SQUARES

8" RAD.   6" RAD.

CURVED-SEAT BREAKFAST NOOK

Pointers for Building

Glue together several sheets of wrapping or other paper to make a single sheet at least 26″ x 41″ in size. Carefully rule this into 2″ squares and transfer to it the squared end pattern shown. Project the bottom of the pattern to include the full height of the seat.

To make each of the four end frames required for the two seats, cut a piece 40″ long from the 2″ x 6″ lumber. Exactly 18″ from a squared end of this piece lay off a line for the upper edge of a notch 1¾″ deep into which one end of a 22″ length of 2″ x 8″ stock will fit snugly. Notching must be accurate to planed-down dimensions of lumber. Then, following the angles and dimensions indicated on your full-size pattern, cut the two 1⅝″ x 3⅝″ members (at the bottom and front) needed to complete the end framing. With the 2″ x 8″ horizontal member temporarily in place in its notch in the vertical 2″ x 6″ piece, transfer the contour of the seat and back rest to the two pieces, following the pattern closely. Be sure that the radii of the bends are not less than those shown. After sawing the pieces to the contour lines, cut out the indicated notches to take the 2″ x 4″ cross members of the seat—three notches on the upper edge of the 2″ x 8″ member and one in the rear bottom corner of the upright. The four members of the end frame can be joined with mortise and tenon or doweled joints glued and clamped. However, the pieces could also be butted and fastened together with long wood screws, set deep in counterbored holes where necessary. Coat the mating surfaces of the wood with glue before turning in the screws. Complete four end frames this way.

For each seat, then saw to length the ten 2″ x 4″ cross members required. Saw five to the full 48″ length of the seat. These go into the notches. Reduce the length of the other five to fit between the end frames. Then assemble the frame with screws, countersinking the heads. Plane off the edges of the cross frame members, as indicated by the plan, to the seat and back contour.

After cutting the ³⁄₁₆″ tempered hardboard panels to approximate size, it is necessary to increase the moisture content before bending. Do this by scrubbing warm water with a broom into the screen, or back, side until the board turns a dark chocolate brown. Then stack the four panels in pairs, smooth sides together, with wet rags or several thicknesses of wet newspaper separating the two pairs and **under** and on top of the stack. Allow to stand about 24 hours.

In the meantime, you can cut and apply ¼″ tempered hardboard to the back, front and ends of the seats. Cut the end piece to the exact shape of the end pattern. Fit the front and back panels to cover the edges of the end piece. When you are ready to curve the seat panels in place, let them also extend over the edges of the flat panels already in place. This will avoid down cracks.

It is a simple matter to apply the seat panels. Do it while they are still moist. Start nailing each panel at a corner to one end of the frame and wrap the panel snugly against the frame as you drive the nails. In the plans, notice that the seat and back-rest panels are butted together over the 2 x 4 frame member at the rear of the seat. Bring these edges into moderate contact.

Cement the sheet of black tempered hardboard to the table top and apply aluminum molding around the edges. Attach the end of the table to the wall with angle brackets. The 1″ pipe, with floor flanges on each end, supports the other end of the table. The seats can be fastened to the wall and floor with lag screws driven in before the panels are applied.

Dining table is handy to the open end of this U-shaped kitchen built with Louisiana-Pacific kitchen cabinets.

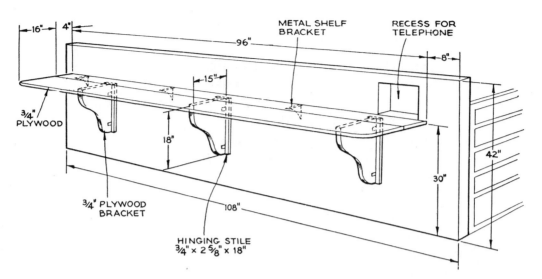

SNACK BAR

Uses

A hinged snack bar like this might be located along any free wall. Here, it backs up a peninsula dividing the kitchen and dining area. Hinging the bar so it can be dropped while not in use makes it a possibility for even a hall or narrow walkway.

Materials

¾″ plywood (4′ x 8′ panel) to make—

    1 pc. 16″ x 8′ — bar.

    1 pc. 4″ x 8′ — ledge.

    3 pc. 15″ x 18″ — brackets.

3 pc. 1″ x 3″ nominal stock 18″ long — stiles.

4 3″ shelf brackets.

6 1½″ x 1½″ hinges (for brackets).

4 3″ x 3″ hinges (for bar).

Pointers for Building

The peninsula should follow standard wall construction, studs and any standard surfacing—lath and plaster, plaster board, etc. On the bar side, the peninsula might be faced with plywood. Frame the telephone recess as part of the peninsula construction.

Position the stiles opposite wall studs and screw them in place. Hinge the plywood brackets so they all swing in one direction. Space the bar hinges so they won't interfere with the swing of the brackets. Include some means of locking the plywood brackets to the under side of the bar when it is up. A hook and eye for each bracket will do, although a catch that latches automatically will be more convenient.

TABLE IDEAS

Door-mounted Breadboard

A large breadboard almost equal in size to a wide base-cabinet door can serve as both extra work surface and breakfast table. Hinge it to the inside face of the door near the top. When the door is open at right angles to the face of the cabinet and the breadboard swung up level from its normally flat position against the door, a hinged wooden bracket swung out from the other side of the door opening will support the breadboard. Make the bracket by joining two equal-length pieces of 1⅝" x 2⅝" stock at right angles and bracing them with a diagonal member. Hinge the bracket far enough inside the cabinet so that, when it is pivoted back parallel to the edge of the shelves, clearance will be provided for the breadboard—allowing the door to close. A snap fastener or hook and eye will lock the bread-board to the bracket in the open position.

Cantilevered Table

Starting with a modern flush-type door, you can install a table that needs no legs, yet is easily moved to the kitchen for breakfast and back to the dining room (or living room) for lunch and dinner. In addition, it makes a convenient sit-down work table in either room.

You can accomplish this by installing the door to slide back and forth in a close-fitting horizontal slot through a base cabinet and wall. Even though about 2½' of one end of the door always remains in-side the base cabinet and wall, the protruding part still gives you a table about 4' long, enough space to serve four persons and possibly a fifth (at the end).

To make up for the lack of leg support, a strong framework of 1⅝" x 3⅝" stock must be installed in the base cabinet. Since down pressure on the free end of the fully opened table will multiply itself into considerable upward stress at the other end, the cabinet framework must be strong above the table as well as below. Assemble the frame with glue and screws, apply diagonal braces on either side (from front to back of the cabinet), and bolt it to the floor. If the slot passes through an existing wall, as well as the cabinet, it will be necessary to cut sections out of at least two wall studs. Nail 1⅝" x 3⅝" pieces across the cut ends of the studs, both above and below the slot, and fasten their ends securely to the adjoining studs. Screw 1⅝" x 1⅝" parallel hardwood guides inside the framework to carry the sliding door. Sand the guides smooth and wax them well. Screw a small block under the edge of the door at each end to serve as a stop. Place molding around the slot at either end.

Instead of using a door, you might build a sliding two-room table in three sections hinged together. If the middle one is made just equal to the combined depth of the base cabinet and wall, the sections on each end can be folded down flat while not in use. The length of the end sections must not, of course, exceed the height of the table from the floor, about 30". A swing-out wooden bracket, hinged like a door, will support the end sections when the table is centered. Folding legs mounted under the end sections will enable you to pull out two sections into either room.

For either of these two-room tables, a pass-through in the wall above will make meal serving easier.

17

Floor-to-Ceiling Cabinets

Although the modern trend is toward exclusive use of wall and base storage units with a streamlined counter arrangement, many kitchens still need cabinets or cupboards that start at the floor and rise most or all of the way to the ceiling. If closets are lacking, tall cabinets are useful for storage of brooms, mops, vacuum cleaners, ironing boards, and the like—if nothing else. In some cases, too, full-height cabinets offer a place to store reserve supplies.

Strangely enough, considering the current emphasis on separate lines of wall and base cabinets, tall storage units have gotten serious attention at some research centers and they deserve to be used in modern kitchens more often than they have been.

On the pages that immediately follow, you will find plans for a swing-shelf storage unit. Its shelves open like the pages of a book. It departs sharply from modern kitchen-cabinet design. The home owner whose heart is set on a new or remodeled streamlined kitchen may not like its looks. It has little in common with conventional wall or base cabinets. Yet for efficiency of storage few cabinets could equal it.

The cabinet is one of several developed at the College of Home Economics of Cornell University during a study of functional kitchen storage. Mary Koll Heiner and Helen E. McCullough, who made the study, have this to say about it:

"The swing cabinet is the most compact example of functional storage here developed. It holds 150 to 175 packaged foods as well as 35 items of major equipment used first at the mix center. Through this device needless kitchen travel and the rehandling of supplies are reduced markedly. Shelving that would necessitate 57 linear feet and would require 9 feet of walking distance (pilot study) was reduced to 5 compact 24-inch units that occupy a quadrant area of less than 4 feet. First-use, ease of visibility, and ease of grasp are readily achieved on shelves ranging from 2 inches to $4\frac{1}{2}$ inches for packaged food supplies. All storage is one row deep, one stack high. Order becomes automatic."

The swing feature and the narrow shelves—just wide enough for the cans or other items to be stored—are ideas that can be utilized in many ways by a home cabinet builder.

SWING STORAGE CABINET

Uses

This cabinet provides space between range and sink for storage of mixing and baking supplies and utensils. It was developed at Cornell University. Their bulletin points out:

"The upper shelves in the right-hand section hold the mixing supplies and those items used first at the sink. The wider cut-back shelves below hold the mixing and baking utensils. Bake pans, muffin tins, and other baking dishes are stored on edge on the bottom shelf and separated by plywood dividers. This eliminates stacking and the unnecessary handling which always accompanies stacking.

"The center panel in the upper part swings between the two outside sections. The small mixing and cutting tools may be hung on the right-hand surface of it and the supplies used first with boiling water are on the left-hand side. All shelves are narrow so that items are stored on them one row deep. They also are adjustable so that they may be moved up or down to fit the items placed on them."

Standing 6' 10½" high, the cabinet occupies only 15¼" x 25½" of floor space. The right-hand section should be fastened to the wall. About 29" of free wall space is needed at the left if the left-hand section is to open fully. If desired, this section can be divided into parts. Divided slightly above the 36" level, the upper part would clear an adjoining base-cabinet work counter. A rolling table could be used in front of the cabinet to provide a work surface.

The university bulletin recommends that if the range and sink are located on the same wall, this cabinet and a work counter should be placed between them. If sink and range are on adjacent walls, the cabinet could be placed in the corner, with the hinge side 7½" from the corner of the room. This will allow the left door to open 90 degrees—flat against the adjacent wall.

Materials

PLYWOOD	HARDWOOD
1 4' x 9' panel ¼".	1 pc. ⅞" x 3" x 6'.
1 4' x 7' panel ¼".	1 pc. ¾" x ¾" x 10'.
1 4' x 8' panel ½".	1 pc. ¾" x ¾" x 8'.
1 4' x 7' panel ¾".	60' ¼" x ½".

1 piano hinge 3' 10" long.

1 piano hinge 6' 6" long.

2 door catches.

12 adjustable shelf standards 6' long.

1 rubber caster 2½" dia.

6 doz. screws for ¼" panels   1"-#6 flat-head.

4 doz. screws for base and shelves   1¼"-#6 flat-head.

3 doz. screws for door jambs   1½"-#7 flat-head.

2 lbs. brads #16.

23 chrome retaining strips 1" x 23½".

SWING STORAGE
CABINET

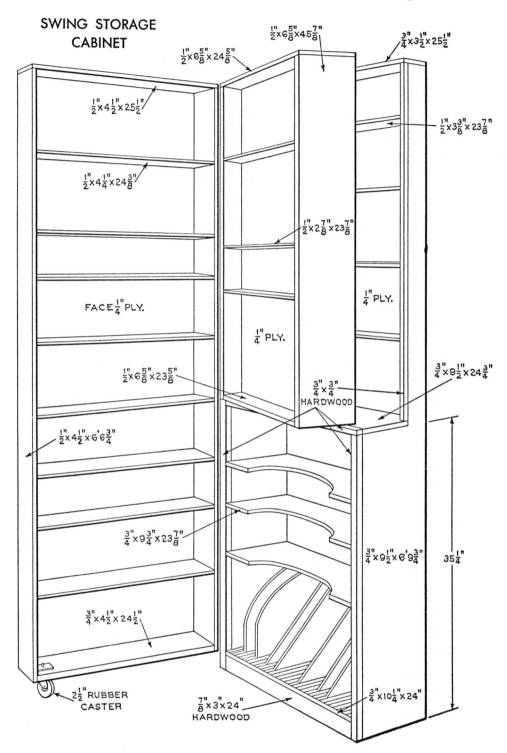

$\frac{1}{2}" \times 6\frac{5}{8}" \times 45\frac{7}{8}"$

$\frac{3}{4}" \times 3\frac{1}{2}" \times 25\frac{1}{2}"$

$\frac{1}{2}" \times 6\frac{5}{8}" \times 24\frac{5}{8}"$

$\frac{1}{2}" \times 4\frac{1}{2}" \times 25\frac{1}{2}"$

$\frac{1}{2}" \times 3\frac{3}{8}" \times 23\frac{7}{8}"$

$\frac{1}{2}" \times 4\frac{1}{4}" \times 24\frac{3}{8}"$

$\frac{1}{2}" \times 2\frac{7}{8}" \times 23\frac{7}{8}"$

FACE $\frac{1}{4}"$ PLY.

$\frac{1}{4}"$ PLY.

$\frac{1}{4}"$ PLY.

$\frac{1}{2}" \times 6\frac{5}{8}" \times 23\frac{5}{8}"$

$\frac{3}{4}" \times \frac{3}{4}"$
HARDWOOD

$\frac{3}{4}" \times 9\frac{1}{2}" \times 24\frac{3}{4}"$

$\frac{1}{2}" \times 4\frac{1}{2}" \times 6'6\frac{3}{4}"$

$\frac{3}{4}" \times 9\frac{3}{4}" \times 23\frac{7}{8}"$

$\frac{3}{4}" \times 9\frac{1}{2}" \times 6'9\frac{3}{4}"$

$35\frac{1}{4}"$

$\frac{3}{4}" \times 4\frac{1}{2}" \times 24\frac{1}{2}"$

$2\frac{1}{2}"$ RUBBER
CASTER

$\frac{7}{8}" \times 3 \times 24$
HARDWOOD

$\frac{3}{4}" \times 10\frac{1}{4}" \times 24"$

Pointers for Building

After cutting the sides, top, and two fixed shelves of the rear unit, screw and glue the four ¾″ x ¾″ hardwood edge strips in place to serve as door jambs. For conservation of material, the three cutaway shelves in the base can be cut from the panel of ¾″ plywood. However, some builders may prefer pine stock here. Cut the indentations in these shelves 3¾″ deep, centering the cutouts 5″ from each end and rounding the inner and outer corners to a 1½″ radius.

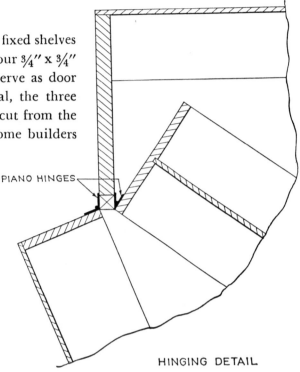

PIANO HINGES

HINGING DETAIL

The base frame consists of two 24″ lengths of ⅞″ x 3″ hardwood, installed between the sides and covered by a fixed shelf. Grooves for the shelf dividers are easily made by bradding strips of ¼″ x ½″ wood to the shelf and ¼″ plywood back. However, builders with power equipment may prefer to cut grooves in the shelf itself. Make the dividers from ¼″ plywood. Two shapes are indicated, each with a 9″ base dimension. Make the curved dividers 12″ high and curve the upper edge to a 9″ radius.

The middle swing unit is partitioned by a 24½″ x 45⅞″ panel of ¼″ plywood. Glue the edges of this panel into grooves cut in the top, bottom, and sides. Shelves 3⅜″ wide are used on the side not visible in the drawing. In the original cabinet, two rows of utensil hooks are placed across the bottom part of the unit on that side. In the rear unit, two of the shelves are cut back to a 2″ width for storage of spices. For these, you can substitute ¼″ material in place of the ½″ indicated.

Install metal shelf strips in all units to support the shelves and make them adjustable. Vertical grooves may be cut in the sides for flush-mounting of the strips, or they may be screwed directly to the sides.

Chrome strips on the shelf edges serve two functions. They cover the raw plywood grain and, projecting above the shelf surface, they keep supplies from falling off.

CANNED GOODS STORAGE CABINET

Uses

In a modern home, this spacious cabinet can take the place of the old-time pantry. Its shelves and door racks will hold most of the canned goods, bought or home-produced, that the average housewife today will want to store.

Projecting only 12½", the cabinet will fit anywhere in the kitchen or adjoining hallway that you can find 48" of free wall space. Cut down in width to suit, it is an ideal cabinet for a narrow wall space between two doors that pass through the same wall.

As shown, the inner shelves are in fixed positions. However, it would be simple enough to make part or all of them adjustable. Use the metal strips available at hardware and building supply stores.

A box step for reaching the upper shelves fits sideways under the bottom shelf. Omit this if the kitchen has a step stool.

Pointers for Building

Nominal stock needs only to be cut to length to give you most of the parts for this cabinet. A good place to begin is at the front. Cut the two vertical facing boards from 1" x 9" stock and the top one from 1" x 4"; cut the jamb and door stop pieces. Make a trial assembly of these pieces around the flush door placed flat on the floor. Then measure the overall width of the assembly. This will enable you to take into account any local variations in the stock and show whether you should adjust other dimensions of the cabinet, especially the length of the shelves.

Screw all cleats to the back, sides, and front members. Begin assembly of the unit by screwing or nailing the ¼" back to the wall. The sides, facing, studs, header, and top can then all go into place.

CANNED GOODS STORAGE CABINET

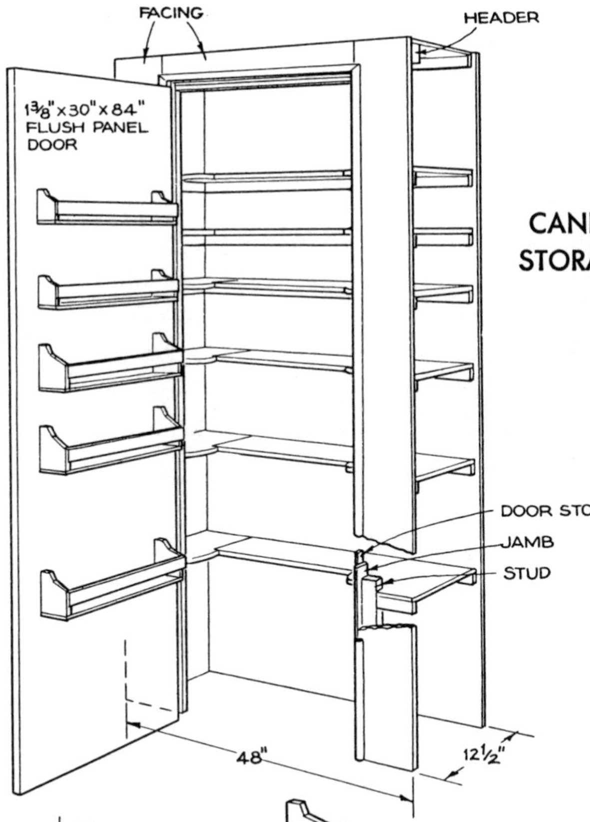
FACING
HEADER
1⅜" x 30" x 84" FLUSH PANEL DOOR
DOOR STOP
JAMB
STUD
48"
12½"

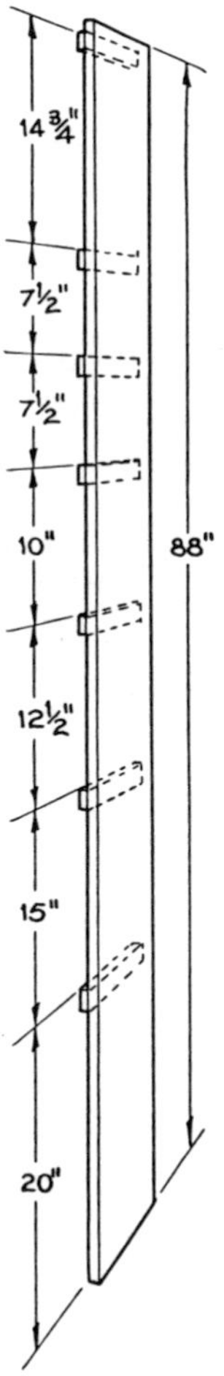
14¾"
7½"
7½"
10"
12½"
15"
20"
88"

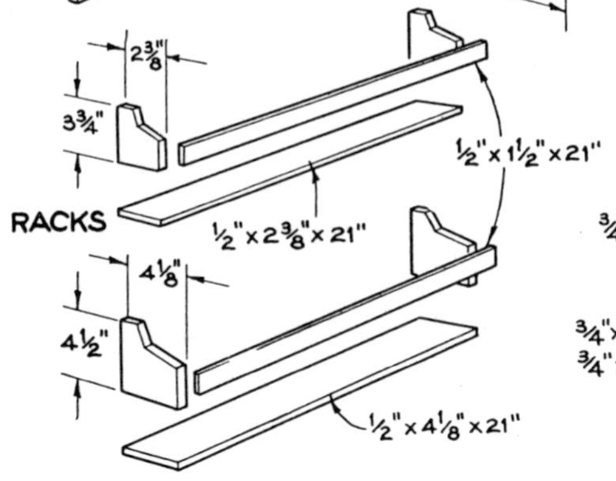
2⅜"
3¾"
RACKS
½" x 2⅜" x 21"
½" x 1½" x 21"
4⅛"
4½"
½" x 4⅛" x 21"

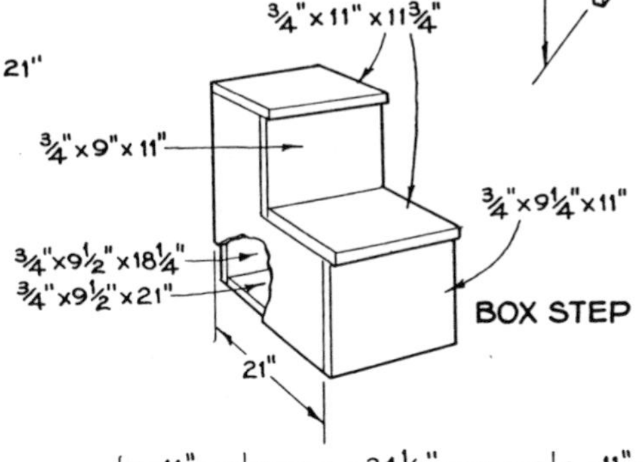
¾" x 11" x 11¾"
¾" x 9" x 11"
¾" x 9¼" x 11"
¾" x 9½" x 18¼"
¾" x 9½" x 21"
21"
BOX STEP

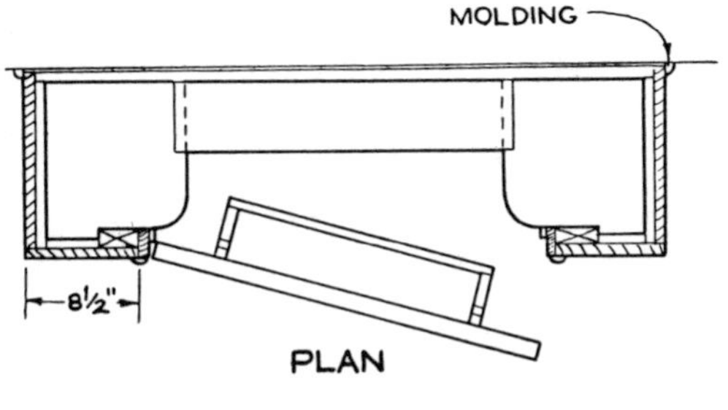
MOLDING
8½"
PLAN

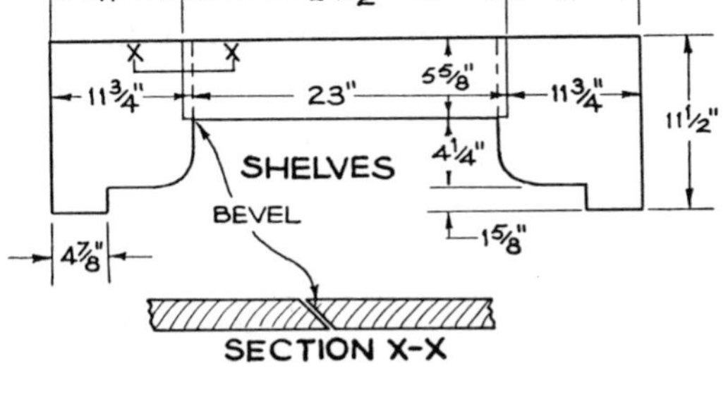
11"
24½"
11"
X
X
5⅝"
11¾"
23"
11¾"
11½"
4¼"
SHELVES
BEVEL
1⅝"
4⅞"
SECTION X-X

UTILITY CABINET

Uses

As shown, this tall cabinet provides space for broom, mop, cleaning supplies, and perhaps a vacuum cleaner. Shoe cleaning and polishing materials, or a child's toys, might go in the bottom drawer. Additional hooks would extend the usefulness of the cabinet to storage of aprons and other small items of clothing. Alternately, an ironing board might stand in the cabinet. If filled with additional shelves, it could be devoted to storage of canned goods and other food supplies.

Materials

1″ x 12″ (nom.) stock (40 linear feet).

1″ x   8″ (nom.) stock (4 linear feet).

1″ x   4″ (nom.) stock (8 linear feet).

1″ x   2″ (nom.) stock (42 linear feet).

1 pc. ¾″ plywood 36″ x 48″.

1 pc. ¼″ plywood 36″ x 88″.

Pointers for Building

Two 88″ lengths of the 1″ x 12″ stock, glued together or simply held by the shelf cleats, will be suitable for each of the cabinet sides. The door might be made of a strip of 1″ x 12″ stock and another of the 1″ x 4″ material. Or you could use ¾″ plywood. Use ¾″ plywood for the cabinet top, the floor, and the two shelves, supporting them on cleats cut from the 1″ x 2″ stock. Two 88″ pieces of 1″ x 2″ stock also are needed for the vertical face strips. Cut ¾″ x 1⅝″ notches in the front corners of the top, floor, and the bottom drawer framing so the verticals can be inset. The drawer is standard construction. Additional pieces of 1″ x 2″ stock should be attached (not shown) to the sides just above the bottom drawer-supporting frame to act as drawer guides.

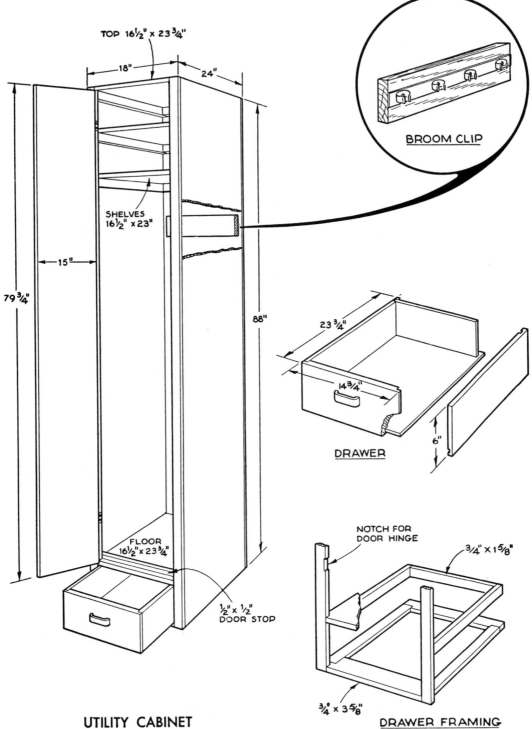

TOP 16½" x 23¾"

18"

24"

BROOM CLIP

SHELVES
16½" x 23"

15"

79¾"

88"

23¾"

14¾"

6"

DRAWER

FLOOR
16½" x 23¾"

½" x ½"
DOOR STOP

NOTCH FOR
DOOR HINGE

¾" x 1⅝"

¾" x 3⅝"

UTILITY CABINET

DRAWER FRAMING

IDEAS

Door Shelves

Useful storage space can often be found on inside doors, particularly the inner face of those opening into closets, stairways, and the like. Narrow shelves, with retaining strips along their edge, can be used for storage of various packaged and canned goods. The shelves can be placed between two vertical frame members, perhaps one-by-fours, mounted a short distance from each edge of the door. A shelf plus a retaining strip about 6″ above (nailed across the outer edges of the verticals) makes a handy place to store pan lids, trays, etc. A similar arrangement might also take an item as bulky as an ironing board.

Roll-out Cleaner Cabinet

A tall, narrow cabinet could have a roll-out unit in its base to store and transport a tank-type vacuum cleaner, standing on its end. Equip the unit with three or four rubber-tired casters and it can be used to move the cleaner and all accessories into other rooms of the house. Let the back of the unit serve as the cabinet door like some of the units shown and described in the chapter on vertical pull-out racks. A roll-out unit like this might also fit into a niche in a storage wall.

18

Installing
Your Cabinets

When your cabinets (either commercial or homebuilt) are on hand, you face the task of installing them correctly. The sketches and instructions on the following three pages are distributed by the Weather-Seal Division of the Louisiana-Pacific Corporation of Portland, Oregon, with the kitchen cabinets it markets.

Attach all cabinets to wall studs with large screws, never nails. Also join the cabinets into a unit by running screws through the front frame of one into the adjoining cabinet frame.

The tools you need include a level, an electric drill with a pilot bit to suit the screws, a countersink for the drill, and, if possible, a power screwdriver (or reversible drill). Begin by locating and marking each stud on the wall where the cabinets are to go. A dull sound when you tap with a hammer indicates a stud. Test by driving in a small nail. Studs usually are 16 inches apart. Nail-test each location. Remove any wall mouldings that might prevent a good cabinet fit. If the baseboard remains in place, trim the back of each base cabinet to fit over it.

Floors seldom are level—but your cabinets must be. Locate the highest point on the floor along the cabinet wall and measure up 84 inches, the customary height for the top of wall cabinets. Start installation in a corner. Have a helper hold each cabinet while you check that it is level in all directions—sideways, and front to back. Use shingles to shim each cabinet, splitting them into narrow strips and then using a section that is the proper thickness. If you install the base cabinets first, protect the counters with cardboard while you install cabinets above.

The following sketches were developed for Weather-Seal cabinets, but most of them should apply to your particular cabinets.

BASE & WALL CABINET INSTALLATION

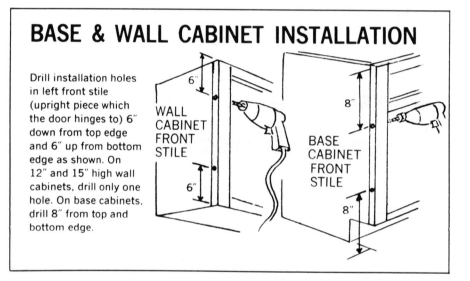

Drill installation holes in left front stile (upright piece which the door hinges to) 6″ down from top edge and 6″ up from bottom edge as shown. On 12″ and 15″ high wall cabinets, drill only one hole. On base cabinets, drill 8″ from top and bottom edge.

FASTENING TO WALL

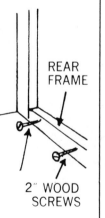

Next, fasten the cabinet to the wall. Shim base cabinets at center between back of cabinet and wall. Attach with 2″ screws through the rear frame of cabinet into the wall. In wall cabinets, do not use holes in rear side stiles—they are for shelf adjustment.

SHIM BETWEEN CABINETS

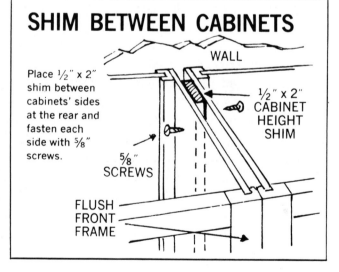

Place ½″ x 2″ shim between cabinets' sides at the rear and fasten each side with ⅝″ screws.

JOINING FRONT FRAMES

Next, make sure front frames are flush on front surface and bottom edge. Drill through existing holes into stile of adjoining cabinet 1″ deep with 3/16″ drill bit. Fasten cabinets together with #8 x 2½″ flat head screws. Countersink for screw head.

#8 x 2½″
FLAT HEAD
WOOD SCREWS

COUNTER-TOP INSTALLATION

Base cabinets have metal gusset plates in each corner. These plates add strength and are used to fasten the counter-top. To attach, run a screw through each plate into the counter-top.

METAL GUSSET PLATES

FLOOR AND WALL SHIMMING

IMPORTANT:

If walls and floor are not plumb and true, base and wall cabinets must be shimmed to the highest point as indicated. This will insure proper alignment and prevent undue strain.

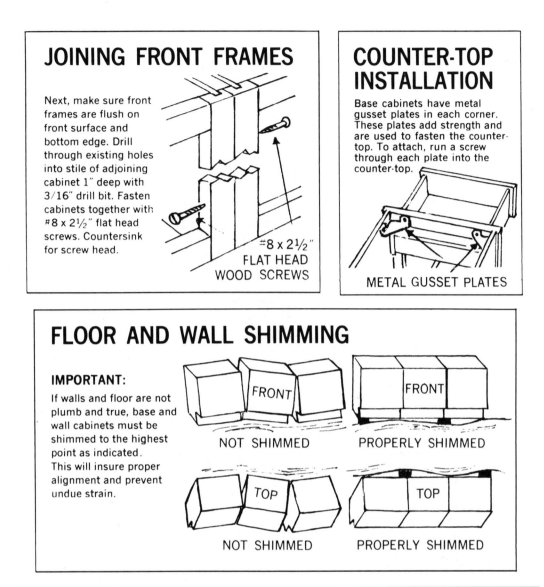

FRONT — NOT SHIMMED

FRONT — PROPERLY SHIMMED

TOP — NOT SHIMMED

TOP — PROPERLY SHIMMED

CEILING HUNG PENINSULAR CABINETS

Locate ceiling joists above cabinet. Drill two (2) 3/16″ diameter holes through each top frame in line with joists. Secure with #8 x 2½″ flat head wood screws. Countersink for screw head.

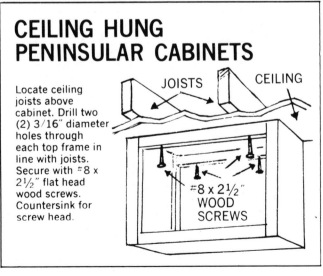

JOISTS

CEILING

#8 x 2½″
WOOD SCREWS

RANGE FRONT PANEL

May be trimmed to width and height and adapted to most drop-in ranges. Base fillers may be cut down and used on the sides. Range front panel consists of one (1) hardwood panel 9½″ x 30″, one (1) white pine bottom filler and one (1) white pine toe board.

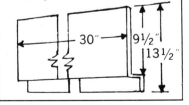

30″   9½″   13½″

BLIND CORNER WALL CABINET

Follow the normal instructions except always use a 3" filler. Use the two (2) holes you drilled into the side stile of the standard cabinet and attach the filler.

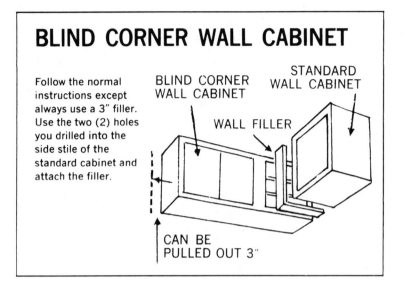

BLIND CORNER WALL CABINET

STANDARD WALL CABINET

WALL FILLER

CAN BE PULLED OUT 3"

BLIND CORNER BASE CABINET

Position the standard cabinet, with filler against the blind corner cabinet. Drill two (2) 3/16" diameter holes through center support of blind corner cabinet and secure with ≠8 x 2½" flat head woodscrew.

NOTE: Blind corner base and wall cabinets may be pulled up to 3" from wall for additional length.

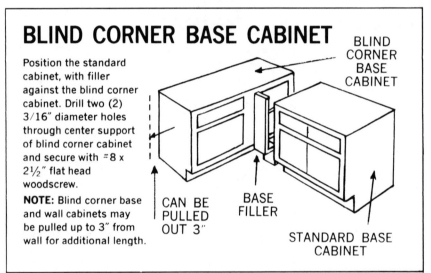

BLIND CORNER BASE CABINET

CAN BE PULLED OUT 3"

BASE FILLER

STANDARD BASE CABINET

SHELF INSTALLATION

Insert plastic shelf clips into predrilled holes. There are three (3) holes, 2" apart for each shelf. Use center hole for equal spacing.

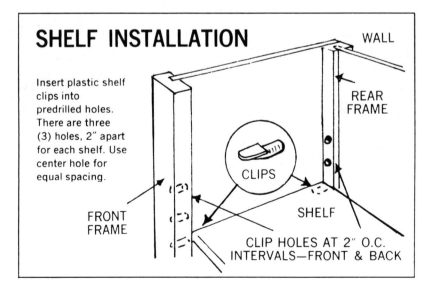

WALL

REAR FRAME

CLIPS

FRONT FRAME

SHELF

CLIP HOLES AT 2" O.C. INTERVALS—FRONT & BACK

OPEN CORNER BASE CABINET

Base cabinets may be installed with an open corner, using a corner base filler.

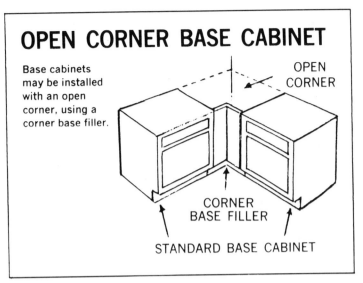

OPEN CORNER

CORNER BASE FILLER

STANDARD BASE CABINET

DOOR ADJUSTMENT

Loosen adjustment screws on each hinge. Make adjustment up and down or side to side and tighten screws. To remove doors, loosen screws until door can be lifted off.

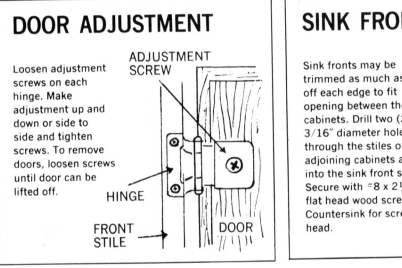

ADJUSTMENT SCREW

HINGE

FRONT STILE

DOOR

SINK FRONT INSTALLATION

Sink fronts may be trimmed as much as 2½" off each edge to fit opening between the two cabinets. Drill two (2) 3/16" diameter holes through the stiles of adjoining cabinets and into the sink front stiles. Secure with #8 x 2½" flat head wood screws. Countersink for screw head.

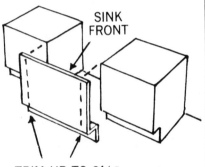

SINK FRONT

TRIM UP TO 2½" OFF EACH SIDE

CABINET ACCESSORIES

Molding is available to trim walls, appliances and ceilings. It is ¾" x ⅜" and available in 4', 5', 6' and 8' lengths.
If a valance is desired, it is available in a ¾" x 5" size and in 4', 5', 6' and 8' lengths.
End shelf units are available for both base and wall units. Various factory finished fillers are available as detailed.

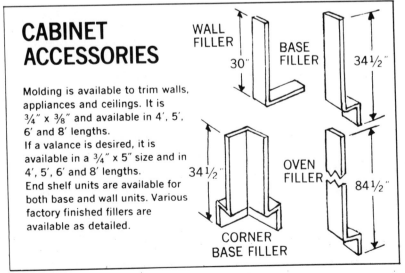

WALL FILLER
30"

BASE FILLER
34½"

34½"
CORNER BASE FILLER

OVEN FILLER
84½"

19

Kitchen Desks

A desk in or adjoining the kitchen is the control center from which the modern homemaker can operate a home smoothly and efficiently. Equip it with a telephone, intercom, and space for storing housekeeping bills and records, cookbooks, recipes, and writing materials. Cabinet manufacturers offer a beautiful variety of desks, but building one is where the do-it-yourselfer can shine. Desk facilities can often be provided in a unit designed as part of the base cabinets.

One of the simplest consists of a projection of the work counter at the end of a line of cabinets. This can be supported by one or more legs of metal tubing or hardwood dowel rod (clothes-pole size) or perhaps by a tier of drawers or an open-shelf whatnot. When the desk surface is supported by tubing or dowel legs, the necessary desk drawer space probably can be provided in the adjoining base cabinet. Depending on the location of the desk, it may be possible to build a telephone niche into the wall. (Amateur builders might like to note that mail-order houses sell these niches as assembled units.) It usually will be possible to locate a shelf for cookbooks on or near the desk.

The builder should give thought to the height of the desk surface. If placed at average counter height, a stool will be needed to raise the user to an easy working level. If a chair is to be used (a more desirable objective) the desk surface should be dropped to correspond. Give thought, too, to secondary use of the desk as a breakfast bar. A kneehole space in a peninsula arrangement of cabinets offers seating facilities for two.

A base cabinet drawer can be adapted to desk use too by hinging the drawer front to swing down. Support it by a metal elbow bracket or length of furnace chain. A pressure catch will keep the front secure while the drawer desk is closed. Use ⅜" or ½" stock for the drawer bottom and mount it with the under side flush with the bottom edges of the drawer sides so as to produce a full closure at the front when the hinged front is closed. A top drawer about 6" deep devoted to such a desk will give a writing surface at a height convenient for a person seated in an ordinary chair.

What looks like a drawer actually can be a desk. This clever pull-out unit has a drop front that increases writing space. It is offered as part of Louisiana-Pacific Corporation's kitchen-cabinet line. Notice the slots for storing cookbooks (flat), recipes, and other materials. If the desk has a depth of 6 inches (up and down) under a counter 36 inches high, the writing surface falls at the ideal height of 30 inches.

Wall-hung home planning center in one corner of the kitchen can be assembled and installed in half an hour—by just about anyone. The makers of Kirsch shelf brackets and finished shelving assembled this one to show how easy it all is. Add a telephone and/or intercom and what more could you want? You'll find Kirsch products at hardware and building supply stores.

Sliding doors hide the contents of this counter-hung desk while not in use, yet open easily when you want to telephone or do a bit of menu planning. Frame it with one-by-two's, install a piece of ¾" plywood as the base, and use plastic sliding-door tracks available from building supply stores. The clever desk was designed by the makers of Marlite paneling. The desk is covered with the same Marlite textured oak paneling that was used on the accent wall and beams. The sliding doors are sheets of the same type of textured hardboard in a leather pattern. Damp-wiping quickly cleans this plastic-finished hardboard.

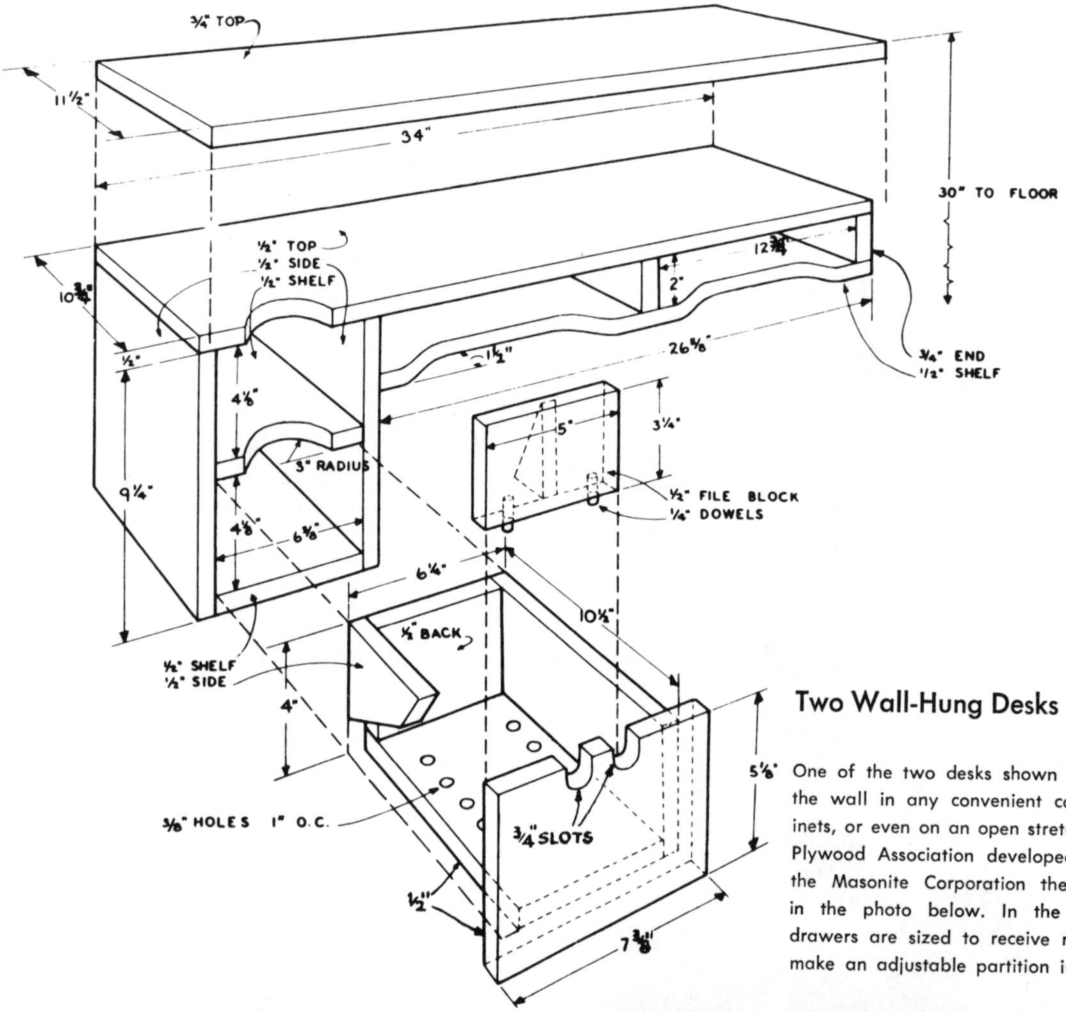
3/4" TOP
11 1/2"
34"
30" TO FLOOR
1/2" TOP
1/2" SIDE
1/2" SHELF
12 3/4"
10 3/4"
2"
1 1/2"
26 5/8"
3/4" END
1/2" SHELF
1/2"
4 1/8"
3" RADIUS
9 1/4"
4 1/8"
6 3/8"
5"
3 1/4"
1/2" FILE BLOCK
1/4" DOWELS
6 1/4"
10 1/2"
1/2" BACK
1/2" SHELF
1/2" SIDE
4"
3/8" HOLES 1" O.C.
3/4" SLOTS
1/2"
7 3/8"
5 1/8"

Two Wall-Hung Desks

One of the two desks shown here can be attached to the wall in any convenient corner, between two cabinets, or even on an open stretch of wall. The American Plywood Association developed the plans at the left, the Masonite Corporation the slightly different desk in the photo below. In the plans notice that two drawers are sized to receive recipe file cards. Dowels make an adjustable partition in each drawer.

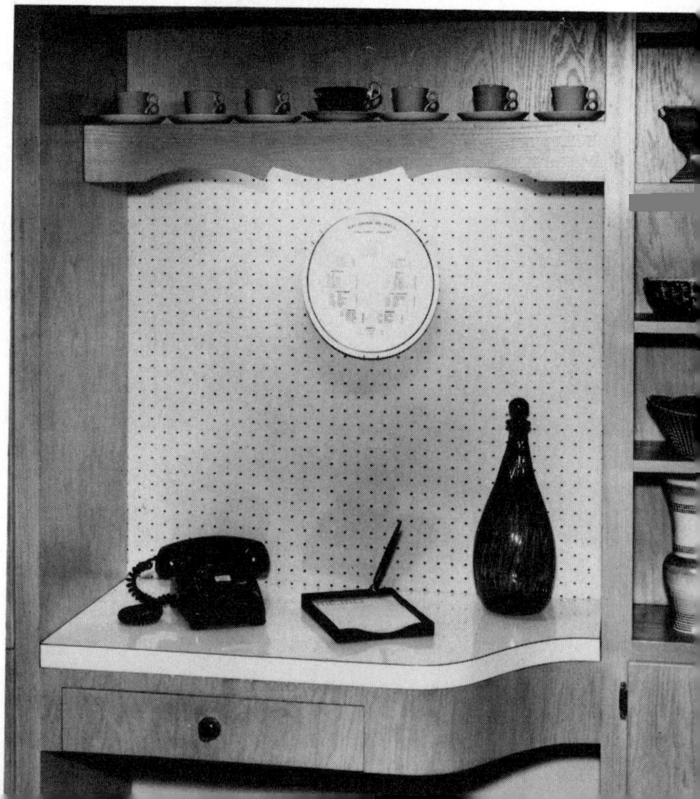

20

Handy and Decorative Accessories

Well-chosen accessories, whether they are functional or merely for looks, give the finishing touch to a kitchen. You can buy some, build others.

A small breadboard screwed to the inside of a breadbox lid puts a cutting surface conveniently at hand. A cutting board resting on narrow cleats near the upper edges of a drawer can be used in place when the drawer is pulled out—or be picked up and carried to another part of the kitchen.

Mounted on a center pivot under a utility-cabinet or closet shelf, a wood disk will support mops, brooms, and cleaning brushes on hooks around its edges. Revolve it, and you can easily reach the one you want. In a dish cupboard, a similar revolving disk will store cups out of the way.

Metal pull-out racks available at hardware stores can be mounted inside a cabinet to hold towels or pots and pans. Ready-made metal shelves screwed to the inside of cabinet doors take a wide range of articles. A narrow shelf suspended from a fixed shelf will store low

239

cans and make use of space that otherwise would be wasted. A narrow shelf resting on cleats between two fixed shelves will do the same. Metal file racks bought and placed on a shelf or door will store pot lids upright, keeping them in order in less space. Dishes, too, can be stored this way. Metal racks also are made to hold bottles on their sides, again in less space.

Units with narrow stepped shelves, bought or made at home, will bring order out of chaos in the spice and glassware departments if simply rested on a suitable cabinet shelf. Triangular shelves mounted in the corners of a cabinet that has fixed shelves spaced too far apart will help increase the storage space.

If you have no other place for the rolling pin, install hooks on the wall above the mixing counter and keep it there.

A unit with ends curving down and back to the wall, fitted under the wall cabinets, can have shelves decreasing in width from top to bottom.

Place bins about 4″ deep and the same dimension front to back against the wall at the rear of a work counter. Handy for storage of many small items—and the space won't be missed from a 24″ counter. Hinge a forward-slanting lid on the bins.

If the refrigerator stands alone, perhaps in a narrow space between two doors, see if there isn't room beside it for a counter-high shelf a few inches wide. The cook will bless you forever after. Put it on the refrigerator door-opening side, of course. A simple wood rack screwed inside a base-cabinet door, the sink cabinet perhaps, will take the paper bags that every housewife likes to collect.

A platter of awkward size will be safe and easily accessible if given its own special place under a shelf. To a narrow, fairly thick strip of wood, nail another wider strip to make an L-section assembly. Make two of these and screw them to the under side of a shelf with the protruding boards facing in—and just far enough apart so the edges of the platter can rest on them and slide in and out.

It is easy to put paper into a waste basket mounted on a shelf on the inside of a sink-cabinet door if you cut a horizontal piece about 5″ wide out of the door above the basket and hinge the cut-out piece back in place at its top edge. Push the paper through, and the hinged flap drops back in place.

These are only a few of many accessories that can be made or bought for installation in a kitchen. By bringing ingenuity into play, you will be able to dream up many more.

CHOPPING BLOCK AND KNIFE DRAWER

Uses

The original of this installation was designed to fit into a base corner cabinet with revolving shelves. But both the chopping block and drawer could be worked into a straight base cabinet 20″ wide and 24″ deep without any changes. The housewife will find many uses for a maple chopping block in preparation of food. The cutting surface is raised $\frac{1}{4}$″ above the counter to prevent damage to the latter. The reason for locating a drawer for storage of sharp knives near the chopping block is obvious. Storing the knives with the cutting edges up lessens the chances of dulling them.

Materials

1 pc. laminated maple 1$\frac{3}{4}$″ x 18″ x 18″.

1″ x 2″ (nom.) stock — cabinet framing.

1 pc. $\frac{3}{4}$″ x 4″ x 16$\frac{3}{8}$″ plywood — drawer front.

1 pc. $\frac{3}{4}$″ x 6″ x 15$\frac{1}{8}$″ — handle rest.

$\frac{5}{8}$″ plywood to make—

    2 pc. 4″ x 22″ — drawer sides.

    1 pc. 4″ x 16$\frac{3}{8}$″ — drawer back.

1 pc. $\frac{1}{4}$″ x 16$\frac{3}{8}$″ x 22″ plywood — drawer bottom.

1 pc. 1$\frac{1}{2}$″ x 3″ x 15$\frac{1}{8}$″ hardwood — blade holder.

1 pc. 2″ x 3″ x 15$\frac{1}{8}$″ channeled wood — paring-knife holder.

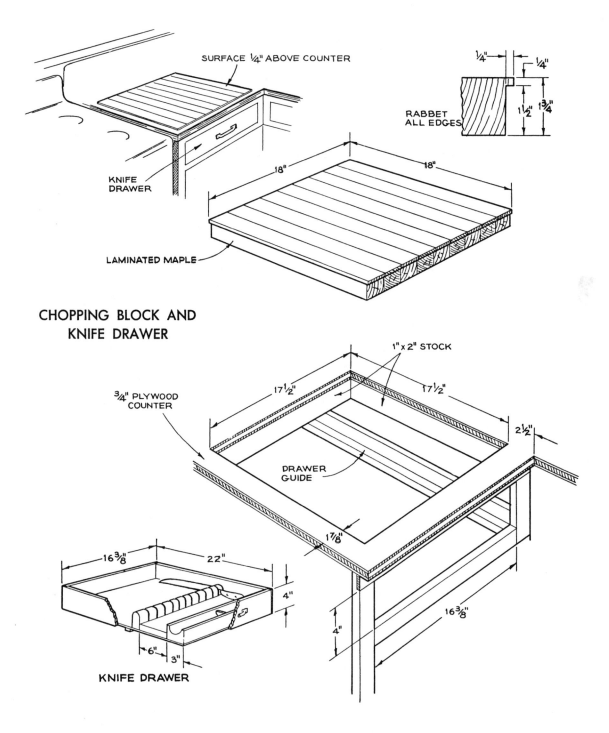

SURFACE ¼" ABOVE COUNTER

¼"   ¼"

RABBET
ALL EDGES

1½"   1¾"

KNIFE
DRAWER

18"   18"

LAMINATED MAPLE

CHOPPING BLOCK AND KNIFE DRAWER

1" x 2" STOCK

¾" PLYWOOD
COUNTER

17½"   17½"

2½"

DRAWER
GUIDE

1⅞"

16⅜"   22"   4"

6"   3"

4"

16⅜"

KNIFE DRAWER

Pointers for Building

The block and drawer can be fitted into any base cabinet built as suggested in this book. Construction of the drawer is conventional, as is its framing. If your lumber dealer cannot provide the channeled paring-knife block, a shop devoted to millwork undoubtedly can. Round off one edge of the $1\frac{1}{2}''$ x $3''$ x $15\frac{1}{8}''$ hardwood strip with a plane and/or a sander. Saw slots $2''$ deep into the $3''$ dimension to take the knives. With the drawer in place in the cabinet, screw a cleat under it to keep it from opening enough to expose the sharp blades.

Hard maple strips already laminated into blocks of various sizes are available from mail order sources and building supply dealers for kitchen counter use. Trim to size, rabbet the edges, and set the block into a hole cut in the counter, adjusting it to a snug and solid fit. Leave the block without permanent fastening so it can be removed occasionally for cleaning by reaching into the opened drawer and pressing the block upward.

UTILITY CART

Uses

This wheeled cart is a kitchen convenience with many uses. It is designed for storage in a base-cabinet recess about $23\frac{1}{8}''$ wide, its back flush with the fronts of the adjoining cabinets. Rolled out, it provides extra work surface anywhere in the kitchen. It hauls supplies wherever you want them. Its tray and shelves are spacious enough to carry an entire meal to the dining room—or the backyard—in a single trip. It makes clearing the table easier too. The tray is removable for use alone. When the cart is in place in its base-cabinet niche, the shelves offer storage almost equal to those in a base cabinet of the same size. Just roll it out to reach the shelves. Located near the range, the cart alone might fill most of the functions of a kitchen serving center.

Materials

⅜″ exterior plywood or tempered hardboard (4′ x 4′ panel) to make—

  1 pc. 20¼″ x 26½″ — back.
  1 pc. 19″ x 22″ — tray.
  2 pc. 16¼″ x 19¼″ — shelves.
  2 pc. 4″ x 5½″ — tray handles.
  2 pc. 1½″ x 5″ — axle supports.
  2 pc. 3″ x 19¾″ — cleats.

1″ x 2″ (nom.) stock (40 linear feet) — framing.

1″ x 4″ (nom.) stock (4 linear feet) — base, handle brackets.

1″ quarter-round (8 linear feet).

1 broom handle or dowel — handle.

½″ dia. x 22″ steel rod — wheel shaft.

2 6″ dia. rubber-tired wheels.

2 axle clamps.

4 furniture glides.

Corner irons, flat corners, screws, etc.

Pointers for Building

Cut the framing pieces to length and cut ¼″ x ⅜″ rabbets in all except those intended for the tray support and the two end verticals. Join the frames with end laps or other joints as desired. Cut the plywood or hardboard panels and fit them into the frames. If desired, the vertical back panel can be set into a deeper rabbet and edged with quarter-round molding. For an easier and quicker job, some builders may prefer to make one-piece panels of plywood, without the framing. The tray frame and middle shelf are mounted with the ⅜″ x 3″ x 19¾″ cleats sandwiched between them and the back panel.

As shown, the tray is simply a plywood sheet with the quarter round mitered for the corners and mounted around the edges. Nail and glue the handles into notches cut in the end. The brackets for the cart handle can be shaped from 6″ lengths of ¾″ x 3⅝″ stock.

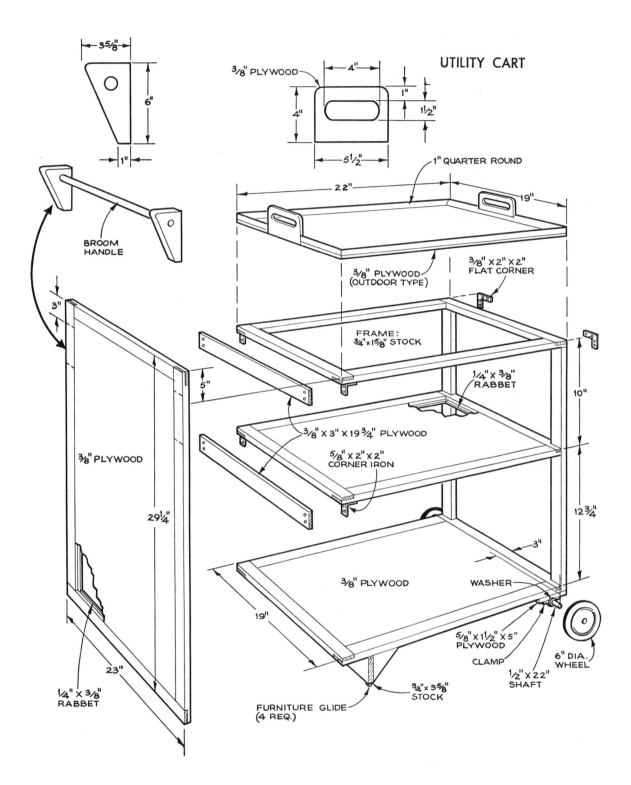

UTILITY CART

$3\frac{5}{8}$"

6"

1"

$\frac{3}{8}$" PLYWOOD

4"

4"

1"

$1\frac{1}{2}$"

$5\frac{1}{2}$"

1" QUARTER ROUND

22"

19"

BROOM HANDLE

$\frac{3}{8}$" PLYWOOD (OUTDOOR TYPE)

$\frac{3}{8}$" X 2" X 2" FLAT CORNER

3"

FRAME: $\frac{3}{4}$"x$1\frac{5}{8}$" STOCK

$\frac{1}{4}$" X $\frac{3}{8}$" RABBET

10"

5"

$\frac{3}{8}$" X 3" X $19\frac{3}{4}$" PLYWOOD

$\frac{5}{8}$" X 2" X 2" CORNER IRON

$\frac{3}{8}$" PLYWOOD

$12\frac{3}{4}$"

29$\frac{1}{4}$"

$\frac{3}{8}$" PLYWOOD

3"

WASHER

19"

$\frac{5}{8}$" X $1\frac{1}{2}$" X 5" PLYWOOD

6" DIA. WHEEL

CLAMP

$\frac{1}{2}$" X 22" SHAFT

$\frac{1}{4}$" X $\frac{3}{8}$" RABBET

23"

FURNITURE GLIDE (4 REQ.)

$\frac{3}{4}$" X $3\frac{5}{8}$" STOCK

The handle is set in suitable holes drilled into or through the brackets. Attach the brackets by screws driven through the rear face of the panel frame. The one-by-four base is strengthened by two right-angle blocks cut from $3/4''$ x $3\frac{5}{8}''$ material. Set this baseboard in far enough to give a toe recess equal to that in the base cabinets. Four glides spaced along the lower edge of this will make the cart easier to move in and out of the niche. Use spacer blocks under the bearing or clamp that supports the wheel shaft so as to bring the bottom of the wheel on a line with the furniture glides. Drill the ends of the rod for cotter pins to retain the wheels or thread it for axle nuts.

KNIFE RACK

Transparent plastic on one side allows a view of the knives for a quick selection from a knife rack that is used in the step-saving U-kitchen developed by the Department of Agriculture. The opposite side is $5/8''$ plywood. A rack like this can be mounted with the plywood side flat against the kitchen wall, or against the side of a wall cabinet or base cabinet.

Both the plastic and plywood are cut to the shape of a right-angle pie segment, that is a quarter circle with a radius of about 11 5/16". The knives are stored blade down in suitable slots cut crosswise in a curved piece that separates the curved edges of the plastic and plywood sides by about $1\frac{1}{2}''$. A piece curved to fit can be bandsawed from a wood block and the plastic and plywood sides can then be bradded to it. Wood separators of equal width would of course go between the straight sides of the quarter-circle rack. You could also use hardboard 3/16" thick for the curved cover. Cut the knife slots first and then moisten the hardboard before bending it.

The portable glass-ceramic Counter-Saver marketed by Corning Glass Works can be used for cutting, carving, and slicing, as well as a place to put sizzling hot pans directly from the oven or rangetop. The Counter-Savers have tough, white surfaces that are nonporous and won't absorb odors. They come in two sizes—11 by 15-inch, and 16 by 20-inch, either in plain white or decorated.

Corning Glass Works has provided a solution that reduces repair costs when a countertop is damaged. It's the built-in glass-ceramic Counter-Saver. It provides a place to cut, slice, dice, and carve, and a place to put hot pans directly from oven to rangetop.

Where can you place a kitchen radio so it's out of the way? Here's one designed for mounting under a wall cabinet. This one comes from Sears—or maybe you can contrive a bracket to mount another one in the same manner.

You can make several useful accessories for your kitchen using Plexiglas acrylic sheet available from local dealers. At the left is a cookbook easel, at the right a recipe card holder. Plans for making these and other useful items are available. See your Plexiglas dealer for the details or write to Rohm and Haas Company, Philadelphia, Pa. 19105.

Kitchen accessories can be both decorative and useful. In this photo, notice the wood tools hanging on the wall and the cabinet in background for display of decorative china. Porcelain knobs ornament the doors and drawers. The photo is supplied by Magic Chef.

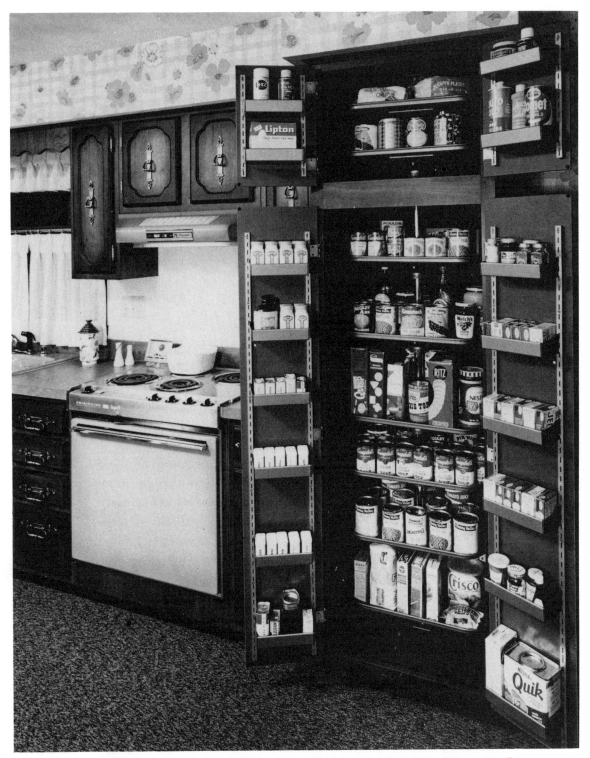

Looking for real storage convenience and capacity? You can load all the shelves and still have easy access to every item, if you install Amerock's "Pantry Pak" in your own standard cabinets. In the installation pictured here, you see 22-inch diameter revolving shelves in the center, and handy shelves 8 inches long and 3½ inches wide (front to back) that adjust up and down on metal standards attached inside the doors. Amerock is a major supplier of cabinet hardware. See a local dealer or write to Amerock Corp., 4000 Auburn Street, Rockford, Ill. 61101.

21

Cabinet Hardware

Visit a hardware store, or glance through a catalog or the advertising columns of a home or mechanics magazine, and you will see that as a cabinet builder you have a wide choice of hinges, catches, and drawer and door pulls and knobs. Not only must you choose from general types, but you must decide on styles and materials as well: whether you'll use flat butt or concealed hinges, in plain or ornamental styles of brass, bronze, steel, chromium, wrought iron; whether you prefer a combination door latch and pull; whether you want pulls or knobs on the drawers, and in what style.

It is wise to make your hardware choice before you begin work, for it may affect design and construction. For instance, hinges must suit the type of door, that is whether it is flush, offset, or overlapping, with or without an inset.

The familiar square or rectangular butt hinge comes in two general types, swaged or flat, and with loose or fixed pins. The leaves of a swaged butt are mortised into the edges of the door and the cabinet frame. To permit the leaves to come together when the door closes, they are depressed slightly from the knuckles. As its name suggests, a flat butt is designed for mounting against the face of the door and cabinet with both leaves showing. The leaves consequently are joined to the knuckles so they form a straight line when open. Butt pins come with a variety of tips—ball, bullet, steeple, cone, button, and others.

If you want to use flat butts on a flush door, you can get them in many decorative styles. Strap, T, H, and HL hinges operate on the same principle as the ordinary butt. All of these are also available with the leaves offset for use on overlapping or lipped doors. Offset hinges usually are bent or curved to suit doors offset $\frac{3}{8}''$ from the cabinet face.

Builders who prefer not to make hinges a display item of their cabinets can either hide them entirely or in part. Semiconcealed hinges include butts with one leaf outside and the other mortised in the edge of the other mounting member. The inside, or swinging leaf, also may be extended to wrap around the inside surface of the door, whether it is flush or lipped. For a lipped door, such hinges must suit the size of the rabbet on the rear edge. If a door overlaps without an inset, you can use semiconcealed hinges made especially for it. The swinging leaf is attached to the rear surface of the door, the fixed one to the cabinet frame outside. The swaged, or double-mortised, butt also has variations worth noting. In one, the swinging leaf is extended and bent at 90 degrees against the inside surface of the door. Another has both leaves to one side for lipped doors. This makes edge mortising unnecessary, the door rabbet being cut wide enough to provide adequate clearance for the hinge leaves when they are closed.

The pivot hinge, sometimes called a concealed hinge, is mounted in gains cut in the top and bottom edges of the door and in the frame. The edges or pivot may show. But a type with meshing leaves and lugs set into deep mortises in the vertical edges of the door and frame is truly invisible. These enable you to build cabinets without apparent hinges.

The selection of door and drawer knobs or pulls is mostly a matter of personal taste and style to suit the cabinets and type of finish. But rather than buy, you may prefer to make your own. For instance, 3″ or 4″ lengths of large-diameter dowel rod screwed horizontally to drawers and vertically to doors will give you effective pulls in modern style. The dowels can be raised from the surface, if desired, by placing blocks under them. Finger grips also might be hollowed out of the sides of rectangular blocks; or blocks of suitable size can be placed on top of smaller ones. For concealed pulls in wall-cabinet doors, hollow out finger grips at the rear of the bottom edge—if the cabinet construction permits.

Door catches may be separate, or operated by a push-button on the pull. The latter may be reversible, for right- or left-hand doors, and are available for both flush and overlapping doors. Strikes can be mounted on the door frame or under a shelf. When separate door knobs or pulls are used, various types of inside spring catches are available—for installation on the door and frame, or on the door and under a shelf. These all release automatically when the door is pulled—as do the handy new magnetic catches.

Improved hardware for installing Lazy Susan shelves in wall or base corner cabinets is offered by several companies. This hardware usually comes as a complete package, including the necessary bearings, center shaft, and two or more metal shelves. The shelves are either a full, three-quarter, or half circle, always with a restraining outer lip.

Major suppliers of such hardware include Ekco Building Products Co., 1250 Bedford Avenue S.W., Canton, Ohio 44710, and the Amerock Corp., 4000 Auburn Street, Rockford, Ill. 61101. If a local hardware store can't show you the products of these companies, write and ask for descriptive literature.

You should definitely not miss the "Kitchen Organizers" offered by Rubbermaid, Inc. These include useful turntables, slide-out racks, and fruit and vegetable drawers.

Metal drawer slides are of several types. Some move on small nylon wheels, some on ball bearings, and some on a combination of both. Most are made for installation on the sides of the drawers, but others go underneath, either single or double.

As a mail-order source of cabinet hardware and other supplies, the cabinet builder would do well to have on hand current catalogs from one or both of the two major firms that deal in supplies for wood craftsmen. Send a quarter with your name and address to Albert Constantine & Son, 2050 Eastchester Road, Bronx, N.Y. 10461, for the

Constantine illustrated catalog. For the second catalog send thirty-five cents to Craftsman Wood Service Company, 2727 S. Mary Street, Chicago 60608. You can buy many of the same items from both firms, but each has some exclusive items.

For example, the Constantine catalog has an informative section on cabinet finishes, what they are and how to apply them. From this catalog you can also order such items as hardware for a pop-up mixer shelf, pull-out racks for pans, towels, and wastebaskets; and patented hardware (called a "Binswing") for swinging out storage bins of various size from within a cabinet. The bin tilts as you pull it out, providing access into the top.

If you'd like to give your cabinets the popular Provincial styling, you'll want to know about an item in the Craftsman catalog—Decramold hardwood moldings. Inward-sweeping quarter circles are included in this molding for use at the corners of square and rectangular molding layouts that characterize the Provincial style. Straight runs of the molding can be cut to suit the size of the drawer or door. Photographs elsewhere in this book show how such molding is used. The Craftsman catalog also has dropleaf table hinges, hardware that you will find useful for folding breakfast bars.

In considering Colonial hardware for your cabinets, you should know that some authorities will tell you that there are two general types. The original hand wrought hardware used in the early days, they say, was generally very plain, in square simple designs, and tended to be somewhat rough and unfinished in appearance. One source of such plain hardware is Acorn Manufacturing Company, Mansfield, Mass. This company makes square end, smooth steel forged hardware. Edges are dimpled to simulate the old hand forged hinges. The shapes were taken from old styles. On request, the Acorn company will send you folders showing and describing their products.

Quite a number of highly reputable manufacturers produce the more common style of Colonial hardware. This is more ornate, the steel having a rough rolled texture. Hinges have points, or steeples.

Amerock makes beautiful hardware in a variety of styles, including the popular Provincial. Included in the latter are offset hinges, graceful drawer pulls, and the rosette door knobs customarily used with the decorative molding of this cabinet style. This company also offers decorative corner plates for use with Provincial-style knobs. These are for doors and drawers where pulls might seem too large.

Stores have handy plastic or aluminum track for bypassing sliding doors made of $\frac{1}{8}''$, $\frac{1}{4}''$, $\frac{1}{2}''$, and $\frac{3}{4}''$ materials. The track comes in 4', 5', and 6' lengths, packaged in sets containing pulls and screws or brads. The track is easily cut to the length you want. For a free booklet illustrating ways of using sliding-panel cabinets, write Stanley Hardware, Dept. PID, Box 1800, New Britain, Conn.

Ekco Building Products, through its Washington line, offers one of the widest selections of kitchen accessories. Especially worth noting are the following Washington items:

Sliding flour sifters and sugar dispensers. These are square steel hoppers that you mount under a shelf. A lever permits flour or sugar to flow out of the bottom.

Fruit and vegetable drawers molded of polystyrene. You mount these in base cabinets. The bins glide out smoothly on steel slides.

Metal drawers with self-opening lids for storage of sugar, flour, bread, and pastry. The company also has tin drawer liners for bread and pastry storage. These have sliding lids.

A pop-up refuse container for mounting inside the door of a sink cabinet. The lid opens automatically when you open the cabinet door.

Sliding racks for hanging up towels, pots and pans, and cups.

Two types of pop-up mixer shelf hardware. (Amerock has such hardware that locks at two levels—for sitting or standing.)

Slide-out towel racks that mount on the side of the cabinet interior are a specialty of Knape & Vogt Manufacturing Co., Grand Rapids, Mich. The company also has racks that mount under a shelf or on the "ceiling" of a base cabinet, as well as racks for pans and cups.

Macklanburg-Duncan Company, Oklahoma City, Okla., offers aluminum tracks for by-passing sliding doors in a wide selection of sizes. The tracks will take sliding panels of glass, hardboard, plywood, or perforated panels. Material thickness can be $\frac{1}{8}''$, $\frac{1}{4}''$, $\frac{3}{8}''$, $\frac{1}{2}''$, and $\frac{3}{4}''$. The $\frac{1}{2}''$ and $\frac{3}{4}''$ tracks include nylon glide buttons for the door bottoms.

For by-passing doors of the size used in kitchen cabinets you might think that overhead hangers would seldom be necessary. However, the John Sterling Corporation, Richmond, Ill., does offer a hanger with ⅜″ offset and an appropriate hanger track for doors made of ¾″ material. Grant Pulley and Hardware Corp., West Nyack, N.Y., fills in with hangers to suit the lesser thicknesses. Overhead roller supports for sliding doors of ¼″, ⅜″, and ½″ are a Grant specialty. The Sterling company also has locks for sliding doors.

Are you stumped about where to find metal frames for installing a kitchen sink? The B & T Metals Company, 425 West Town Street, Columbus, Ohio 43215, is a major supplier of such frames, both aluminum and stainless steel. Write and ask if there's a retail outlet near you. This company has also marketed a useful hardwood cutting block, already framed in metal, for installation in the kitchen counter, especially where the original surface has been damaged.

22

Applying the Finish

It is axiomatic that a wood finish is never better than the base to which it is applied. For a finish of which you'll be proud, start with a glass-smooth surface, one on which your finger tips can detect no flaw. This calls for careful and thorough sanding of the wood. A power sander, rented if necessary, eases this job on surfaces as extensive as those of kitchen cabinets. Leave off all fasteners, pulls, and knobs until the finishing operations are complete. Use progressively finer paper. When you are satisfied that the surface is glass smooth, dust it with a brush or a cloth moistened with turpentine. If you refinish old cabinets to match new ones, clean down to the original surface first.

The finish you apply to your cabinets should be determined largely by what wood you have used for the visible surfaces and the styling you have given to the cabinets, that is early American, provincial, or modern. The best commercially-made kitchen cabinets nowadays rank with fine furniture. Yours can too. To achieve this, it's best to limit your use of fir plywood to inside parts of your cabinets. Use solid wood or a hardwood plywood for visible surfaces.

Applying finishes to wood is a complex subject and the scope of this book doesn't permit coverage of all possibilities for kitchen cabinets. But it is possible to offer some guide lines. The job actually is simple. The problem is to choose the finish most suited to the cabinets you have built.

For the early American style of cabinets that have been popular now for two decades, you want the finish to complement the original beauty of the wood used. Most frequently this has been knotty pine, either in the form of solid wood paneling or plywood. You can do this very simply by applying two thinned coats of white shellac, plus a final coat of satin varnish. Let the shellac dry for a full day and then rub it down with the finest steel wool before applying the next coat. The varnish provides the waterproofing that all your cabinet surfaces should have. It is well to apply two or more varnish coats on end wood, for this is always a source of moisture absorption that can cause doors and drawers to stick. Always apply exactly the same finish to opposite faces of cabinet doors.

Whatever your finishing problem—early American, modern, or provincial—you can solve it with one of the penetrating finishes that have come on the market in the past decade or so. A clear penetrating finish applied as directed on the container (often by wiping) will give you exactly what you want if your objective is to retain the original beauty of the wood while giving it protection. You can use this on any good wood As the name suggests, the finish penetrates the wood—and seals it. The surface will look very much as it did before.

Penetrating finishes also are the answer if you want a finish that simulates a wood other than what you have used. Birch plywood is a favorite for kitchen cabinets. This finishes beautifully in its own right. But you can also turn it into the fruitwood, cherry, walnut, or one of the other popular finishes now found on commercially made cabinets. You do this with appropriate stains. Most of the major paint makers now have a wide choice of stain colors in penetrating finishes. Minwax is a member of this family. You get the color you want, plus protection, in one simple application. What could be simpler?

23

Kitchen Lighting

Artificial lighting in a kitchen should include both general illumination and direct light where it is most needed—at the sink, range, and mix center. Incandescent and daylight-type fluorescents can be combined to drive out the shadows.

Because there is no lighting superior to natural daylight, kitchen planners nowadays strive for the maximum in window area. This should never be less than 15 to 20 percent of the floor area, and up to 25 percent if possible. But a compromise with storage needs is sometimes necessary.

General illumination of a kitchen may be achieved in several ways—by one or more overhead lamps, attached to the ceiling or hanging; by recessed lighting, perhaps above a suspended ceiling; by cove lighting, or by fluorescent installed in built-in beams installed across the ceiling. The latter is one of the most recent lighting ideas. Plywood on wood framing across the ceiling simulates a solid wood beam. Lamps installed inside shine through a strip of translucent material that serves as the bottom of the beam.

Cove lighting provides illumination at the edges of the ceiling, utilizing hidden fluorescents. Coves may be used along one or two walls—or may completely encircle a room.

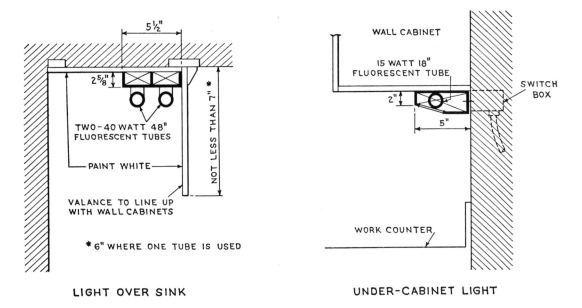

5½"

2⅝"

NOT LESS THAN 7" **

TWO-40 WATT 48"
FLUORESCENT TUBES

PAINT WHITE

VALANCE TO LINE UP
WITH WALL CABINETS

** 6" WHERE ONE TUBE IS USED

LIGHT OVER SINK

WALL CABINET

15 WATT 18"
FLUORESCENT TUBE

SWITCH
BOX

2"

5"

WORK COUNTER

UNDER-CABINET LIGHT

SECTION DRAWINGS—COURTESY WESTINGHOUSE

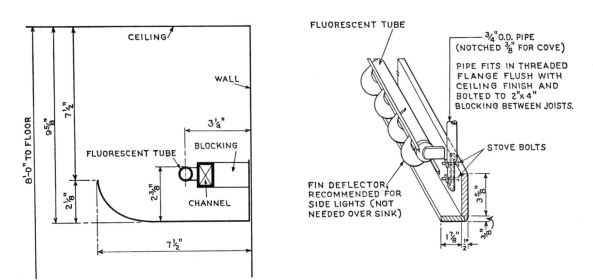

CEILING

WALL

8'-0" TO FLOOR

9⅝"

7½"

3¼"

BLOCKING

FLUORESCENT TUBE

2⅛"

2⅜"

CHANNEL

7½"

WALL-MOUNTED COVE

FLUORESCENT TUBE

¾" O.D. PIPE
(NOTCHED ⅜" FOR COVE)

PIPE FITS IN THREADED
FLANGE FLUSH WITH
CEILING FINISH AND
BOLTED TO 2"x 4"
BLOCKING BETWEEN JOISTS.

STOVE BOLTS

FIN DEFLECTOR;
RECOMMENDED FOR
SIDE LIGHTS (NOT
NEEDED OVER SINK)

3⅝"

1⅞"

½"

⅜"

CEILING-MOUNTED COVE

Coves are sometimes used for indirect lighting alone. For this, a cove can be attached directly to the wall or the front surface of a drop ceiling (soffit) when the latter is used to fill space between the top of wall cabinets and the ceiling. The fixture can be attached to the wall or soffit face, with blocking behind it to bring the centerline of the fluorescent tube out about $3\frac{1}{4}''$. For the cove, attach a $3''$ strip of wood at right angles to one edge of a length of stock $7''$ wide and mount the latter at right angles to the wall about $2''$ below the fixture, using small shelf brackets placed above. The $3''$ front strip should point upward to hide the fixture.

To avoid glare, secondary kitchen lights should not be in the direct line of sight. A sink light can be hidden behind a valance, or can be mounted in a soffit board; or perhaps a combination of valance and soffit can be used. A bridging soffit above the sink offers a natural place for a recessed light. Various fixtures are available to shine light downward through an opening in the soffit board. Although not required, a decorative valance may be desirable below the soffit flush with the adjoining wall cabinets. A valance may be used, too, either with or without a soffit, to conceal a long fluorescent light. The handyman builder can cut a valance in a variety of designs. If unable to find a suitable pattern, he should have no difficulty creating an original design and sawing it out. Or he can buy valance boards by the foot at a local lumber yard.

Some modern ranges have built-in lights. If yours doesn't, you should consider whether there isn't some way to place one above or near it without robbing the cook of storage space or interfering with installation of a ventilation system. In many cases a fluorescent fixture can be attached to the bottom of a shelf or cabinet directly above the range.

At the mix center and other strategic spots along the work counter, conceal fluorescents under the wall cabinets, locating them back against the wall. Each of these should have its own control switch.

The final touch in kitchen lighting, one that is not used as often as it could be, provides illumination inside the cabinets, particularly in the dark recesses of cupboard-type base units. Space usually can be found for a small incandescent light. Let the hinge side of the cabinet door operate a spring-type door switch—like the one in your refrigerator—and you will have real convenience.

Suspended ceilings have become popular for kitchens in recent years, and there's no better place to locate your kitchen lighting than above the ceiling tiles—as you see in the National Gypsum photo above. In the kitchen at the right, note how fluorescents were hidden in a boxed-in area along one entire wall of the room. In this kitchen the sliding-doors are faced with panels of Marlite, a colorful plastic-coated hardboard.

24

Ceilings, Walls and Floors

Before a kitchen modernization is complete, you must redecorate or cover all of the surfaces not covered by cabinets—the ceilings, walls, and floors. You can, if you prefer, contract to have all of this work done by a professional, but actually all three surfaces are prime do-it-yourself areas.

Satisfactory ceiling and wall surfaces or coverings may already be in place. If so, perhaps all you will need to do is redecorate with paint or wallpaper, your main problem being to make the choices that will produce a cheerful and attractive room with surfaces that are easily cleanable. If you decide on paper or other wall covering, consider one that comes with a matching fabric for curtains or valances.

For both the walls and ceilings you might consider paneling—boards, plywood (prefinished or not), and plastic-coated hardboard or plasterboard in one of the many available decorative patterns. If the idea of paneling the ceiling surprises you, be reminded that tongue-and-groove pine paneling was frequently seen overhead a century or more ago. Such paneling is still suitable for a kitchen with cabinets in a Colonial style.

Shutters close off the pass-through that leads from the kitchen to this eating area when the space is being used for purposes other than meals. Everything you see here is a simple do-it-yourself project. The wall paneling is Masonite's attractive Royalcote Sable Walnut.

On either walls or ceilings, the large panels are easily applied with cement or nails, sometimes both. Your supplier may have specific instructions for the material you buy.

Suspended ceilings are both popular and practical—and many do-it-yourselfers have installed them successfully in kitchens. Large squares of the ceiling material (tiles) are suspended on a supporting grid dropped below the original ceiling. If you choose a suspended ceiling, take the opportunity to improve your overall room illumination, too. Special fixtures are available for use in place of or above one or more of the grid squares. Check your local supplier or a mail-order catalog to see what's available. Sears, for instance, has offered ceiling fixtures that match cabinet styles—Provincial, Mediterranean, Contemporary, or Country.

Marlite's Mossy Pecan Woodgrain paneling was used on the walls of the dining area in this home. In the kitchen, the eye-catching Riviera tile on the wall between the wall cabinets and counter is actually panels of the plastic-finished hardboard. A damp cloth wipes it clean.

You might borrow several interesting ideas used in this model kitchen—the table-style peninsula, the simple molding-edged cabinet doors and decorative porcelain knobs, as well as the Azrock vinyl asbestos floor tile. Azrock Floor Products supplied the photo.

Here's a light fixture (Tilemate) made for installation as part of a new ceiling. Get information about this and other Armstrong Cork fixtures from local dealers. Instructions for installation may also be available.

Do-it-yourselfers are successfully installing floor coverings, too, and the manufacturers cater to this trend by offering attractive materials that are easy to put down. It is not always necessary to take up an old resilient tile floor, either. Armstrong Cork, for instance, offers a wide vinyl material that goes down quickly over any old surface without adhesives. Check your local supplier for this and other flooring materials.

Carpeting is sometimes put down in kitchens, but consider well before you follow suit. Carpeting can be very attractive—but it is not as easily cleaned as conventional kitchen floor materials.

High style can go into the floor as well as the cabinets and appliances of a modern kitchen. In this model kitchen, notice how the beautiful Kentile flooring pattern has been used to edge the sink island and as a backdrop for the planter in the island's end. Visit a local floor covering shop to see other interesting Kentile patterns.

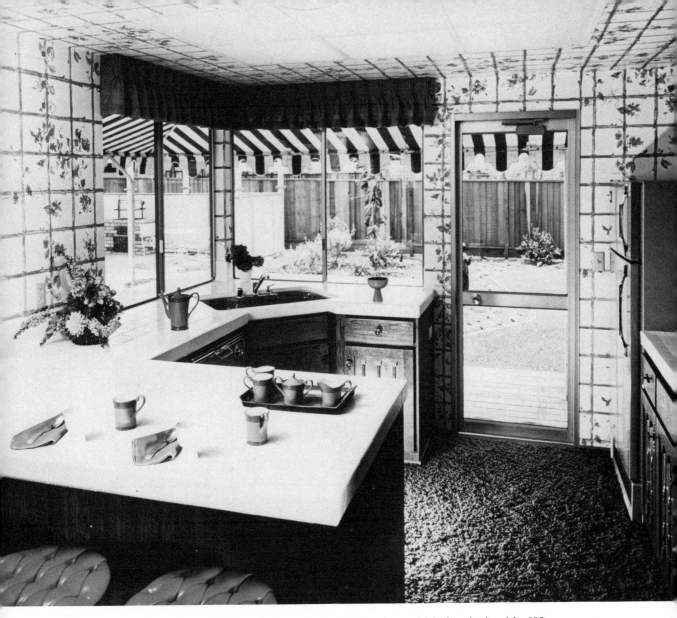

Kitchen modernizing ideas galore are seen in this view of a model kitchen developed by PPG Industries. Notice those big sliding windows that look out on the backyard, the sink placed on the diagonal, and the carpeting on the floor. See also the climbing vine pattern on the walls and ceiling.

In your decorating choices for walls, ceiling, and floors you will, of course, be concerned with colors. Actually, you will have made some color choices long before this, perhaps when you decided about the appliances for your new or remodeled kitchen.

The first kitchen appliances of the modern era all came in coats of antiseptic white—and some still do. Even now you may prefer these. There is a growing realization, however, that appliances in soft colors usually are more pleasant to live with—and manufacturers now offer several colors. Some even make it possible for you to interchange front panels and switch your entire kitchen decorating scheme from time to time.

You can carry color throughout the remainder of the kitchen too—to the cabinets, the walls, the floors, the accessories—to achieve the most you-pleasing kitchen. But do this with care and taste. Seek color advice wherever you can find it—but settle only for what really satisfies you.

Tappan's *The Kitchen Book,* mentioned in a previous chapter, offers excellent advice—in full color—on the subject of color.

SKETCH YOUR OWN KITCHEN PLAN HERE

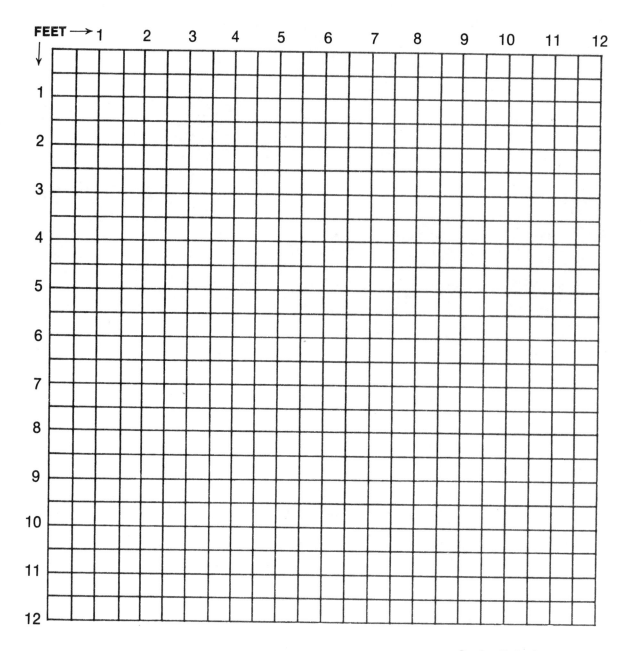

Scale: ½ inch = 1 foot

SKETCH YOUR OWN KITCHEN PLAN HERE

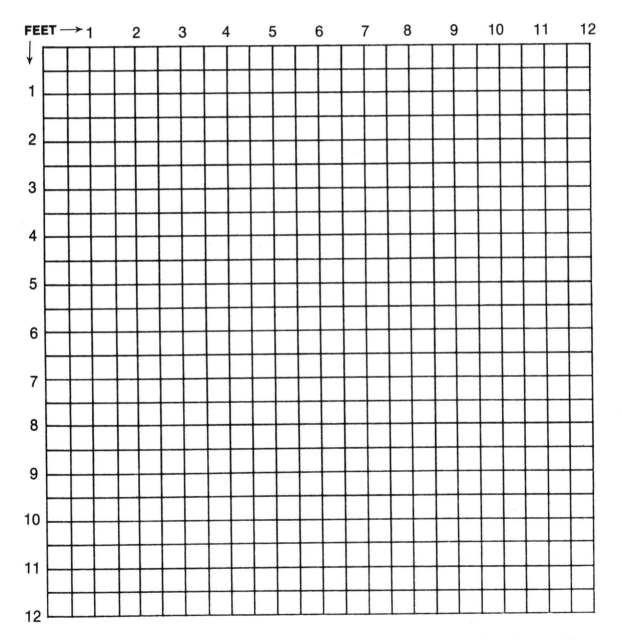

Scale: ½ inch = 1 foot